studies in jazz

Institute of Jazz Studies
Rutgers—The State University of New Jersey
General Editors: *Dan Morgenstern & Edward Berger*

Studies in Jazz No. 16

Metuchen, N.J., & London, 1993

The Scarecrow Press and the Institute of Jazz

Traditionalists and Revivalists in Jazz

Chip Deffaa

Studies, Rutgers—The State University of New Jersey

Other works by Chip Deffaa from Scarecrow Press:

Swing Legacy (1989)
In the Mainstream (1992)

British Library Cataloguing-in-Publication data available

Library of Congress Cataloging-in-Publication Data

Deffaa, Chip, 1951–
    Traditionalists and revivalists in jazz / Chip Deffaa.
        p.   cm. — (Studies in jazz ; no. 16)
    Includes bibliographical references and index.
    ISBN 0-8108-2704-2 (acid-free paper)
    1. Jazz—History and criticism. 2. Jazz musicians. I. Title.
    II. Series.
    ML3506.D433   1993
    781.65′3 —dc20   93-1875

For "Earf"

Contents

EDWARD · BERGER

Editor's Foreword

In this, his third volume in the *Studies in Jazz* series, the indefati-
gable Chip Deffaa turns his astute eye toward a corner of the
jazz world largely ignored by other writers. The notion of how
to play improvised music within a traditional context takes on
added relevance today with the growth of the jazz repertory
movement and the new attention paid to the "tradition" by
younger artists. The issues raised by Deffaa and his subjects
become even more pressing with the unfortunate but inevitable
loss of direct links to the music's creators. For the first time,
younger players working within the traditional jazz framework
will have to learn their craft without benefit of the kind of master-
pupil relationship so well described here by Terry Waldo (with
Eubie Blake), Joe Muranyi (with Louis Armstrong), and Orange
Kellin (with many of the New Orleans pioneers).

While many fans and writers view "traditionalism" as one
homogeneous movement, it is clear from these pages that there
are many approaches to playing classic jazz, ranging from the
proponents of note-for-note re-creation (Vince Giordano, for example) to the reinterpretationist school of a Terry Waldo or a
Marty Grosz.

One of Deffaa's strengths is that he lets his subjects speak
freely; his own comments are always to the point and never

ix

interrupt the flow. As a result, after reading one of these profiles, one truly gets a feel for the subjects. As usual, the author has chosen his interviewees well. Here we have an intriguing cross-section of artists who have not been overexposed in the jazz press; Deffaa understands that the most fascinating tales are not always told by the biggest "names." Among the many interesting and illuminating pieces are a moving vignette of Louis Armstrong by Joe Muranyi, a refreshingly sympathetic portrait of Benny Goodman by Dan Barrett, and a frank discussion by Richard Sudhalter of the attitudes of black and white musicians toward playing traditional jazz. Several of the chapters present insiders' views of the music business, including the change in types of venues, the phenomenon of the "jazz party," and the sporadic flirtations with mass popularity of traditional jazz and ragtime revivals.

Finally, Deffaa turns a welcome spotlight on some unsung heroes who keep the tradition alive in a very different way: the wizards of the recording laboratory who painstakingly restore the original 78 rpm discs for reissue. Deffaa has once again produced a work that is as entertaining as it is instructive.

EDWARD BERGER
Institute of Jazz Studies
Rutgers—The State University of New Jersey

Traditionalists
and
Revivalists
in Jazz

Introduction

In this book you will meet 14 traditionalists and revivalists in jazz. I've enjoyed their contributions and I respect them. They're not, for the most part, in it for the money. Or the glory. They're simply making music they believe in. They're trying as best they can—and it isn't always easy in a world where rock and rap predominate—to keep certain older traditions of music alive. Some, like bassist Vince Giordano and trombonist Dan Barrett, are only in their 30s today. Others, like clarinetist Joe Muranyi and guitarist Marty Grosz, have now reached their 60s. But all are enthusiastic for styles of jazz that originated "before their time." Typically, they got hooked on records made before they were even born. Most of these musicians have worked—in many cases quite often—with one another. None, with the exception of Grosz, has ever before been profiled in a book.

As individuals, their specific stylistic preferences naturally vary, although all favor styles that pre-date the advent of bebop in the 1940s. Trumpeters Dick Sudhalter and Peter Ecklund would have been right at home in 1927, respectively digging the new sounds of Bix Beiderbecke and his Gang, and Louis Armstrong and his Hot Five. Had Joe Muranyi been around at that time, he would have been checking out Armstrong too, of course, but also the likes of Johnny Dodds and Jimmie Noone.

Pianist Terry Waldo, by contrast, would have been paying especial attention to Jelly Roll Morton back then; he also has a fondness for the ragtime greats of earlier years. And while showman Vernel Bagneris shares Waldo's affection for Morton, his interests take in the whole of black show biz in that era, from musicians to dancers to singers. The pioneering black jazz and blues singers of the '20s and '30s are the particular inspirations for big-voiced vocalists Carrie Smith and Sandra Reaves-Phillips.

Swedish-born clarinetist Orange Kellin would have been in paradise if only he could have played in New Orleans at its peak as a jazz center. Marty Grosz would have fit right into Jazz Age Chicago; he's still disappointed that the scene which existed in Chicago in the '20s wasn't there when he reached the city in the '50s. By contrast, though, banjo player Eddy Davis believes that he *did* get to experience at least a little of what the old Chicagoans had, both by playing with those few holdovers from the '20s who were still active in the late '50s and early '60s and by working in mob-run Chicago clubs. Hard-driving cornetist Ed Polcer was, unfortunately, born too late to have been part of the famed Eddie Condon jams; he seeks to keep alive their feisty spirit today. Though clarinetist Stan Rubin first gained renown as a king of collegiate Dixieland, he has achieved his greatest success playing swing music of the '30s and '40s. Vince Giordano's passion is for the earlier hot dance music and jazz of the '20s and '30s.

Because this is a collection of profiles, the reader should not expect too many unifying threads. And yet certain issues and themes do recur in various profiles, as musicians address issues of common concern. How best should vintage jazz be revived? Should the emphasis be on accurately re-creating what has been played before? How much artistic freedom should traditionalists and revivalists have? How can young audiences be attracted? What future is there for the traditional jazz that these musicians love?

The profiles have been sequenced so that artists associated with one another follow each other. The book opens with Giordano, whose dedication to preserving valued aspects of our musical heritage is unsurpassed. The three musicians whose stories

4

immediately follow Giordano's—Waldo, Davis, and Ecklund—have all played in Giordano's band. Ecklund works regularly today with Grosz, whose story is told next. Because Grosz has so often teamed up with Muranyi and Sudhalter, their profiles follow his. Barrett has played with both Sudhalter, whose profile precedes his, and Polcer, whose profile follows. Polcer got his start with Rubin, whose history is related next. The final four profiles bridge the worlds of jazz and theater. Smith and Reaves-Phillips have been doing parallel things, singing classic jazz/blues numbers both in clubs and on stage. Reaves-Phillips, Kellin, and Bagneris have all worked together in shows that Bagneris has devised.

In contrast to my previous jazz books, most of the subjects of this book happen to be white. Lest any of my friends and relatives who are black raise eyebrows at that fact, perhaps I should make clear that it simply reflects the situation in the world of traditional jazz today. Although jazz was to a considerable degree a black invention, and is often thought of as primarily a black art form, most of the traditionalists and revivalists on the current scene are white. Why this is so and whether this is likely to change are additional questions that musicians I've interviewed have pondered.

I'm glad that I've had an opportunity to preserve some of these artists' thoughts and recollections. I don't mean to imply that the 14 musicians I've selected are by any means *all* of the important players in their field today. (Some fine revivalists have emerged in recent years in New Orleans, for example, whom I hope to include in a future book.) But I think these subjects make up a lively and representative cross section. And with the resurgence of interest in older forms of jazz that we've witnessed in recent years, perhaps the time is right to focus some attention on them.

Earlier, shorter versions of about half of these profiles were originally published in *The Mississippi Rag*. I've also written articles about a few of these musicians in such publications as *The New York Post*, *Coda*, *The Princeton Alumni Weekly*, and *Down Beat*. Several profiles have been written exclusively for this book. Each profile is written in the present tense, with conditions described being those at the time of the original interview, the date of which will be found at the end. Where pertinent, I have added in footnotes or parentheses significant developments that have occurred since the original interviews took place.

I don't necessarily agree with all opinions expressed by these musicians. (How could I? They don't always agree with one another.) I've simply tried to convey as accurately as possible their range of opinions. And it should not be inferred that those musicians given more space are necessarily more important than the others; some simply had more good tales to tell. But enough of my words. Let's listen to theirs.

CHIP DEFFAA
November 1992

VINCE · GIORDANO

Reclaiming the '20s

Somewhere out there, Vince Giordano will tell you, are aging musicians, or their children, who have arrangements from 50 and 60 years ago. And Giordano intends to find them, to save those arrangements, and to play them. For Vince Giordano is a man with a mission. He's the leader of the Nighthawks, which may well be the world's foremost revival orchestra: a 12-man group that specializes in re-creating the jazz and dance music of the 1920s and early '30s.

Night after night, Giordano's men offer the likes of "Clementine" and "My Pretty Girl," just the way Jean Goldkette played those numbers, "Ida," exactly as Red Nichols and the Five Pennies handled it on their million-selling record of 1927, and "The Creeper," as done by the young Duke Ellington. They revel in King Oliver's "Snag It," the California Ramblers' "Zulu Wail," Ben Pollack's "Waitin' for Katie," and Bennie Moten's "Small Black." And when Giordano introduces even the most obscure of pop tunes, he does so with a real respect and affection for the material.

He has spent countless hours, plus countless thousands of dollars, in his quest for the original charts—both stock and special arrangements—played by the orchestras of the '20s and early

7

'30s. No other individual owns nearly the number of vintage arrangements Giordano does.[1]

Eddie Cantor used to say: "Sometimes it takes 10 years to become a star overnight." Giordano's band has been kicking around New York, under various names, for that long. But in the last year and a half, it has been "discovered" by New York's society crowd, which is helping to put Giordano on firmer financial footing. The William Buckleys, for example, hired the orchestra for a private party that Mrs. Buckley called the best party she ever had. The Nighthawks have been booked for black-tie galas of the Metropolitan Museum of Art, the Friends of the Library, and the New York City Ballet. They are finally getting the recording offers and quality bookings, including concert appearances, they have long deserved.

September 16th, 1984. It is opening night at the Cafe Carlyle. Rene Peyrat of the Carlyle, surveying the packed room, remarks that he had not expected so large a turnout. In recent years, this has for the most part been a piano room. But now it is being turned over on Sunday and Monday nights to Vince Giordano's Nighthawks. Giordano's tuxedo-clad musicians have barely sufficient space, in the front of the room. Superb pianist Dick Wellstood—not a regular member of the orchestra, although he plays in it from time to time—jokes that maybe Henry Kissinger will show up. Kissinger *has* danced to the music of the Nighthawks on occasions recently, along with the likes of Brooke Astor, Mica Ertegun, and Bill Blass; "Suzy" and Charlotte Curtis have said so in newspaper society pages.

The house lights are dimmed. The only illumination comes from the flickering candles on the salmon cloth-covered tables around the room, and from the lights on the musicians' stands. Giordano kicks off the band, and the saxes—phrasing in a brisk, clipped manner, with Andy Stein's violin above them adding an unutterable touch of sweetness—take the melody on the Nighthawks' theme, "The Moon and You."

---

[1]As of 1992, Giordano's library includes, rather incredibly, more than *30,000* arrangements.

From one of the tufted corner love-seats, a man in his 40s, wearing a tux, and a woman in her 20s, wearing a 1920s-style turban, long black dress and black gloves, rise to approach the tiny parquet dance floor. They execute a highly stylized Peabody. During a break in the music, James Lake and Deborah Grisorio explain that since discovering the Nighthawks, they have become almost groupies of the orchestra. "It's the best orchestra to dance to. The best," Lake insists. Over the course of an evening, the music affords dancers a chance to try everything from the lindy, the Charleston, and the fox-trot, to the varsity drag, the shimmy, and the black bottom.

Through a megaphone, vocalist John Leifert is now singing: "There's something wild about you, child, that's so contagious / Let's be outrageous / Let's misbehave. . . ." And in the dimly lit room, for a moment, you can imagine it's 1928.

Vince Giordano will tell you that in his own mind, he has been leading this orchestra since he was five. That was when he first discovered the 78s in his grandmother's attic. "I'd go to her parties in Brooklyn, for Christmas and Thanksgiving, and I'd run upstairs and crank up the old Victrola. She had about 2000 old records, everything from Caruso to King Oliver. And I just fell in love with what those people were doing. That sound and style," Giordano says. The best jazz and dance band recordings of the 1920s and early '30s, Giordano says, contain subtleties that took him years to appreciate fully.

Giordano makes no effort to hide his contempt for the way 1920s music is usually re-created on TV, in movies, and in various clubs. "The arrangers get in every corny lick," he declares. "It's overdone—very 'New Year's Eve party-type music'—which if you go back to the old recordings, it wasn't like that at all. It was sophisticated dance music."

And it was played with style. For the 1920s was a period of high style, high spirits, and extravagance. On Broadway, Flo Ziegfeld mounted some productions so lavish that he knew neither he nor his backers could ever make money on them; he simply assumed he could always find new financial backers for future shows. (Otto Kahn was at times even more extreme; he once refused to put his money into a Gershwin musical because he said it was certain to be a hit.) In the late '20s, Paul Whiteman's orchestra, the most popular of the era, swelled to 27 musicians, plus vocalists—an enormous economic burden for anyone trying to make a weekly payroll.

Giordano's band takes its name from the long-gone Coon-Sanders Nighthawks, a spritely '20s dance band whose 10 members, at the band's zenith, traveled from engagement to engagement—each in his own Auburn roadster rather than in a bus. *Style.* . . . Even when Vince Giordano's men were playing in scruffy rock clubs and near-deserted bars in the outlying boroughs a few years ago, Giordano always insisted they wear tuxedos.

Over the years, Giordano's bass saxophone, tuba, and/or string bass have been heard everywhere from Broadway's *Doctor Jazz* to the soundtrack of Woody Allen movies. He has recorded with such varied types as Max Morath and Leon Redbone. He toured briefly with veteran trumpeter Clyde McCoy. He has appeared in concerts and on TV with the late, lamented New York Jazz Repertory Company. He has accompanied the Twyla Tharp Dance Company. With various groups, he has played at the Newport and Kool Jazz Festivals, the St. Louis Ragtime Festival, the Breda (Holland) Jazz Festival, and so on. He is seen and heard briefly, too, in the film *The Cotton Club*.

Giordano started learning tuba while in seventh grade, and soon followed that with string bass, banjo, and drums. He began collecting old records, too, amassing thousands of his own.

"I just didn't care about school anymore. It was music that I really wanted," he recalls. "In about a year and a half, I was working my first gigs on tuba, and working with a banjo band out on Long Island. I was in the eighth grade and I was gigging, Friday and Saturday nights. And then I heard a Bix Beiderbecke record with Adrian Rollini playing bass sax, and I said, 'I got to get a bass sax.'" The bass sax, virtually extinct today, was a key instrument on many of the '20s jazz recordings Giordano admired so much. Simply finding a bass sax took some doing. He got one from an old-timer, and studied it with pride.

"And then there was a book in the library, *Jazz: The New York*

Scene. I was always pretty much into the Whiteman band and all that stuff, and they were talking about an arranger in there, Bill Challis. I had joined the union when I was 14 or 15 years old. So I got a union book and just started flipping around, reading it—and there was this fellow, William Challis," Giordano remembers. "I called him up and said, 'Are you the same William Challis that used to work with Whiteman?' He said, 'Yes I am.' So I asked him about arranging. Oh, I was nervous as hell, let me tell you. So I went down to meet him. We spent a good three or four years, going over things, every Saturday morning. The majority of the sessions were just talking—him telling me about the old days, about Bix and Frankie Trumbauer and Goldkette days. Some of the funny things that used to happen in the Goldkette band, crazy things. It was kind of rough, because I'd have to work as a musician until three in the morning on Friday night. Then I'd go to see Bill, 11:00 on Saturday. And then I worked Saturday night too, in another place. I wanted to go and learn how to arrange. But he wanted to teach me the Schillinger system, which was a system Gershwin used and Glenn Miller used. It's a very hard system; I don't particularly enjoy it," Giordano says. But Challis' tutelage gave Giordano the personal connection, the permanent link to the era he loved so much. And Challis (whom I profiled in *In the Mainstream*) proudly says, "Vincent was my star pupil."[2]

After a stint in the Navy, Giordano established himself as a full-time freelance musician in New York. He chanced to tune in one Sunday to Rich Conaty's *Big Broadcast*, a weekly radio show on WFUV-FM featuring classic jazz and pop from the '20s and '30s. On the air, Conaty invited musicians interested in running through some arrangements of the original Paul Whiteman orchestra to meet him at Fordham University. Giordano was one of a mere handful of musicians who showed up.

The Whiteman charts, which had been preserved in the

---

[2]In 1988, Circle Records released *Bill Challis' The Goldkette Project* in which the Nighthawks, co-conducted by Challis and Giordano, play music that Challis had originally arranged in the 1920s for the Goldkette Band, including several numbers never recorded back then.

Williams College library, had been written for as many as 25 to 30 men. But some of the numbers, Giordano felt, could be played with a few alterations by 10 or 12 men. He helped Conaty get that many musicians to rehearse together, and to play a few engagements. That band, fronted for its initial bookings by Conaty, and playing under a variety of names, was the beginning of today's Nighthawks. Conaty soon went back to concentrating on his radio activities; Giordano threw all of his energies into building up the band.[3] In 1976, Giordano's band—then known as "the New Orleans Nighthawks"; it would eventually drop the "New Orleans"—started a weekly gig at the Red Blazer Too, a gig that has continued (with relatively brief interruptions) to this day.[4] The band worked private parties as well. (The band *can* fulfill requests for hits from the Swing Era—Giordano has a number of those charts, too—but Giordano's own strong preference is for older music.) Though in the early days musicians might vary from date to date, as the band got more bookings its personnel began to stabilize. Through constant practice, the musicians came to develop a feel for the idiomatic phrasings of the 1920s and '30s—something that star-studded orchestras put together for one-time-only concerts could not duplicate.

Getting vintage charts has been Giordano's obsession. He recalls: "To get arrangements, I was advertising in the musicians' union papers, and putting posters up in the union halls and in rehearsal studios. I was asking for both the stocks and specials, things that were written out by guys. And I just was getting all kinds of calls and letters from people all over the country. Pretty soon, boxes of stuff were arriving. Sometimes guys were just happy to get rid of this stuff. Musicians in their late 70s, early 80s. I'm mean they'd given up the horn 30 years ago, and all this stuff is kicking around in their garages, in their basements, in their attics. They know it's going to get pitched eventually.

[3]Conaty has remained the band's greatest booster, giving it frequent plugs on his radio shows; as of 1992, he still on rare occasions will front the band for Giordano when Giordano is unable to make an engagement.
[4]As of 1992, the band is the best-known and most popular attraction of the Red Blazer Too, 349 West 46th Street in New York City, playing every Tuesday and Friday.

They'd rather see somebody getting some use out of it." Giordano clips obituaries of older musicians, too; after an appropriate interval, he or an associate will write the heirs to see if the deceased musician may have left behind any old music. And he spends a good deal of time on the phone with older musicians, in search of material.

One important early goal for Giordano was to track down the arrangements of cornetist Loring "Red" Nichols. Though often overlooked today, from 1926 to 1931 Nichols was tremendously popular and influential. He was constantly recording, using such gifted jazzmen as Miff Mole, Jimmy Dorsey, Arthur Schutt, Vic Berton, Jack Teagarden, Benny Goodman, Gene Krupa, Charlie Teagarden, Eddie Lang, and Pee Wee Russell. His records, featuring an excellent mix of arranged passages and improvised solos, were sought out with equal fervor by musicians and laymen alike. Nichols' star faded in the '30s and '40s. But he enjoyed a resurgence of popularity from 1959 until his death in 1965, after Danny Kaye portrayed him (with Nichols, of course, doing his own playing on the soundtrack) in the film *The Five Pennies*. Suddenly in demand again, Nichols took his modern Five Pennies everywhere from England to Afghanistan. And he recorded steadily. He offered rearranged versions of most of his old hits, too. Giordano was interested in the classic arrangements from Nichols' early period, as well as the charts Nichols used in the final years of his career.

"I started calling all the sidemen that I could, who recorded with Nichols. Abe Lincoln and a few other guys, Bobby Hammack I think. And finally I got a hold of Heinie Beau. And he says the stuff's up in Eugene, Oregon, at a college up there. He says—'But, you're going to have to go through Mrs. Nichols. *But* don't go through Mrs. Nichols. Because she doesn't like to be bothered anymore with the old times and talking about *Loring*— not "Red" but *Loring*. And it would be just too upsetting for her.'

"So, I really wanted to see these arrangements, but it wasn't worth it to upset this lady. And I had written to the college and they had told me the same thing: I had to go through her if I wanted to make a few copies. . . . So, almost a year and a half passed by. And then I got this letter from them: 'We've considered your case, and you can come out and look at them and copy them.' They were really nice about it; maybe they had asked about me or something." Giordano saved up to make a research trip to Oregon, to stay a week or two, to search through what he imagined would be the almost limitless treasures of the Nichols archives.

"I did go out there," Giordano recalls, "—and 99.9% of the stuff that was out there was kind of disappointing." Where are the classic Nichols charts? According to Giordano, not in the Nichols archives. Much of the material had to do with Nichols' 1935 stint as bandleader on a commercial radio show, *Kellogg's College Prom.* "There were boxes—I mean boxes—of every college alma mater and fight song that they played on that show, that had absolutely nothing to do with jazz. And why *this* stuff was preserved there, I don't know," Giordano says.

Giordano had hoped to find complete original charts for "Indiana," "China Boy," "Dinah," "The Sheik of Araby," and the other Nichols favorites. "The stuff that *was* there was in fragments," Giordano notes. "'The Sheik of Araby'—there'd be a third alto and a drum part, or some stupid thing like that. I mean, I photocopied anything I could copy. But it was really disappointing.

"I did get a few 1920s-era arrangements. I got a couple that Sam Lanin did. Some pretty advanced scores by, I think, Fud Livingston. They're uncredited, but they sound like Fud Livingston's writing: 'One Step to Heaven' and 'Too Busy.'" Giordano realized that if he wanted to re-create some of the finest old Nichols material, he had no alternative but to listen to the old 78s and attempt to make note-for-note transcriptions.

Giordano's search for the charts Nichols played in the later years of his career proved totally fruitless. Those later arrangements may not have been important in jazz history, but they had been tasteful, professional—and certainly more colorful than the head arrangements that the average Dixieland pick-up group tends to come up with.

Giordano notes: "I couldn't find those charts either. That was another search. Occasionally I get calls to put together a Dixieland group. I love Dixieland or traditional jazz. But I'm kind of disappointed with a lot of the repertoire, and the attitudes of these guys that take these jobs. Nobody rehearses anymore. And nobody even plays in the same band anymore together. It's 'freelance city.' Everybody grabs a job and then they fill it in with the guys they know. You kind of scoot around, and you play the same tunes, tunes that everybody knows. And that was one of my reasons to go out there to that Nichols archive. Because he had everything written out. With room for jazz improv solos. So, this way you could have a bigger repertoire—still play your jazz, but have an ending, and a beginning, little modulations, and that's what's missing in today's traditional or Dixieland jazz.

"Heinie Beau did some of that arranging for Nichols, a fellow Bobby Hammack did some arrangements, Red did a few. Heinie assured me that they are up there. They're not there. I went through that. I spent two weeks up there, working like from nine to five. As soon as the door opened at the library, until they had to push me out of there, that's how much stuff there was up there—recordings too," Giordano says.

Giordano says that in many cases, with band after band, the old arrangements simply were not saved. The Nighthawks often play, for example, "Birmingham Breakdown," which Duke Ellington recorded in 1926. Giordano had this arrangement transcribed from a record. People might assume, he says, that the Duke Ellington Orchestra would have all of the early Ellington charts.

"But they don't have them. Jimmy Maxwell, who used to do some arranging for them, said there's hardly anything—just fragments, little scraps of paper—left from the early days. They just didn't save it. When a tune got old . . . I mean, a tune from 1927—in 1931, they didn't play it anymore: 'It's *out*. Get rid of that old thing!' Even though it's a masterpiece. It was *old*. I guess Duke didn't care or whatever, and that stuff was just thrown out," Giordano says.

"I've spent many thousands and thousands of hours and dollars in putting these things together, these arrangements. Finding them, advertising for them. I have people working for me now, to help sort, collate all these things. Two to four people per day come over, plus myself."

15

Giordano will go to almost any lengths to obtain vintage material. Since this interview took place, for example, Giordano traveled to St. Louis, where he put in six 12-hour days rummaging through the shuttered and neglected Ambassador Theater, seeking arrangements of vintage pop tunes and show tunes and vaudeville numbers. The theater's roof leaked, and the heat was off. Taking inspiration from homeless people he had seen in New York, Giordano constructed a makeshift igloo to keep out some of the cold and the damp and the grit in the air, and he methodically went through the contents of some 900 boxes stored in the theater, dating back to vaudeville days. He came away with 58 boxes of oldtime arrangements he could use, for which he paid more than $6000. The theater's owner suggested cynically that Giordano was probably planning to resell those arrangements for bigger bucks in New York. Giordano could only laugh. For who would place a higher value on such old charts than he would? He simply didn't want that music rotting in an abandoned theater; he wanted it to be heard.

"There's still a lot of music that I don't have," Giordano declares. "One of my pet projects right now is the music that was used in the Hal Roach comedy shorts, like the Little Rascals and Laurel and Hardy. It was great stuff, written by a very talented guy named Leroy Shield in Los Angeles around 1930, '31. And I've been trying to find that stuff.

"I put an ad in the Los Angeles musicians' paper—it cost me $325 for a full year: 'musician/historian seeks piano arrangements and musicians who worked with Leroy Shield at the Hal Roach studio, 1930–34.' I gave my phone number, said please call collect. You know how much response I got? Zip.

"Leroy Shield was a kind of interesting guy. He was an A&R [artists and repertoire] man for Victor. He supervised a lot of Whiteman recordings Bix was on. When he was in Chicago, he supervised the recordings there. He went to Los Angeles in 1930. I got his last will and testament; that's how much research I've done. Going into the Victor files, calling up ASCAP. Calling people all over the country," Giordano says.[5]

---

[5]Giordano has now transcribed a great deal of Shield's music from film soundtracks and is in the process of recording it at his own expense.

Vince Giordano (photo by Chip Deffaa).

*Vince Giordano, with the string bass, bass sax, and tuba that he plays profession-
ally (top photo, courtesy of Vince Giordano), and the piano that he plays at home
(bottom photo, by Chip Deffaa).*

Veil. I talked with Tex Brewster, who was in the Goldkette
n 1924. . . . I used to talk with Joe Tarto a lot. He was a
d bass player with all the Red Nichols sides, and a pretty
guy, back in the '20s and '30s," Giordano says.
you never know what might turn up when, he adds.
months ago, for example, Joe Tarto rediscovered some
ents he had written for Fletcher Henderson's Band in

transcriptions that we do of Whiteman, the California
Duke Ellington, Bennie Moten, Isham Jones, the Hal
ic—those are note-for-note re-creations, *including the*
t were performed on the records back then." Some
tion Giordano's policy of re-creating classic solos
letting his own soloists express themselves freely.
owever, "The musicians today don't go home after a
d up the phonograph and listen to Frankie Trum-
or Louie or Coleman Hawkins. They're into all
c. They'll listen to a little bit of that, but they'll be
other things. Which is all fine and well. But what
o is do a *repertory band* that sounds like music from
he jazz should be of that era too. If you just put
in the solo spots, which I used to do, and the
a 1927 chart but the soloist is playing Coltrane
does that make sense? No. So I have the solos
the guys play them as the guys played them
a great solo, it's worth rehearing. We're paying
ds." But, he adds, "I do give some freedom to
play like one or two Dixieland numbers a set.
on that, and I also let the guys blow on other
up."
cts: "The amount of time I spend on this,
crazy—Why don't you just forget about this
e a rock 'n' roll musician or something like
much easier for you.' I say, 'Yeah, but my
It's like when they asked Stan Laurel what
ilms so great. And he said: 'All the love we
e same with what we're doing."
currently consist of Randy Sandke and

22

*Disc jockey Rich Conaty of WQEW-AM and WFUV-FM, a longtime supporter,
greets Giordano in the top photo. The bottom photo shows the Nighthawks in
full swing at New York's Red Blazer Too (photos by Chip Deffaa).*

John Leifert (at right) assists Giordano in the filing of Giordano's vintage arrangements. Giordano now owns more than 30,000 arrangements, and his library is still growing (photo by Chip Deffaa).

Giordano notes, too, that in the
dard practice for bands to play s
bands simply played stock charts,
them to suit their purposes.

"Advertising in the past fiv
picked up anything that was *spec*
stock arrangements, stuff that y
music store. When a tune came
bands all over the country pl
arrangement, in the exact sa
little bit, put some solos in it,
were master editors back the
Fred Rich—I don't know w
the California Ramblers. O
tic editor. He would take
with it in 15 minutes, y
the stock; he'd disguise
Even the Goldkette ba
ment of 'I'm Looking

"We do a chart
Ramblers, which is
the Coon-Sanders B
because he was on
But it is not a stoc
It's perhaps goin

Giordano's
arrangements,
recordings. Th
know where t
talked to Mrs
I've talked t
the survivir

"Ther
who used
away. I
player w
Raymo
The se

Herb
band i
tuba an
famous
But
Just a fe
arrangen
early 192
"The
Ramblers,
Roach mus
hot solos th
might ques
rather than
He notes, h
gig and win
bauer or Bix
kinds of musi
influenced by
I'm trying to d
that era. And
chord symbols
band is playing
licks in there—
written out and
back then. If it's
homage to the g
my musicians. W
I let the guys blow
stocks that we cut
Giordano refle
People say, 'You're
old crap and becom
that, and that'd be
soul is not into that.
it was that made his
put into them.' It's t
The Nighthawks

John Marshall, trumpets; Joel Helleny, trombone; Chuck Wilson, Bill Overton, and Mel Keller, saxes; Andy Stein, violin and baritone sax; Vince Giordano, tuba, string bass, bass sax, and occasional vocals; Jim Lawyer, banjo and guitar; Herb Gardner, piano; Arnie Kinsella, drums; and John Leifert, vocals.[6] Kinsella, a real master of early drum styles, plays a drumset that actually dates back to the 1920s, since modern drums and cymbals do not sound the same. Stein often solos on a vintage Stroh "phonofiddle," with an attached phonograph-type horn that was designed to project the sound in premicrophone days. Helleny produces mellow tones blowing his trombone through a megaphone of the sort once used in Jean Goldkette's Orchestra.

After 10 years, Giordano is on the verge of getting some of the recognition from the general public that he has long received from his peers. On the day on which Giordano opened at the Cafe Carlyle, cornetist/jazz historian Dick Sudhalter commented: "The entertainment business right now is full-to-brimming of people who have gotten rich and famous very fast on very little talent and very little effort. . . . And when you get a guy like Giordano who actually knows his field and believes in it, and has labored and suffered, and really hung in there for a long time—and is, by the way, the best person in his field for doing a specific thing—then you sure as hell want him to succeed. I don't know anybody who plays the music better on his instrument, and who has been more tenacious, and has had more integrity in his belief in that music."

Tonight in the Cafe Carlyle, Vince Giordano is bringing to life the music he first discovered as a child listening to the Victrola in his grandmother's attic. Three clarinets work their way in unison through the melody of "Sugarfoot Stomp." Then the

---

[6]Among performers who have been featured in the band in the years since this profile was written are trumpeters Jon-Erik Kellso and Peter Ecklund, reedman Mark Lopeman, pianist Jeremy Kahn, and vocalist Johnny Crawford (whom some will recall as a young actor on the *Rifleman* TV series of the late '50s). Giordano has recently signed record contracts with the Stash and Stomp Off labels.

cornetist stands to punch out Joe "King" Oliver's original solo—with the whole band shouting the words heard on the first recording of that tune: "Oh, play that thing!" And Giordano's face radiates true satisfaction. Oh, play that thing indeed.

1984

Still Raggin'

Legendary ragtime pianist/composer Eubie Blake affectionately called him "my ofay son." Legendary talent scout John Hammond—who had launched the recording careers of everyone from Billie Holiday and Count Basie to Aretha Franklin and Bob Dylan—was certain he would have "an enormously successful career." Thus far, however, Terry Waldo—a romping ragtime pianist and authority in early pop music in general—has had a career marked by an inordinate amount of bad luck and what-might-have-beens. Although he is well-known and respected in the field of traditional jazz, he is frustrated that he has been unable to make a name for himself outside of that field, frustrated that his financial situation has often been precarious. Time and again he has felt he was just on the verge of greater success, of reaching a broad audience, but it never quite happened.

In April 1991—to give one minor, fairly recent example—Waldo opened at prestigious Michael's Pub in New York for what was supposed to be three weeks. An unexpected hit, his ragtime show ran for two solid months, the longest run the club had seen in several years. Waldo received excellent press coverage, was working steadily, and appeared to be building a following. A breakthrough! After a three-week breather, he returned to launch, for what he hoped would be another equally prolonged run, an all-new show, "Sporting House Revelries: An Authentic Look at Bordello Music." The show, inexplicably, failed to catch on, and soon closed. Waldo has gotten used to— which is not quite the same thing as "accepting" or "understanding"—such reversals. Unlike most other traditionalists and revivalists I've met, who seem resigned to the fact that in today's rock era the music they love strongly appeals to a rather limited audience, Waldo is convinced that if only the music were marketed properly—if record companies and radio and television people gave it real support—it could win a great following.

When Waldo talks in that vein, the thoughts that first come to mind are apt to run along the lines of Don Quixote and the windmills. But sometimes—just sometimes—Waldo is so earnest, and his love for the older music comes through with such conviction, that I too start wondering what might happen if the music ever were to receive some real major-label support. Not that it's ever likely to happen. But I've repeatedly sat in audiences and seen Waldo win people over, playing—and sometimes singing—spritely vintage curios that are undoubtedly new to most (or perhaps even all) who are listening. I've seen him offer ragtime piano numbers with depth and beauty surprising to many of today's listeners. And I've heard remarkably fine small-band recordings he has made, using the best current players of classic jazz, that have been ignored by most of the jazz press, which concentrates on newer styles. I can understand, at least partially, his frustrations. He's got so much expertise in the older forms of popular music and knows from experience that— if given half a chance—he can usually get audiences to share his delight in such music. Why must he be on the extreme periphery in today's entertainment world?

That's a question to ponder at length later. The thing I want to know first, though, as I visit with Waldo at his Upper West Side Manhattan apartment, is how a fellow who—judging by appearances—probably came of age in the 1960s managed to avoid becoming hooked on rock music. Waldo points out that he's actually just old enough to have begun forming his musical tastes in the prerock era. I invite him to tell me about it, and he's more than happy to oblige.

"I was into music as a kid," Waldo notes. "I was born in 1944 in Ironton, Ohio, a small town along the Ohio River. And in the late '40s and early '50s, the music scene was such that you had a whole bunch of different kinds of music. You were hearing tunes like 'Cement Mixer—Put-Ti Put-Ti'; you were getting Teresa Brewer doing sort of ragtime hits; you were getting all kinds of novelty things; you were getting jazz; prerock; and it was all on 78 rpm records. So you got this terrific cross section of stuff. And I had a neighbor who must have had the only extensive collection of classical music. So when I was three years old, four years old, I used to go down and play his classical records along with Spike Jones records and stuff like that. I remember when I was four years old, I got—for a dollar you could send away and get a hundred 78 records that they had just taken off the jukeboxes. So you'd get a box of these things and go through them and every one was different. And I got Bob Wills—Texas swing—and just all kinds of stuff. Something like 'Steel Guitar Rag' was a big hit. And then you'd have—who did it?—'I'm sending you a big bouquet of roses. . . . ' I remember that as a kid. You had the Jimmy Dorsey things. And Spike Jones, which made a big impression on me. I used to listen to Glenn Miller records when I was three years old and, you know, I just loved them. Just all kinds of stuff.

"We did not have television when I was first born. So everybody used to sit around after dinner. You'd rock back and forth on the front porch and watch the cars go by and tell stories. So I was raised, at first, in that sort of semirural, really all-American, quintessential small-town kind of an upbringing. Then, in 1950, we moved to Columbus, Ohio. We got a piano when I was in third grade and I took about three years of classical lessons. Then about sixth grade I discovered ragtime. I think it was Big Tiny Little that I heard play 'The Maple Leaf Rag' on *The Lawrence Welk Show*. I got the music for it and I started collecting some other ragtime things. My piano teacher encouraged me to quit playing piano because I wasn't keeping up with the classics. She just didn't understand what I was trying to do, and she knew that I was not really giving good recitals because I was spending more time doing other kinds of music. But I kept on playing it—I couldn't stay away from it. And then we moved up to Upper Arlington and I took some other instruments; I played trumpet, tuba, cello, string bass, tympani. I started a band in high school, in 1961 or '62, called the Fungus Five—'Our Music Grows on You.' And we were on *Ted Mack's Original Amateur Hour* in 1962— between my junior and senior year in high school. That was the first time that I'd ever been to New York. At that time I played banjo with the band. I always took up whatever instrument nobody else would play. And I kept that band together with various personnel through college."

While Waldo's musical tastes remained eclectic, in his teens he focused increasingly on Dixieland. He particularly liked the music of West Coast revivalist trombonist/bandleader Turk Murphy. "Turk Murphy knocked me out. The first time I heard Turk I was in high school and I was sick. I had the mumps and— because it was later in life—they went down to my testicles. So I'm laying in bed in pain and agony, and out of school. And I'd gotten some records from the library, and one of them was a Turk Murphy record, with Don Ewell playing piano, called *New Orleans Shuffle*. Wonderful stuff and it just knocked me out. I used to love the Firehouse Five when I was a kid and then I heard Turk's band. I loved that stuff and then I, you know, I read about the Lu Watters things and I started collecting the Lu Watters stuff. I really liked that kind of two-fisted banjo-and-tuba kind of stuff. It was close in a way to what Spike Jones was doing, I think. It had that kind of feel and it was akin to ragtime; there was a lot of ragtime stuff in it. The fire and the humor of that kind of music got to me."

Waldo found opportunities to play the kind of music he liked, professionally, too. "I used to play with Gene Mayl's Dixieland Rhythm Kings, a midwestern revival band that had made records for Riverside in the late 1940s. There were a number of revivalist bands in Ohio; in fact, there was a whole movement, and they were quite influential in it. Carl Halen, who played like Bix Beiderbecke, came out of that band. And Marty Grosz was involved with Carl Halen; did a record with him at some point. And at one time in Dayton, Ohio, which was near Columbus, there were six Dixieland bands playing six nights a week, in the early '50s. It was that popular.

"You know, there was kind of a Dixieland revival for a while, nationally. Lu Watters and all of those people were sort of gaining popularity on the West Coast. And Turk Murphy was kind of coming into his own. And on the East Coast you had Bob Wilber and Wellstood and some of those people in the revival mix." Although the Dixieland revival had been strongest in the 1940s, it continued into the 1950s, enjoying a particular appeal in America's heartland. And even after rock 'n' roll attained a near monopoly on many radio stations, coast to coast, occasional numbers with a Dixieland sound periodically broke through. For example, in 1958, Waldo recalls, clarinetist Joe Darensbourg (who had played with the likes of Jack Teagarden, Kid Ory, and Louis Armstrong) and his Dixie Flyers scored a pop hit with a fresh recording of W. C. Handy's 1928 composition "Yellow Dog Blues." It reached number 43 on the *Billboard* pop charts. Among new numbers with old-time feels that became hits, Waldo recalls "Midnight in Moscow," recorded in 1962 by Kenny Ball and his Jazzmen, a British Dixieland band, and "Washington Square," recorded in 1963 by the Village Stompers, a Greenwich Village, New York, Dixieland-style band. Both of those recordings rose as high as the number-two spot on the *Billboard* charts. "These things used to pop up. Radio stations would play a variety of things and so every once in a while you'd get a little Dixieland hit. And there were some radio shows that played Dixieland, where you got a lot of that stuff. There were still bands that were doing it. And I used to play with some of the older guys. Gene Mayl had Bill Rank [a trombonist known for his 1920s work with Jean Goldkette, Paul Whiteman, and Bix Beiderbecke]; I used to play with him in Ohio quite regularly. I played with Pops Foster [a veteran New Orleans–born bass player associated with Louis Armstrong, Kid Ory, Sidney Bechet, and others] out in San Francisco, and with [trombonist] Spiegle Willcox, who used to play with Goldkette. These guys were still around and I played with a few of them. And I was very fortunate that Gene Mayl worked so much, and I got to play with his band.

29

"This was after high school, when I played with him—it was very shortly after I went into Ohio State University, where I also had my own band and was playing ragtime stuff. And I was playing with these guys during college. I played ragtime and I did this on the side. Basically, I'd go to college for maybe three quarters of the year and then I'd go out someplace. I went down to New Orleans when I was 20 years old and played down there for Jack Dupen and they used to play with the Preservation Hall guys. I used to play with Frog Joseph, Alvin Alcorn, Kid Valentine, and Johnny Wiggs. I played piano mainly, although I did play tuba. The following year, around 1967, I went out to San Francisco for the first time. I took six months off from college and went out there. I was thinking of living there. I had a room for a dollar a day—$30 a month—over on top of Earthquake McGoon's. And the first time I went out there, I was playing with the Red Garter Band. And I played tuba with Ted Shaffer's Band out there, which was doing two-trumpet King Oliver kind of things. I occasionally played banjo with Turk out there."

When he arrived in San Francisco, it was at the height of the hippie era. "I didn't know about it. I didn't know what was happening," he says. But the anything-goes atmosphere of the times even touched the world of traditional jazz. "When I first hit San Francisco, I'm 21 years old, and Dick Lammi—the bass player from the Lu Watters Band—was playing with the Red Garter Band. And he was crazy; he was doing all these kind of drugs and stuff. A wonderful man. He was the real Emperor Norton of San Francisco. At that time, San Francisco was such an open city you could do any damned thing at all and everybody dug it. They loved eccentrics. And the more eccentric the better. I remember the army baked a cake—the *army* now—baked a cake for Beethoven in the shape of a grand piano and then gave pieces of cake to everybody. This is the army at that time. And they had, you know, cable car bell-ringing championships in the afternoon and just all stuff like that. The drugs were part of that. And Dick Lammi was right in that tradition—one of the real eccentric characters. And the first night I played with the Red Garter Band and I started talking to him about the old records and talking about Lu Watters and so forth, and he said, 'Well, come on over to my apartment.' So this was four o'clock in the morning. I got out of work real late. We go over there and his apartment is filled with all kinds of television sets and coats and just all sorts of things. And this guy keeps coming in every half hour, bringing in some more stuff; he'd come in with an armload of clothes and then he'd go out again. And I didn't know who he was. Dick Lammi was doing some kind of drug; I don't even know what he was doing. He was shooting up something that he was melting in a spoon, it was a yellow pill or something. I couldn't tell you what it was. And I was amazed by all of this—some kid out of the midwest, you know. About two days later, Dick Lammi got arrested for grand larceny. And it turned out he was just letting this guy store stuff at his apartment. I mean, Dick Lammi would never steal anything. The trial came up for this guy and Dick Lammi came up to testify and he got everybody so confused that they threw the case out. He says, 'Well the guy was just my friend and he's got a wife and . . . ' and he goes on and he's absolutely guileless. Dick played a number of instruments. He played tuba for Turk, but he used to be, like, humping the tuba when he'd play it, so Turk had to take him off the tuba and put him on banjo. Turk had a great band and Clancy Hayes was singing intermission. That's what was going on. And living there was really terrific.

"Then I moved back. I was married. I ended up getting my master's degree in communications from Ohio State with an emphasis in film. Then in 1970, I had to go to active duty for the reserves because it was the time of the Vietnam thing. I was 26, the oldest guy in my unit. I'm a guy with a master's degree and there's some sergeant saying, 'This is how I learned ya and this is how I want it did.' I was in the reserves, based in Ohio. I played tuba—'Offensive tuba,'" Waldo says, chuckling, as he recalls his military service.

Afterwards, Waldo still had to decide what he wanted to do with his life. While he enjoyed playing old-time music, he initially treated that as a kind of sideline. Playing piano and banjo and singing at a local Shakey's Pizza Parlor, which he did for five years, didn't bring in much money and was sometimes demoralizing. It was often hard to get patrons, who were more interested

31

in eating and drinking than in listening, to pay attention to him. Occasionally, out of sheer frustration, he would change keys at inappropriate times or deliberately sing badly. He taught courses at Denison University in film (1970–71) and the history of jazz, blues, and ragtime (1971–78). He also sought to develop a career in the film and television industries for himself. "But there wasn't too much going on in Columbus, Ohio, and when I was a film editor, I was doing flash-frames. And the people I was working for, doing commercials and stuff, considered that too radical. They use that technique all the time in MTV now, where you just get a split second of a scene and a split second of something else. But when I was trying to work in Columbus as a film editor and film-maker, they considered that kind of editing to be too radical; they considered *me* a radical. And that has happened a lot of times with stuff I have been involved with; it was ahead of its time."

Waldo would occasionally get gigs as a musician, either on his own or with a small Dixieland band, and periodically also got opportunities to play and sing his vintage songs on television. "I did a lot of television shows for various channels in Columbus," he recalls. He served in the 1970s as the musical director of a daily local TV amateur show and as the host of another show, *Columbus Then and Now*, in which he got to play numbers of his own as well as accompany guests, and he also wrote and hosted some specials. Making music, he gradually came to realize, meant more to him than teaching in college or making a name for himself as a TV host.

"The ragtime thing just kept pulling me. I was very interested in it and I kept doing more of it and I started getting more and more of a reputation doing it. And I started making some records. I guess in '69 we made the first Gutbucket Syncopaters record. That was for GHB, one of George Buck's labels. And then I think about '71, I did a solo album called *Vaudeville and Ragtime* for Fat Cat Records. And in '71, we reorganized the Gutbucket Syncopaters. Frank Powers and I decided that we would get the best guys and arrangements we could get. And he decided that I should lead the band, actually. We came up with title Waldo's Gutbucket Syncopaters because we played gutbucket, you know, with that kind of a fiery sound, but we were also enamored of

TERRY WALDO

big bands, King Oliver's Syncopaters. And they did have sort of a connection with ragtime, with that kind of a feel. We made our first album with the reconstructed band, which included some guys who had been with another band, the Salty Dogs. So we had Frank Powers, who was from Cincinnati, and Roy Tate, who was also from Cincinnati, and then we brought in Jim Snyder, Wayne Jones, Mike Walbridge, Bob Sunstrom—all Salty Dogs guys. And the personnel changed somewhat over the years and we started bringing in Eddy Davis to play banjo for a while. And then we started using Hal Smith on drums." He wanted players who could get the kind of *sounds* early jazzmen did. "One thing we always did—which a lot of other bands that play older music miss—was the tone coloration. Roy Tate, playing trumpet, is a throwback to the early '20s, those old New Orleans guys. And he's one of the guys who really understands Louis Armstrong and understands the spirit of Louis Armstrong, and the coloration and the bending of notes and the phrasing. He's still in Ohio. But that was always important to me. You know, we picked out guys that really understood the subtleties of the music, the rhythmic and the tonal color."

Waldo's Gutbucket Syncopaters existed, off and on, over a span of a dozen years. But although the band took its inspiration from old records, Waldo stresses, it did not strive to strictly *recreate* those records. Nor, for that matter, have the bands Waldo has led since then. Waldo thinks of old records as being akin to snapshots, capturing—sometimes quite casually—performances musicians happen to have given at particular times. "I've always been less likely to try to do note-for-note copies of records, although I do it sometimes," he says. "Generally, I try to get musicians that understand how to play and improvise in the style, and then *create* jazz recordings—which is what Jelly Roll Morton or Louis Armstrong or any of those guys would have done. None of them would have recopied themselves or done note-for-note copies. But you get into violent disagreements with other people that are in the trad jazz world about that. My recordings—I won't say all of them but most of them—are unique creations by jazz musicians. If I had one of Jelly Roll Morton's original jazz charts and the trombone plays four bars here—you

33

know, certain things are written out and so forth—that's the way we would do it. We would do it like it was Jelly Roll's original jazz chart and then everybody would be free to improvise what they want to do, in their spots. That's sometimes. Now sometimes, playing jazz, we'll go further than that, and change the order and all that kind of stuff. The stock arrangements of *ragtime* music that were published at the time were a little bit more towards the classical thing—fixed in form. Now what I'll do a lot of times is add piano choruses to them, where I can free them up a little bit and give them a little bit more flexibility." Waldo is not so much interested in showing exactly how the music was played in the past as he is in giving a vivid, creative reinterpretation of the music.

Often, Waldo's piano will play a bit more prominent role in a performance than did the piano on the original recording that served as an inspiration. As a player, he tends to establish the musical character of any band that he is in (more overtly than, say, a Vince Giordano, who keeps his own presence unobtrusive when necessary to ensure authentic re-creations of vintage recordings). Waldo notes of his bands' performances: "Generally on all of them, the rhythmic concept will come off of the piano. When I play something, I've got rhythmic concepts that I don't think anybody's got. Eddy Davis calls it flex-time. When it's working right, sometimes the rhythm will stay the same but I'll be lagging, I'll be behind the beat or ahead of the beat or on one side of it. Or maybe I'll be stretching something—a classic rubato. The newer ragtime players think rubato is if you slow down a phrase, you know; I think Scott Joplin has been inflected to death by the Juilliard jerks. But in the old sense, which I'm trying to aim at, you would maintain a strict beat but play within that context, so you might cheat on one note a little bit and so forth. You would give it a little bit of expression that way. What I'm doing is not a unique concept to probably older performers but I don't think there's many that do it now.[1]

---

[1]Some musicians find it difficult to work with Waldo because of his unsteady beat, though. One, who would rather not be identified, commented: "As a solo pianist, Waldo's got his own style, which is him, and there's something to say for it. But as a band piano player, he doesn't belong. He'll skip beats, jump beats. I'd rather work with a pianist whose time is right on the money. For Waldo, 'Time' is a magazine."

"I don't know exactly where I got that way of playing from. Maybe a bit came from Eubie [Blake]. I have certain influences among piano players. One, Paul Lingle, I think does some of that, a wonderful, very expressive San Francisco piano player. There's another piano player named Bob Wright—an astounding player out of Chicago—who maybe has a little bit of that. Incidentally, I'm producing an album of Bob Wright solos.

"I think in some of the King Oliver things you get some of that, a little bit in Clarence Williams' records; it's hard to trace, but I know it'll make a difference in a band. I'll be playing like single lines around the trombone range for instance, which is the way Jimmy Durante used to play, and that's one style; they called it thumbing. And I'll always do that in accompanying and also in the band parts; you play little syncopated things and that's what really gives a band a goose. And that's the way I can make a difference in a band. Whatever band I'm playing in, I'll play these little syncopated things and give the rhythm some interesting complexity.

"If you listen to a lot of these old black bands, they had that. Some of them used to—like, some of the musicians, maybe the lead might be playing in threes with kind of a swing concept, but then the rhythm section would be playing straight up-and-down ragtime. And you'd get all these things happening and it's a polyrhythmic sense. And that's one thing that makes old records more interesting than newer ones. You know, when you hear somebody re-creating a Louis Armstrong or a Bessie Smith thing but they're all swinging, it isn't nearly as interesting as when they had different rhythmic concepts going. And so I ended up doing that, filling in those kinds of things. A lot of times I'll do it on piano. And one of the great things about the Syncopaters was that they all did that, too. They all intuitively understood and played that kind of thing.

"In terms of my playing solo, the ragtime stuff, I try to get a great variety of dynamics, which I also think is important. This is what ragtime was. When you heard Eubie and stuff, you'd hear loud and soft, you know, it was music. And a lot of that's been lost. But I think that's true about classical music, too. I think if you would have heard Beethoven and Mozart and all these people, they would have been like jazz players; they improvised.

They would have been fiery and ballsy and bending the rhythm here and there, and you would have heard all that emotional stuff, which I think largely gets lost in most of the interpretations of classical music."

If vintage jazz, pop music, and ragtime are played with spirit and life—as they should be—Waldo sees no reason why they cannot grab young listeners today. He notes, "I've had a million different projects I've been trying to do to get this stuff marketed and get it into the pop market." While in Ohio, for example, he shot a pilot for a proposed television "magazine" show, *Waldo's Attic*. The idea was to mix in all kinds of things that appealed to him, from new performances of old songs by his Gutbucket Syncopaters (plus guest trumpeter and novelty vocalist George Rock from the original Spike Jones Band), to vintage clips, both musical and humorous. Keep the pace snappy. A taste of an old black swing band, then perhaps a Spike Jones clip (Waldo has a weakness for Jones' hokum), or an "amateur hour" sequence in which an outrageously bad performer gets a hook. "I think the show would go now, actually, because it's funny and it has the same kind of surrealistic Dada approach to mass media as David Letterman has. We had all these strange little film clips, and I think it would be very hip right now. I thought it was hip then but nobody understood what to do with it. I said Scott Joplin would be popular a year before it was and then, you know, this thing came along. And I think there's a market now for this kind of music if it's presented as [popular music]. I think Leon Redbone is starting to get into the possibilities of all this stuff. I think this music is at the heart of American popular music. Leon Redbone is sort of doing jazz. His records are in the rock 'n' roll bins. Go down to Tower Records; you'll see they put his records in 'rock 'n' roll'—which is now a pseudonym for pop music."

If Waldo ever needed any evidence to bolster his theories about the revivability of older forms of music, it came in the early 1970s, when Joshua Rifkin recorded three solo-piano albums of Scott Joplin's rags for a classical label, Nonesuch Records, which unexpectedly made the best-seller charts. Conductor/arranger Gunther Schuller then successfully recorded band versions of Joplin numbers for Angel, which got airplay on both pop and classical radio stations. The publication of *The Collected Works of Scott Joplin* put Joplin's music in the hands of pianists nationwide. In 1974, the producers of the Academy Award–winning film *The Sting* opted to go with an all-ragtime score: the soundtrack featured six Joplin rags (arranged by Schuller and adapted by Marvin Hamlisch). The main theme of that enormously popular motion picture, Joplin's "The Entertainer," enjoyed a 16-week run on *Billboard's* pop charts, peaking in the number-two spot— an incredible achievement for a 72-year-old piece of music. Joplin's long-forgotten ragtime "folk opera," *Treemonisha*, was successfully mounted on Broadway in 1975. Pianist Dick Zimmerman made the first recording of Joplin's complete works, for Murray Hill Records. Small record labels such as Biograph, Yazoo, Herwin, and Folkways—all capitalizing on the popularity of *The Sting*—rushed out ragtime reissues; it was obvious the slower-moving major labels wouldn't be far behind. For a spell, ragtime enjoyed a vogue, the likes of which it hadn't enjoyed in decades. Young aspiring pianists were taught to treat it with respect as a serious musical form, rather than as old-fashioned, good-time honky-tonk music. Assorted classically trained pianists tried their hand at ragtime. The heightened interest in the genre also had the effect of shining a spotlight on nonagenarian Eubie Blake (born 1883), the last major surviving pianist/composer from the original ragtime era (roughly 1897–1917), giving him legendary status for the remaining 10 years of his life. Blake had composed his first piano rag, "Charleston Rag" (also known as "Sounds of Africa"), in 1899, and had gone on to compose such popular tunes as "I'm Just Wild About Harry" and "Memories of You." Although Blake's various contributions were known to jazz and ragtime revivalists, he had lapsed into obscurity until *The Sting* revived mass interest in ragtime.

Waldo struck up a friendship with Blake circa 1970, well before Blake's rediscovery by the public. A fellow ragtime pianist suggested Waldo write Blake for guidance as to how to play one of Blake's compositions. Waldo was skeptical about writing someone so prominent out of the blue. But he did it, and Blake responded with great generosity—requesting only that Waldo give him a mention when playing his music. "I wrote Eubie for some manuscripts and then I learned how to play 'Charleston Rag.' And at that time, nobody knew who he was. So he was real thrilled that anybody bothered to learn that stuff. Then I met him at the St. Louis Ragtime Festival and played the thing for him and he was just thrilled. So we got to be good buddies. We hit it off." Waldo often stayed at Blake's home in Brooklyn. Blake taught Waldo, measure by measure, how to correctly play rags. And Waldo—whom Blake described as an extension of his musical self—wound up transcribing and arranging a folio of Blake's rags, which Marks Music published.

"Around 1972, I did a radio series for National Public Radio, *This Is Ragtime*—26 half-hour shows—and I interviewed Eubie for it. And then I brought him to Columbus, Ohio, as a guest lecturer. I was teaching at Denison University at that time—early '72. And I got him a bunch of television performances and stuff like that. He came in by himself. I used to travel a lot, and there was a bunch of festivals. Around 1974, the Scott Joplin thing was very popular; in 1974, there was a Scott Joplin Ragtime Festival in Sedalia, Missouri, celebrating the 75th anniversary of 'The Maple Leaf Rag.'

"About that time, there was a lot of ragtime around. Eubie did a lot of things and I did a lot of things. I remember, we played four festivals in one summer—St. Louis Ragtime Festival, the Sedalia Festival, there was a ragtime festival down in Texas, and I think there was one out on the West Coast. I performed in New York with Eubie Blake at the Theater De Lys and we did a concert. He had several of his protégés there. He sponsored a bunch of us. I ended up being, I guess, the star protégé, because I stuck with Eubie. We were lifetime buddies."

In the meanwhile, Waldo recalls, "Somebody came and asked me if I knew anybody who could write a book on ragtime. I said, 'Well, I just did this series on NPR.' So they said, 'Write a sample chapter,' and I wrote one. They bought it. And so I wrote the book *This Is Ragtime*. I interviewed all the people who were doing it: Dick Wellstood and Max Morath and Eubie Blake and Lu Watters, Turk Murphy, Joe 'Fingers' Carr, Lou Busch, Dick Hyman, Joshua Rifkin, Dick Zimmerman. The only guy I could not get to was Marvin Hamlisch, who at that time was in the middle of writing *A Chorus Line*. It took about a year to write. It was published in 1976 by Hawthorne Books, and has since been reprinted by Da Capo." It got good reviews. The *New York Times* gave it a good review. It won the Ohioana Book Award for Sociology: the best book by an Ohio author in *sociology*—which surprised me. That came out of nowhere. And we were supposed to do a big publicity campaign. But the two people who were doing publicity quit by the time the book came out. Eubie Blake and I were going to do some shows together. I was supposed to be on *The Today Show* with Eubie. But none of that happened. They never gave it a publicity push." Waldo's voice, as it periodically will, takes on a darker, I-was-wronged coloration.

But Waldo's future as a pianist looked promising indeed. When he appeared as a guest soloist with the Columbus Symphony Orchestra to play selections of ragtime, he earned what *Columbus Dispatch* reviewer Sara Carroll described (October 22, 1974) as "one of the most prolonged and enthusiastic standing ovations we have ever witnessed." Waldo, she wrote, was "fast gaining attention as the foremost exponent of ragtime now performing" and had not just the musicianship but also the "dry wit, stage presence and, yes, charisma" to be a fascinating entertainer.

Although Waldo continued to base himself in Columbus through the 1970s, he made periodic forays into New York. Particularly important to him was a month-long engagement in the fall of 1974. John S. Wilson reported in *The New York Times* September 21, 1974: "In a year when the Academy Award went to a film score based on piano rags by Scott Joplin and when the New England Conservatory Ragtime Ensemble is one of the hotter attractions on the concert circuit, it is not surprising that someone has finally had the notion of putting ragtime into a New York nightclub." The 70-year-old Village Corner, a bar on the corner of Bleecker and La Guardia Place in Greenwich Village, announced it was changing its name to the New York Ragtime Center, to become a "permanent" home for ragtime. That "permanence," of course, lasted only as long as did the fickle public's infatuation with ragtime. Waldo was offered as its first featured attraction. Wilson described Waldo as "a versatile and personable entertainer who does full justice to the piano rags. But he never allows his performance to become so esoteric that he loses listeners just beginning to discover there is a lot more to the pop music of the first quarter of this century than was on the soundtrack of *The Sting*." Waldo not only performed the rags by Joplin and Eubie Blake that one might expect, Wilson noted, but he also introduced a brand-new rag of his own, "Watergate—A Real Slow Drag," and played a cakewalk from just before the ragtime era, as well as some vaudeville tunes from the period just after it, numbers like "Evolution Mama (Don't You Make a Monkey Out of Me)" and "How Could Red Riding Hood Have Been So Awfully Good (and Still Kept the Wolf from the Door)?" In reviewing Waldo, *Variety* suggested in December 1974 that his "sparkling piano" and "charming" personality would be a natural for a ragtime TV series. So many opportunities seemed just over the horizon for Waldo.

He says of his 1974 gig at the Village Corner: "I got a lot of good publicity in New York. So much so that John Hammond offered me a 10-record contract at Columbia. And so did RCA. It was my last day in New York, after playing a month at this Village Corner gig. John Hammond had sent word that he wanted to see me. And so did Peter Munves, the head of RCA's Red Seal division at that time. I saw them both the same day. John Hammond wanted me to record with Columbia. Then I went to see Peter Munves at RCA in the afternoon; he offered me a 10-record contract, including the five-record set that Dick Hyman eventually did for them: the complete Scott Joplin. They offered me that job, plus five more albums." What a heady feeling it was for Waldo, having the two biggest record companies bidding for his talents!

He was tempted to accept RCA's offer. But then, he recalls, "John Hammond said that they could give me the same thing at Columbia, and the records would be in print longer. And they would do more publicity-wise for me." If Hammond, who for four decades had been one of the most revered discoverers of new musical talents in the country, declared Waldo had a future at Columbia, that was certainly good enough for Waldo. The economic recession at that time was making companies think twice before committing themselves to any new artists, but Hammond expressed confidence he could get around that potential obstacle. "But then he had a heart attack," Waldo recalls. "He had his secretary call me and say hold on, because as soon as he was going to get out of the hospital, he was going to pursue this thing and there was a big meeting of Columbia executives."

On December 16th, 1974, Hammond wrote Waldo:

"Until Thursday I was certain we had a deal at Columbia . . . but on Friday afternoon there was a staff meeting which I was unable to attend. At that meeting—believe it or not—the word came down from the 35th floor that there was to be no signing of new artists until further notice. This hit everybody right between the eyes and has made me wonder whether there is any real use for my own position here.

"When I talked to you this morning I had not heard the results of the meeting and I was still sure that we had not only a deal, but a good one. Needless to say, I am embarrassed beyond belief and I will take this up again at the very top level of the company in case things don't work out immediately at RCA for you.

"My humble apologies and best wishes for what I know will be an enormously successful career. I might as well tell you that you are the first and only ragtime pianist I ever really enjoyed and I think that, particularly in these lousy times, you have a real future."

Over a period of time, Hammond made further attempts to help but, Waldo recalls, "he was never able to do anything. So I went back to RCA. But by this point, Peter Munves had left. And Dick Hyman had been signed to do the Scott Joplin project, and so I lost both opportunities to record. I thought it was very sad." Having a major-label recording contract—something Waldo has never managed to obtain—would have made an enormous difference in his career, Waldo believes. Knowing how close he came to having got one still gives him a twinge of discomfort.

Others, however, continued to see in Waldo the same bright future that Hammond had seen. After all, ragtime was still going strong, and Waldo appeared to be riding the crest of the wave.

Among those who happened to catch a concert Waldo gave with Eubie Blake was Tom O'Horgan (director of the acclaimed musical productions *Hair* and *Jesus Christ Superstar*), who was then a very hot name in the theater world. "Tom asked me to write the music for a show about Warren G. Harding, to be called *Warren G*. In '74, I started writing the music for it," Waldo recalls. The show had its first workshop production in 1976, by which time the public's interest in ragtime music had begun to dissipate. *Warren G* was clearly not yet Broadway material, but the principals involved continued to rework it. (At the time of our interview, 16 years after work on the show had begun, Waldo was still hoping for a major New York production of the show, which had been greatly revised in the intervening years.)

If Waldo's involvement in the proposed Harding musical did not bring him the Broadway success he might have hoped for, it wound up bringing him something else he valued highly: a relationship with a woman who became his partner, both personally and professionally. (His marriage had ended in divorce.) He explains: "The producer of the show, Mack Gilbert, who was from Ohio, had a date with a singer, Susan LaMarche, whom he had met at some lounge. She was working there with a touring band that did all your favorite rock 'n' roll tunes, like 'Proud Mary' and all that kind of stuff. Well, he had a date with her and then brought her over to my apartment to meet his composer, you know, who was working on his show. I played a couple of tunes that I was writing—and I fell in love with her. I asked her out and then she ended up leaving the rock 'n' roll band and moving in with me. I started working with her as a duet, in Ohio. Then we toured Germany. I had a vast collection of this old music, so she started singing, learning this stuff, and then we worked together for years.

"I brought her into the Gutbucket Syncopaters as a vocalist, to the consternation of everybody in the band. Everybody thought we didn't need a woman—'This is a man's kind of band,' you know. They all bitched about her being in the band at first," Waldo recalls. From his point of view, they were all quite clearly and definitely in the wrong, and he wasn't about to listen to them. But a bandleader in love isn't always the best judge of whether the woman he loves is the best singer for his band. I have had mixed feelings about LaMarche's contributions. It seemed to me, on some of her early recordings, as if she were patronizing the old-time material she sang—treating it with an "isn't this a cute old song, and isn't it cute the way I sing it" attitude, which the top artists who first sang those songs certainly never had, and which I found off-putting. (Listen to, for example, her 1983 recording of "What Cha Gonna Do When There Ain't No Jazz?" on the Stomp Off album *Waldo's Ragtime Orchestra: Spectacular Ragtime*.) She didn't sound, to me, as if she took the songs as seriously as the musicians in Waldo's bands generally did. She seemed, at times, almost as if she were doing a caricature of an old-time singer. (*Mississippi Rag* reviewer William J. Schafer described her as a "Boop-voiced singer.") But there's no doubt she had appeal for many listeners. It's easier to reach people, generally, with vocals than with instrumentals, and she has helped bring to light some wonderful old songs from the repertoires of Sophie Tucker, Marion Harris, Bessie Smith, and Jane Green, which would otherwise languish in obscurity. Waldo found songs for her that sometimes sounded suprisingly contemporaneous. So even if the band's style of playing was obviously from an earlier era, when she'd sing an old-time line relating to "reefers" or to her need to take things "slow and easy," she would bring home the fact that interest in drugs and sex didn't originate with modern youth; she would help make the old-time music seem more relevant to contemporary listeners. In reviewing the album *Vamp 'Til Ready* (Stomp Off Records), which LaMarche made with Waldo's Gutbucket Syncopaters, Chris Albertson of *Stereo Review* (May 1983) applauded her originality; he liked the fact that her rendition of the bawdy "I Got What It Takes" was not a copy of Bessie Smith's famous rendition, and that her "Blues My Naughty Sweetie Gives to Me" did not sound like anyone else's he had heard. Albertson liked, too, the way LaMarche's voice could "cut through a roomful of loudmouths" when needed, then drop to a "cat's purr." In recent years, she has learned to sing the old songs perfectly straight (listen to

"Here Lies Love" on the Stomp Off album *Terry Waldo's Gotham City Band: Footlight Varieties*), which I greatly prefer to camp treatments.

Waldo says that eventually the other musicians in the Gutbucket Syncopaters "all came up and apologized to me because we turned out some wonderful albums with her singing on them." But his personal enthusiasm for her may have blinded him to the validity of criticisms of her work from other members of the band. Waldo says: "Susan had had a bit of classical training. She had a great ear and she could hear everything that was happening. And she could sing rock 'n' roll; she sang great. See, that was my theory. Most of the singers who are doing traditional jazz music are people that are not in pop music. You know, they're sort of nostalgia freaks; they're generally not good singers. I always thought that if you found somebody who was really a good singer and had the same kind of power and pizzazz that you get in pop music, that they could learn this stuff and really do a good job with it. Because jazz was once pop music, you know. It really was pop music. And Susan had that kind of ear. And taught me a lot about singing. She was great; she had great pitch and could do great arrangements. She did all three Boswell Sisters parts on a couple of tunes we did; she triple-tracked them. 'Minnie the Moocher's Wedding Day.' Incidentally, those things are being rereleased by Musical Heritage. She was great at picking up that stuff and understanding about the music. She understood what I was trying to do. We were really close there.

"I brought Susan in because she was really sexy and made the music come alive and so forth. At her best, she could be very raucus. She was kind of like a traditional-jazz Cyndi Lauper. She was young and into rock 'n' roll and understood the connections between pop music and the ways of doing it. And I always thought the music could be presented like pop music. If it were presented using the same kind of budgets that you have for any other videos and, you know, marketed right. . . ." That's always been his dream. He notes the way Bonnie Raitt can connect with young audiences whether singing a new song or an old blues. He believed LaMarche could do likewise—if given proper chances. Waldo's theory, that a brilliant rock or pop singer could interpret

44

old-time material with an audience-grabbing flair, is a good one. Whether LaMarche, who had previously sung with an obscure rock band covering other groups' hits, was the ideal singer to test that theory, though, was another question. My first impression of her was of a decent singer, without the stylistic distinctiveness needed to really grab an audience. (I've been much more impressed by her work in more recent years.) Waldo's enthusiastic assessment of her as a "traditional-jazz Cyndi Lauper," seems clearly influenced by his love for Susan. LaMarche recorded both with the whole band and with only Waldo's piano accompaniment, for small labels such as Dirty Shame and Stomp Off Records, which received but limited distribution. And Waldo continued to record, in formats ranging from solo piano (albums such as *Snookums Rag* for Dirty Shame and *Wizard of the Keyboard* for Stomp Off) to a full old-style ragtime orchestra, including violin, cello, and piccolo (albums such as *Smiles and Chuckles* and *Spectacular Ragtime*, both for Stomp Off).

Waldo also continued to make occasional visits to New York, playing unaccompanied, for example, for a stretch of Sundays and Mondays in 1980 at the Cookery. *New York Times* reviewer John S. Wilson wrote approvingly of Waldo's matter-of-fact "Midwestern casual" way of singing, noting Waldo offered "Blue Skies" "with a simplicity that is so unexpected that it is stunning." Wilson reserved highest praise for Waldo's work as a pianist, observing, "He plays Eubie Blake's 'Charleston Rag' with a stompy vigor that once delighted Mr. Blake so much that he exclaimed, 'If he was a woman, I'd marry him.'" In *The New York Post*, Richard S. Sudhalter described Waldo as "an excellent craftsman, whose personal charm and infectious elan easily compensate for any lack of subtlety in his approach to such more-than-meets-the-ear works as Joplin's 'Pineapple Rag.'" He praised Waldo for combining musical virtuosity with a keen understanding of the importance of *entertaining* audiences—something Sudhalter found all-too-lacking among many jazz musicians. He warmed to the sense of ease Waldo projected on stage. Waldo returned home to Ohio following such visits with renewed self-confidence.

Meanwhile, friction was mounting within his band. He was

not always sensitive to the dissatisfaction of other members of the band. "The Gutbucket Syncopaters were always plagued by disasters of various kinds," Waldo says. "It was always an emotional band. Everybody in the band was always very emotional and very excited about playing the music and had ideas about how it should be played. So there'd be fights all the time—arguments about style and whether somebody else should come into the band or not. Like Eddy Davis worked with the band for a while. And we ended up where he didn't want to do any vocals. And there were certain tunes he didn't want to do. And so we ended up with fights about that. We did a recording in St. Louis one year after we'd been playing together all week at the St. Louis Ragtime Festival. And we made an album at five o'clock in the morning after we'd been playing. But we had had so many fights that the band was going to break up. Susan LaMarche was lying on the ground crying because she had had her feelings hurt by some things, you know, guys didn't want to do those kinds of tunes and stuff like that. And we wound up making a great album for Dirty Shame Records—our swan song—called *Harlem Hot Jazz*: ballsy, hard-driving, full of the spirit of hatred!" He laughs. "We figured we were never going to play again so everybody was putting everything they had in it.

"Then the following year we came back together to play again, but Roy Tate's son was in an accident, so he had to leave and we had to bring in another trumpet player. And we had some confusion. I kept trying to get Eddy Davis to play banjo. But he brought another band—all-black except for himself—to one of the festivals, so we didn't have him, and everybody was mad about that. It ended up that there were personnel changes and then the guys started playing with other bands, and then finally the last year that we played together the guys in the band got the idea that they wanted to do some other music. Well, they were having secret rehearsals at the St. Louis Ragtime Festival. They had Jim Dapogny playing piano instead of me, and essentially the rest of it was my band with a few additions. They made it into a big band. Vince Giordano, who had played with me at some other gigs, was playing tuba. This was in the early '80s. They started a band called the State Street Aces, but nobody talked to me. They had these rehearsals during the day and nobody told me that this was going on. Because they felt embarrassed about not telling me. Everybody was involved with it except me. It was my whole rhythm section. Hal Smith, who was playing with me, Frank Powers, Jim Snyder, Roy Tate, Vince Giordano, Jim Dapogny, and maybe a couple of other people. I was furious about this when it finally all came together. And so my band came apart.

"I think Frank Powers had the idea of putting together the other band and was talking with Dapogny and they were talking about some tunes they wanted to record. Well, they did King Oliver things and some different tunes and stuff like that. But there'd been so much grousing about, you know, we missed some of our personnel the year before and people weren't sure if they wanted to work with Susan. So they split up. Their repertoire wasn't much different from what we'd been playing. It was just a slightly bigger band. And there were some more unusual tunes."

Was their dissatisfaction with LaMarche a prime factor in their deciding to form their own band?

"It was partially Susan, it was partially the fact that Eddy had another band so we didn't have him to play rhythm. There was grousing about a lot of stuff. The band had been together 10 or 12 years. Well, they went off and formed the State Street Aces and made three or four records. Jim Snyder had started playing with the South Frisco Jazz Band. And you know, Frank formed his own band and so forth. I tried to get the band together, but they wouldn't do it. I called Frank up and he says, 'That's all over with; we're all going to do our own thing.' So my band split up." Waldo had not seen it coming, and he still smarts over the way the other members of his band betrayed him (as he interprets it) by leaving to form another band. Meanwhile, there were other troubles brewing.

"About that same time, I had been working on trying to market the world's largest collection of jazz movies, which belonged to John Baker, who wanted to sell it. And I had also bought a house, a beautiful house in Columbus, Ohio. Well, I spent $50,000 trying to market this collection of jazz movies; I had a year's option on them. I put together a demo of John Baker's collection, which I paid for. I ended up coming to New York and trying to find some investors.

"I talked with [television talk-show host and nostalgia collector] Joe Franklin. Joe had his own collection of films and we were going to combine it with mine. We were thinking about doing some television shows. In fact, we even did a pilot together—I played piano behind Joe and did some things; an investor put up money for the pilot. Then Joe found out, about the same time as I did, the incredible legal problems of trying to market these films and getting everything cleared. The copyright problem, the ownership problem with the old films was the thing that we ran into. It turned out that 90% of the films were illegal prints. I was living in New York and talking to people. Gil Noble, the host of television's *Like It Is*, was interested in the collection—they were mostly black films, jazz—and I had extensive talks with him, too. But his lawyers told him not to get involved because the films were not cleared. And some other people who were partners of mine turned out to be bastards. So I lost about $50,000 by the time I got through. I spent all the money to put the demos together, to come to New York, to spend time, to travel back and forth, to talk to everybody, to live here during that time. I had paid for a year's option for the films, which turned out to be totally useless. John Baker sold the films to Kansas City, which owns them now; they're good for a library or something like that, but the minute you try to make money off of them, you're in trouble. I was just nuts about the films so I didn't think.

"But I lost my ass. I had to sell my house—I had a beautiful house in Columbus—to pay off my debts. And this was about the same time that the band left. Somewhere around 1984, I lost everything. With what money I had left after selling my house, I moved to New York, where I put together the Gotham City Band.

"I'll tell you what made it tough. I thought I was going to be getting some work with some help from Vince Giordano. I mean, he was literally my best friend at that time," Waldo says. Initially, Giordano *did* hire Waldo to do some gigs with his band, which had established itself as unsurpassed in music of

48

the 1920s and '30s. "Like, we did a major concert in Boston with the singer Odetta, and Vince had me put together a band within his band to do funkier stuff for Odetta. You know, we did Ma Rainey and Bessie Smith stuff, and got great applause. I did a few things like that. I was playing gigs with Vince. And I had borrowed some music from him, and he'd given me some stuff. And I was also trying to get work for my own band. I had a different approach than Vince," Waldo says, noting that he likes to give players greater opportunities for self-expression than does Giordano, who generally favors playing music as closely as possible to the way it was originally recorded. Waldo also prefers working with a seven-piece small band, rather than an 11-piece big band, such as Giordano's, which of necessity must rely more on written arrangements. But such distinctions would be lost to the average band booker, who would see Waldo and Giordano simply as both purveying vintage jazz and pop music. Giordano eventually had to wonder if Waldo was encroaching upon his territory.

Waldo notes: "I hit town here and I did only two concerts with my band, the Gotham City Band. I wanted to do small-band stuff. When I hit New York, I figured I couldn't do the King Oliver, Louis Armstrong, Jelly Roll Morton stuff I had been doing because there were no musicians here who were really into that bag like the guys I had in the midwest. There was more of a tradition here of New York music, so the first album I did and the music I was playing was Bix Beiderbecke, Red Nichols—that kind of a feel to it." (One reason, of course, that Waldo found musicians in New York familiar with music of the likes of Bix Beiderbecke and Red Nichols was that Giordano had helped to develop a corps of musicians who frequently got to play such music.) The personnel of Waldo's Gotham City Band in its premiere New York engagement at Folk City, as listed by John S. Wilson in *The New York Times* (May 13, 1984), consisted essentially of musicians associated with Vince Giordano. Waldo had Giordano himself playing bass and tuba, Joel Helleny playing trombone, Chuck Wilson playing clarinet, Arnie Kinsella playing drums, Howard Alden playing guitar and banjo, Peter Ecklund playing trumpet, guest-star Andy Stein playing violin, and Susan

LaMarche singing. Giordano, Helleny, Wilson, Kinsella, and Stein all played regularly in Giordano's band; Alden and Barrett periodically subbed in Giordano's band. LaMarche scored a hit with a Sophie Tucker specialty, "If Your Kisses Can't Hold the Man You Love (Then Your Tears Won't Bring Him Back)," which Wilson noted she sang "in a delivery that had Mae West as well as Miss Tucker in it." The overall spirit of Waldo's show, Wilson wrote approvingly, was "infectiously joyous." Waldo and La-Marche had moved to New York and, with a band culled largely from Vince Giordano's group of musicians, quickly got off to a most impressive start.

Waldo recalls: "Then I had another concert booked that I was trying to bring some reviewers in to see. This time, Vince backed out of playing in my band; he had a gig with his own band or something like that. And I pleaded with him to make it because I had reviewers coming in and I couldn't find anybody to take his place. He suggested some other musicians, who weren't of the same caliber, and it was important to me to really have the guys that could feel it. He says, 'It won't matter; you'll get by with it.' When I did the concert, I made some crack about his not being there, which he found out about. And he had a shit-fit." Which most of us might find understandable.

Waldo continues: "And then I didn't realize it, but Vince had been getting mad at me about a litany of things, which I had no idea about. I had handed out some business cards on some of his gigs and I'd played my album at a party that Dick Hyman had. And Vince got mad. You know, these were his gigs, and Vince considered this kind of music his domain. Vince wouldn't talk to me. He may have had a point about my passing out cards on his gigs. But when I hit town, I was scared to death I wasn't going to get any work, and I was aggressively trying to get a band together and trying to get some things happening."

In his desperation to establish himself as a leader in the field of playing vintage jazz, Waldo had not thought how his actions might have impacted upon Giordano, who would have had every right to resent Waldo's using Giordano's gigs for self-promotion. Was Giordano concerned that Waldo was a potential competitor?

"I think he was—although I wasn't," Waldo says. "Well,

after I gave back to him this music I had borrowed, he never called me again. And refused to talk to me. Except that if I had a concert or something like that, he'd call me and give me hell for using his stuff and stealing his musicians and ruining the music and this and that. And I'd say, 'Well, what do you want me to do, Vinnie? Curl up and die and quit playing?' And he said I used all of his musicians. I didn't. I mean, there's a pool of musicians in New York, and at the time, Peter Ecklund was not one of Vince's musicians, and Alden was not—and Alden got me trombonist Dan Barrett, who was not.

"And if I led a small band, even if I did use guys who had played with Vinnie, it would sound entirely different from his band. My philosophy basically is to let the guys do what they can do and take advantage of the talent you have in the band. When I do a stage show, like, I'll have Andy Stein do his duet thing with Howard Alden or whoever—a Venuti-Lang violin-and-guitar thing. And I'll try to let all the guys do solos and whatever kind of stuff that they do best. And that's where Vinnie and I differ philosophically. He likes to have the charts come first, basically. And I think the musicians come first—whatever you can create. I think when you're doing charts, if you're doing re-creations, you never get it right. You can get all the notes and it's still never as good as the original records. You're always copying and it's a different mindset. You're not creating spontaneously, you're not doing jazz. You have to do something that's already been done and you're doomed to not do it as well as the original recording.

"When I first moved to New York, I was dying here. I was going heavily into debt, which I still haven't come out of. I'm paying off old credit cards and things. Because I didn't know anybody here, except Vinnie. And I ended up not getting work with Vinnie—and Vinnie had so many gigs. I thought I was going to have that, at least, to keep me going financially. He cut off all that stuff!" Waldo exclaims, sounding almost as if he believed Giordano had an obligation to keep him employed. "And then I couldn't hire the musicians because the guys I would want were generally working with Vinnie, and I couldn't offer them enough work to get them to cancel a lot of gigs with him.

You know, there really aren't that many musicians that can do the stuff. There's maybe three drummers in the whole country that are just right for it. The same thing goes for all the musicians. There's not that many guys that make it really work.

"Vince thought I was stealing his musicians and out to take his territory. He wanted to own the Bix Beiderbecke bag and the rest of those kind of things. But I'm not doing the same things as he is. I don't want to have a society band. I'm not really interested in a big band other than using it for a stage show, which is what I've done. You know, I've tried to put in dancers. When I perform, I have Betsy Baytos, an eccentric dancer who's studied with all these old people, and Susan is singing some things, and I work with tap dancers. See, I think it's show biz. That's the way it was—you go back to the old Harlem shows, it was a full show. The songs that Duke Ellington did, they were written for show biz. They had dancers. That's the way jazz used to be—guys used to have a good time with it and it was entertainment; all that changed during the bop era.

"But Vinnie got real bitter towards me. I went out to a Kool Jazz Festival gig he was doing in New Jersey, and I sat down with him and I said, 'You know, we've been friends for too long to do this. This is silly.' And he says, 'No, you have your ideas and I have mine.' The fact that he believes in re-creating music note for note was a big part of it, I think. He told some people that I was ruining the music by not doing the copies of the records. But I was so hurt, I was having nightmares about it. Because I had felt so close to him and I felt like he was my ally. And then he wouldn't talk and he badmouthed me to every situation. And, you know, Vinnie had been part of the group that had taken away my band a few years earlier! I mean, when I had the Syncopaters and they started with Dapogny and so forth, Vinnie had been a part of that group. We were supposedly buddies but he never came to me and said, 'You know, we're doing these rehearsals.' So I decided he had a lot of balls to say that I was trying to steal his band, now." Waldo was so preoccupied with his own problems, he did not see how he might have contributed to the rift with Giordano.

"I'd still love to get together with Vinnie," Waldo says. "I think Vinnie and I could help each other. He's got so much knowledge about the music. And so he knows how to put the bands together. And he's got the music together and he's a great musician. And I think I could help him by giving him a freer— you know, creating stuff and doing original things, which would be very good for him.

"It's been rough working against him in a sense. He never tosses any work my way. If he was offered a job he couldn't make, he would never say, 'Call Terry Waldo.' I mean, after I hit New York, I eventually played a lot of places—the Village Gate, the Village Corner, Hanratty's, the Red Blazer, Michael's Pub, and so forth—but I was really scuffling for work."

Waldo was pleased when he was invited to conduct and perform in a concert of orchestral ragtime music at the prestigious Juilliard Music School with Juilliard students. The concert made a positive addition to his résumé; Juilliard was not a bad name to be able to drop. He was stunned when, a couple of years after giving the concert, he received an angry letter from someone at Juilliard stating: "I'd appreciate it if you would in the future kindly refrain from fraudulently affiliating yourself with the Juilliard School. . . ." To Waldo's horror, copies of the letter had also been sent to a major booking agency and other potential sources of employment for him. Waldo wrote back immediately: "I never claimed to have any affiliation of any kind with the Juilliard School. . . . I have said I once conducted a concert of ragtime music at Juilliard using Juilliard students. As you know, this was at your request. . . . My performance and scholarly credentials in this area are quite substantial. It would hardly benefit me to fraudulently claim to be connected with someone else's organization, and I haven't. I was shocked to receive out of the blue the fusillade of abuse contained in your letter. Similarly I was appalled that you would disseminate those charges so broadly without contacting me at all. If you would advise me of the 'who said what to whom' details of the charges, I'd be willing to help you deal with your problem in this area. If there are individuals to whom you would like me to send copies of your letter and this reply, I should be pleased to do so."

Waldo also telephoned the man from Juilliard who had written him, "and tried to get it settled on the phone, but he hung up on me." Waldo had never dreamed there could be so much pettiness and infighting in the music world. "I hit New York here and I couldn't believe it," he says, adding sarcastically, "I had a *wonderful* few years here when I hit New York."

Although Waldo's anecdotes often seem to accentuate the negative, stressing hard-luck experiences he's had, it should not be inferred that he lacked work for too long after arriving in New York. For as soon as word of his talents got around, he received plenty of job offers. And he created plenty of additional opportunities for himself. Unlike many musicians, when Waldo moved to New York, he never had to take a "day job" outside of the music world in order to pay bills.

Waldo has served quite effectively, for example, as pianist and musical director for various touring productions of Vernel Bagneris' hit show built around black jazz, blues, and vaudeville songs of the 1920s, *One Mo' Time*. (In fact, *The Newark Star Ledger's* Peggy McGlone, reviewing one production of that show, suggested [July 19, 1990] that perhaps its "biggest asset is musical director Terry Waldo, who leads the band from his place at the piano. Under his direction, the band performs the swirling arrangements of the Dixieland standards with a daring, fun-loving flair.") Waldo notes, "I've also worked with Vernel on a show about Jelly Roll Morton, *Mr. Jelly Lord*; Vernel took the dialogue from Morton's Library of Congress reminiscences. We did it as a workshop down at the Village Gate. I did the actual piano playing; he played a dummy piano, and also did some dancing and so forth. It was a wonderful piece. He was trying to get it launched as a regular off-Broadway production."

Waldo himself sought at one point to put together a show built around risqué old songs, which he thought would appeal to today's audiences. "The title of the show was *I Think I'll Shake That Thing*. But I've kind of abandoned it because there was so much of that kind of material in *One Mo' Time* and *Further Mo'*. My show wouldn't be as black oriented as those shows, although we'd probably have a couple black performers in it. I've also been working on a show called *Popcorn*, which is a history of corny popular music—novelty stuff. And the Warren G. Harding show is in very good shape now; Mack has 70% of the money to get it launched in a major way. We did a workshop at the Vineyard and it went over very well. We'd done a larger workshop, actually, back in 1976. We made it an all-black show since that time, and we're calling it *The Capitol Cakewalk*. The plan is to produce it in a major theater in Chicago. And then bring it into New York."

Waldo has served as pianist and musical director for assorted other cabaret and concert productions, ranging from a *Hoagy Carmichael Review* to *No Maps on My Taps*, featuring veteran tap dancers Sandman Sims, Bunny Briggs, and Steve Condos. He has recorded music for commercials, TV shows, and films. He wrote both songs and skits for Children's Television Workshop educational TV. While Waldo often seems, in his discourse, to focus on difficulties he has encountered in his career, there is no denying he has achieved considerable artistic success. Repeatedly he has surprised and impressed both critics and general audiences with his zesty renditions of numbers so old that they're new.

In a 1984 Kool Jazz Festival concert at Carnegie Recital Hall, for example, Waldo delighted in sharing Artie Matthew's five-part series of "pastime rags," which he noted accurately listeners were "not likely to hear anyplace else." With pleasant surprise, John S. Wilson wrote in *The New York Times* (July 1, 1984) that one of those obscure, World War I–era rags "actually sounds as though it might be the work of Thelonious Monk." Reviewing another Waldo Carnegie Recital Hall appearance six years later (June 4, 1990), *Times* critic Peter Watrous similarly expressed surprise at the sophistication of some vintage rags Waldo played. Although he classified Waldo as a "decent if erratic player" (because Waldo fumbled a few passages), he stated that Waldo's "use of dynamics, from a thumping left hand to breathless 10-note chords to whispered arpeggios, was revelatory, taking the compositions out of the realm of kitsch and Americana and putting them in the realm of music, where they belong."

Catching one of Waldo's small-band club engagements in 1989, I noted that having heard over the years so many Dixieland combos trivialize early New Orleans jazz, reducing it to one-dimensional, cheerily raucous music, it was refreshing to hear Waldo's band bring out the beauty in numbers like "New Orleans Stomp," "Why," and "Once in a While." Waldo's was the best New Orleans–ish group I had heard in New York in several years. His six conscientious, New York–based traditional-jazz players found not just joy but—and what a wonderful rarity this has become—also poignancy in the music. There was much to like in their little show—from the very sound of drummer Eddy Davis' vintage cymbals, to the tender interplay of Peter Ecklund's warm cornet (he has grown increasingly expressive in recent years) and Dan Barrett's trombone (first-rate in the idiom), while Orange Kellin added appropriate fills on clarinet.

That night (and on other appearances of Waldo's that I've seen lately), Waldo contributed primarily as a member of the band that he had organized; he did not try to steal the show as a soloist—which I found welcome since he had surrounded himself with such excellent musicians. In fact, he did not strike me as being the most impressive soloist that night; I took much greater notice of Barrett and Ecklund. And John S. Wilson, in *The Times* (December 4, 1989), gave particularly high praise to Kellin, whose clarinet, he felt, slashed "headlong through solos with a commanding presence that fills the room." But whether or not Waldo, as an instrumental soloist, was the band's star that night, it was very much his show. The band would not have been playing the music it played, had it not been for him, for Waldo has a knack for finding vintage music that isn't over-exposed—often offering it, these days, in brand-new arrangements, created by himself or members of the band, that have a genuine period feel. One could not accuse Waldo of copying his rendition of Jelly Roll Morton's little-known "Exit Gloom," for example, from any recording of it by Morton (although Waldo's treatment was appropriately Mortonesque)—for the very simple fact that "Exit Gloom" was never recorded by Morton! Or, for that matter, by anyone else until Waldo recorded it, first with a trio in 1980 and then with a septet in 1987. But Waldo is keeping it alive today, more than a half century after Morton's passing, along with Morton's rollicking "Good Old New York," his haunting, ahead-of-its-time "Freakish," and other wondrous ob-

Terry Waldo (courtesy of Terry Waldo).

*Terry Waldo's bands have included such musicians as (in the top photo) clarinet-
ist Joe Muranyi, cornetist Peter Ecklund, bassist Brian Nalepka, trombonist Joel
Helleny, banjoist Frank Vignola, and drummer Eddy Davis, as well as (in the
bottom photo) trombonist Dan Barrett, violinist Andy Stein, cornetists Peter
Ecklund and Randy Reinhart, banjoist Howard Alden, clarinetist Chuck Wilson,
and drummer Arnie Kinsella (courtesy of Terry Waldo).*

Susan LaMarche and Terry Waldo (courtesy of Terry Waldo).

This edition of Terry Waldo's Gutbucket Syncopators included Hal Davis, drums; Roy Tate, trumpet; Louise Anderson, tuba; Jim Snyder, trumpet; Waldo, piano; Eddy Davis, banjo; Frank Powers, clarinet; and Susan LaMarche, vocals (courtesy of Terry Waldo).

scurities that you hear and think should hardly be so obscure. He also does his part to keep alive the repertoire of Eubie Blake. How many other pianists are you likely to find who play, for example, Blake's "Stuyvesant Rag" (and with echoes of Blake's own performing style, no less)?

When Waldo works on his own, as a solo entertainer in a club or restaurant, he places heavier emphasis on his singing. And while his singing is by no means as distinguished as his playing, he gets by. His approach is casual and unaffected, his dry midwestern sound recalling, very faintly, Hoagy Carmichael. Curious, I ask Waldo who some of his favorite singers are.

The range is actually quite broad, he says. "Of the male singers, you've got to like Bing Crosby. I like Jolson, of course. My favorite pop singer has got to be Nat King Cole. But I mean, I like certain operatic singers and certain rock people; I came up with the Beatles and so forth, so I like all those people." Among female singers, he mentions: "Sophie Tucker, who was really wonderful—her '20s recordings especially—and, of course, Ethel Waters, Bessie Smith. A singer in the late '40s who made some gay '90s tunes, Beatrice Kay, was very good. Aside from that, I like all the great standard singers: Mildred Bailey, Billie Holiday, and all those people. Annette Hanshaw, who called Joe Franklin when she heard one of our recordings, with Susan singing one of the tunes she used to sing; we ended up talking to her on the phone. And of course we always liked the Boswell Sisters. And Jane Green. There were some other early singers, about the time of Jane Green, who recorded like 1918–19. Marion Harris—we've done some of her material, like 'I'm a Jazz Baby'—Nora Bayes, and Fanny Brice. Susan and I did an album where we did a lot of that earlier stuff." Waldo's familiarity with this material is a prime asset. While many singers are familiar with, and have revived, songs associated with Bessie Smith and Billie Holiday, few today are familiar with the work of such gifted, distinctive, but largely forgotten, early singers as Jane Green and Marion Harris.

The breadth of Waldo's interests may be inferred from the stage shows he occasionally has opportunities to mount. In 1987, for instance, he offered "Waldo's 1927 Revue" at Symphony

Space in New York. Not only did his Gotham City Band play old favorites like "Dinah" and "Tiger Rag," and Waldo himself play such familiar solo ragtime vehicles as "Twelfth Street Rag" and "Maple Leaf Rag," but Waldo also introduced "blues balladeer" Patty Holly (who sang "My Daddy Rocks Me with One Steady Roll," a sensuous reminder that folks were doing their own rockin' and rollin' back in the '20s) and self-styled vaudeville vocalist and ukulele player Danny Willis (whose tremulous voice, on "Singin' in the Rain" and "When My Sweetie Puts Her Lovin' On," sounded "eerily like a kazoo," according to reviewer Kevin Grubb of *The New York Native*). The high point of the show, from the audience's point of view, came when eccentric dancer Betsy Baytos, in a flapper dress, sang (in a Carol Channing–ish way) and danced through "Let's Misbehave" and "I Want to Be Bad." She drew an ovation so strong, Waldo asked aloud how he was ever going to be able to follow her—and then gamely forged onward through "The Burning of Rome," a five-minute-long period musical extravaganza, with thanks appropriately expressed to one Todd Robins for taking care of the "special sound effects" needed for a satisfactory Rome-burning. Clearly, Waldo's interests extend beyond an academic appreciation of vintage music. One could question his *taste* at times. (Did he seriously consider Willis a great singer? Or was he bringing him on for the novelty of it, pandering to the presumed interests of the audience?) Sticklers for accuracy might also question why something billed as a "1927 Revue" should have some songs that actually were from 1928 ("Let's Misbehave") and 1929 ("Singing in the Rain" and "I Want to Be Bad"). But Waldo was trying to have fun with the music, not give a strict history lesson. Maybe patrons did not leave the theater discussing the finer points of the music they had heard as they might after a serious concert, but at least one elderly couple broke into an impromptu Charleston under the marquee after the show. And if Waldo could get 'em to feel like dancing—he loves to dance himself—he figured he had done all right.

Keeping the fun in the music is important to him. Oh, it's nice to see ragtime played (with stately execution) by a serious-looking pianist in a concert hall; it means the music has received a stamp of approval from the Establishment. But Waldo knows the music had validity all along, before it was discovered by academic types. He doesn't want us to forget that ragtime was born in whorehouses; he doesn't feel that's something to be ashamed of, or that anyone is necessarily doing the music a favor by bringing it into the concert halls. For him, it's important that a bit of whorehouse spirit stay in the music. To early audiences, he notes, the connections between ragtime and jazz (or "jass" as it was first called) and sex were obvious.

"Yeah. You know, we've gotten away from that so much, and that may be one reason why we're not getting younger people as fans of this music. I think it's important to do it just like it's contemporary music," Waldo says. The rambunctious sexual energy that the best of ragtime and early jazz so often projected is lost in studied re-creations, Waldo believes. "And traditional jazz is a very physical music. When you're using acoustical instruments, it's a physical thing. You play it. I used to play tuba and you get inside this thing, you know, and it's wonderful. And the piano, you've got to beat the shit out of it and so forth. So it has all those qualities to it. The music is sexual. And physical. You know, in rock 'n' roll they certainly make that connection real heavy, but I think it's also true about jazz. And I've always tried to play that way. I've been called sleazy, raunchy, what have you!" He laughs freely now. "But I think—well, I've got a quote from Lu Watters [the trumpeter/bandleader who played a key role in launching the revival of interest in New Orleans–style hot jazz in the 1940s] where he says that playing jazz is like approaching a woman's pussy; some people do it the right way and some people don't.' And I say, yeah, it's like sex. I mean, it has all those elements about it."

Having a richly satisfactory sex life, Waldo believes, helps in achieving a richly satisfactory performing life, and like many of the early ragtime and jazz players he has admired, Waldo is quite candid in acknowledging his pursuit of both goals. His rather free ideas about sex, he notes, brought him into clashes with his family—particularly his businessman father. (Waldo absorbed a good bit of the counter-cultural values that were part of the youth movement of the '60s and early '70s.) In terms of values, he actually found himself more on the same wavelength with Eubie Blake, who was old enough to be his grandfather but was a free spirit, than with his father. In his personal life, Waldo saw himself as rebelling against conventional Establishment standards of his day. The early ragtime and jazz musicians he admired, he notes, had also lived lives that were rebellious compared to the straitlaced norms of bourgeois society in their day.

Living in Ohio, back in the '70s, Waldo recalls, "I was kind of a wild ass then. Boy, there were some wild times! I mean, you'd be standing on the street and some girl would come up to you and say, 'Where you going? Can I go with you?' Oh, it was incredible. And it was about the time Quaaludes hit Columbus, Ohio. They were introduced in Columbus, did you know that? 'Soapers'—that's what they called them in Columbus when they first came out in the early '70s. You know, the sexual revolution was not too long before then. I mean, I can remember having sex with three different women that I'd never had sex with before, in one day. It was just real loose at that time. Of course, I was younger then and there weren't so many diseases around. You could get by with all that. I'm not doing it these days; it's a more dangerous time. But I think the attitude about sex and being open to the sexuality and sensuality and physicality of the music is important. I mean, it shouldn't have a repressive feel about it." The basic idea that a good sex life contributes to a good performing life, Waldo believes, "is still true."

Waldo's comments, I tell him, make me think of comments I've heard from some of the oldest musicians I've known, such as pianist/bandleader Sam Wooding and saxist Benny Waters, whom I profiled in *Voices of the Jazz Age*. Both were in their 80s when I came to know them in the 1980s, and both spoke quite freely about sexual matters. Wooding, like a number of other musicians he knew, had even briefly been a pimp in his youth. Waters remembered going with fellow musicians to "sex circuses" in Harlem in the '20s; a fulfilling sex life, Waters believed, added life to his playing.

"They all talk about it," Waldo says of the older musicians and sex. "Well, Eubie Blake was talking about it. And Eubie Blake was having sex. He came to Columbus. And how old was he? 87, I think. And he'd been on a train all night and he comes in in the morning; the first thing he made me do is to take him over to visit his girlfriend he'd been dating on the sly for 55 years. And he was all the time—you know, he just loved it. He loved women! And that was very good, that attitude, to love women and to love sex and the idea of it—you know, really love. That's one thing I loved about Eubie. You know, you just love—genuinely *love*—women, and then sexuality is a part of it, and a healthy part of it. You don't see that in our culture much, an open embracing of people loving people. So that's always been a message I've had and it should come through in the music." The oldest musicians, Waldo found, all seemed to be open about, and positive towards, sex. "And that's the way I've always felt about it," he adds. "And that's one thing I don't like about rock 'n' roll. I think rock 'n' roll has an unhealthy attitude about sex, because for all its sexuality, it does not glorify sex and love. It's angry and it's looking down on women and it's using them as sex objects. And a lot of it's frustration—not getting it."

Waldo's attitudes towards drugs, like his attitudes towards sex, are generally more positive and accepting than those of most Americans. He sees both good and bad sides to drugs. For example, based on his experiences, he believes that audiences on grass rather than alcohol tend to be more open to the music. As for himself, he adds good-naturedly, "I used to smoke a lot of grass and I can't do it anymore. I guess in my old age I can't drink, I can't smoke grass, I can't do much of anything!" He laughs, but goes on, serious once again, to suggest that he sees connections between the types of drugs a musician will take and the music he will produce, offering some insightful observations. "Well, you can see the '60s, you know; there was certain music that was related to acid. And certain music that was related to marijuana—damned near everything at that time, including music that I was playing. We enjoyed marijuana. Oh, yeah! I was certainly doing a lot of marijuana at that time. Unlike Dan Quayle, I'll admit it! Marijuana had a positive effect. It had a negative effect, too. And I would say that I probably abused marijuana, as I did everything else. I probably abused sex—I was a sexaholic at one time. You know, doing marijuana—I got stoned every evening that I was playing. By the second break I'd get stoned. I can remember one time I sat down at the piano and the keyboard was rolling. It was like waves of keys that were moving up and down, and then I looked at it and it seemed like the keyboard was vertical. That was just from pot. It must have been pretty good pot, I guess! And I was sitting up there on stage trying to hold down the piano. There were so many people doing stuff.

"What's positive about using marijuana? Well, when you listen to music, it cuts down your inhibitions and you can really listen to music and also get into the physical aspects of it. That was probably one reason I might have been into the physical part of it. The marijuana really opened up all that. I mean all the reasons that the '60s were liberating I applied to traditional jazz and ragtime and stuff. That was my lifestyle, you know, and that's the way I approached it.

"I mean, hell, I don't think Louis Armstrong ever made a record when he wasn't stoned! It freed him up. I've done recordings on marijuana. Certain kinds of tunes are more interesting but other kinds of tunes where you have to concentrate— you can't concentrate on what you're doing. So it has that downside. I've made good recordings both ways, but I don't do it [smoke marijuana] anymore at all when I record. I've certainly played enough times when I was stoned and you really enjoy it. You think it sounds so wonderful at the time and it's really great. But you go back and listen to the records you've made and a lot of times they'll sound like shit."

The real downside to using marijuana, Waldo suggests, is that "it does accumulate in your brain cells and gives you a dull feeling and will keep you from accomplishing anything." But it *did* help him to become more creative, he feels. "It opened up certain things. And I did a little bit of acid, not many times, but some—you know, mushrooms and this and that, at times, and I'm glad I did. A little bit. But I also saw people that were just absolutely blown away, and so I mean there's a real downside to all that. And some people use all that stuff as a substitute for really facing their problems and getting their shit together, and that's the problem with it. And *some* people who do marijuana do it all the time and then really waste their lives," he notes. "I've seen people do that—and I can see myself doing that, and not really getting my shit together so I get focused and really accomplish things.

"But I'm dead set against the big deal they're making right now about marijuana. They're cracking down on some person that has a joint! If they're going to do that, then they ought to bust everybody that takes a drink because booze has certainly done more damage than marijuana. I don't listen to anybody who's a drinker, who speaks against drugs. If you drink or smoke cigarettes, which is the most addicting thing that you can do, you haven't a leg to stand on about accusing anybody about drugs. You know, there have been people who have used heroin all their lives in controlled ways, who have functioned entirely well and been very creative and so forth. If you listen to the bop guys, I mean they're starting to get into heroin. So that music has a different feel to it. It's *not* marijuana. Louis Armstrong and the old jazz people—that's marijuana. And then there's an alcoholic thing that becomes real depressing—bullshit Dixieland, you know: 'Let's hear the songs we've heard before.' I think a lot of that comes from alcohol. I don't have a lot good to say about alcohol. I don't know what music has really been great— although I guess Bix Beiderbecke and those guys were drinkers, too, weren't they? And a lot of the musicians have been. But for the most part, I haven't seen musicians inspired to creativity by alcohol. It tends to have a morose kind of effect eventually. It's a downer. But I know a lot of good music came out of marijuana in some sense. So I mean, you know those different drugs and you can understand the sound, how they're related.

"I don't know what good music has come out of crack. Coke dealers have been so prevalent in the music industry in recent years. And you used to see a lot of that. I worked with people who were doing coke and I did not like it. It did not seem to help. I'd be pretty much down on coke—you know, users start getting angry and surly, not really much good. I never got into coke, which always seemed to me to be so wasteful. Marijuana was the main one that I did."

I like Waldo's candor and openness in discussing sex and

drugs. His attitudes are much more liberal, I would suspect, than those of many of the mostly older listeners who support traditional jazz today. He agrees with that assessment, saying he's always been "a radical" in the field of traditional jazz.

Changing subjects, I ask Waldo how he thinks the revival music business is right now. Does it look like things are getting better or worse?

"For me it's been getting better—mostly because I have not really been connected with the mainstream of revival of this music," he responds. "But I think in general it's getting worse because most of the revival bands are amateurs who play Dixieland and the Lu Watters charts; you know, there are a lot of these festivals where they bring out the doctors and businessmen and so forth to play. I don't like most players of Dixieland, traditional jazz, and ragtime. It bores me."

And what does Waldo think of attending festivals that are made up almost entirely of amateur or semi-pro Dixieland bands?

"Oh, I hate it! I hate it," Waldo exclaims. "I like all kinds of music. And I like to hear the best of any particular style. I'll match my ragtime playing with anybody in the world. But I do a variety of stuff; I won't consider myself *strictly* a ragtime piano player. You know, I'll play different types of music, and I'll sing. I'm not *fanatical* about ragtime like most people who play ragtime.

"Most of the Dixieland being played these days isn't being played like *jazz*. I mean, between being codified and played the same way time after time, you know, through re-creating old records, and being played by the amateurs, there's not much left in the way of real jazz spirit."

For Waldo the key goals are to play the music with professionalism, with zest, and with creativity. To keep it lively and appealing. "You can see what I'm trying to do on my new album. I've got Leon Redbone singing on it. And I try to do arrangements that are fresh. I try to get the audience that likes Bugs Bunny cartoons. Because that music is jazz and vaudeville. So we're getting to the heart of where I'm really coming from right now. I'm trying to find ways to tap into that. Because I think there's a tremendous market for it. The people that know that stuff and know the Bugs Bunny and Betty Boop cartoons, and Fred Astaire movies and all those kinds of things—those are all jazz things. And, along those lines, I'm glad to see that Vince Giordano is working on an album of tunes from Laurel and Hardy movies, and I wish him every success; that's great stuff.

"Jazz, I feel, is at the heart of American pop music. That's what I aim for. And I strive to perform it in such a way that it's *entertaining*. That's the way it should be presented. It is not museum stuff. And it's not for amateurs. It's very complicated, sophisticated music that was at the real center of American pop music. And is still valid today. It's not sold that way. But I think that's the way you sell it."

How to sell the music he loves is an important question for Waldo. He is aware that most self-defined jazz fans today—who are apt to be into either bebop or so-called contemporary jazz— have little interest in, or knowledge of, the old-style music he plays. And that's a pity because Waldo offers plenty of terrific music—some of it predating jazz, some from the early years of jazz. And his music can be appreciated on more than one level. The casual listener can readily enjoy, for example, his piquant recording of "Some Sweet Day" (on the Musical Heritage Society CD *Waldo's Ragtime Orchestra: Ragtime Classics, Volume One*) for its innocent charm, much the way casual listeners enjoyed the Scott Joplin rags used as background music in *The Sting*. (And indeed, this kind of music would work wonderfully as film background music, if Waldo were ever fortunate enough to get a major film commission.) But the more sophisticated listener can appreciate Waldo's performance of that number on a deeper level. "Some Sweet Day" dates back to 1917, the year the first jazz recording was made; it stands, one might say, on the cusp between the so-called ragtime era and the Jazz Age. It was published as both a one-step (a dance popular in the ragtime era) and as a more "modern" fox-trot (favored in the Jazz Age). Waldo offers samplings of both of those ways of interpreting the music, taken from authentic period orchestrations, separated by a well-constructed piano solo in which he improvises, he notes, "in the tradition of the composer Tony Jackson." A good bit of musical history is packed into the less than three minutes of that recorded performance—history that very few performers other than Waldo could offer us. Waldo has also recorded that tune (on the album *Footlight Varieties*) in a new arrangement with a classic-jazz feel as a superb showcase for singer Susan LaMarche. She justifies Waldo's long-held faith in her, giving the lyrics an unhurried, sensual, and extremely fetching reading. Beautiful! That whole album, by the way, is testimony to the high standards of musicianship and creativity for which Waldo strives. While most of the numbers date back to the 'teens, '20s, or early '30s, the arrangements by Waldo and members of his band are all new. No performance is an "imitation" of any specific older one, and the soloists, including such laudable players as Dan Barrett, Howard Alden, Ken Peplowski, and Joe Muranyi, express themselves freely. (Economic realities mean that when Waldo gets a club booking, he cannot always hire musicians this good.) Listen to Barrett's swinging, offhand vocal and attractively aggressive trombone playing on "Just an Hour of Love"; he is showcased better on this Waldo recording than on most of his own! Leon Redbone's characteristically warm, engaging vocal on Jelly Roll Morton's "Good Old New York" works for present-day audiences, while connecting with Morton's own style of singing. One of the album's most intriguing numbers is a Waldo original with a hint of a revival-meeting feel, "The Wrong Side." Waldo preaches against hypocrisy, warning that, for example, greedy condominium developers who profit by throwing little guys out on the street, even if they make a show of going to church, are on "the wrong side, brother" (or, as he cleverly varies the phrase in other choruses: "You're on the wrong road, Rocky," and "You're going the wrong way, Corrigan"). The whole performance has a delicious old-time feel to it, yet we can hear in Waldo's warning that "cosmic justice" will catch up for those seeking "obscene wealth" echoes of idealistic, 1960s counter-culture. When I hear appealing Waldo originals like this, I have to wonder—as Waldo does—if he couldn't win a larger following if only he were given greater exposure, if only he had a major record company really pushing him.

"But, you know, I hit a lot of audiences anyway," he reflects. "My stuff is played on classical stations all over the country. I heard this guy on WQXR, the classical radio station owned by

The New York Times, and he says [Waldo goes into a stuffy voice]: 'Now we've just heard Terry Waldo's Ragtime Orchestra playing "Proctology" [a Waldo original]. And now we're going to hear Haydn's *Symphony Number 104*.' You know, it's great. He really did announce it on one of those things: 'Proctology.' And I've been on some of the traditional jazz shows on radio, and I've been on some mainstream jazz things—there are some jazz stations that play my music. But jazz is generally *not* where they put me. They never quite know what to do with me. And I don't quite fit in jazz festivals, either, although they like me. You know, [modern jazz pianist] Roland Hanna has been a fan of mine, and so forth; they all like me. Recently I've been doing cabarets and have gotten good reviews, but I'm not like the cabaret people either, because they have a whole different style. I'm introducing jazz and ragtime into these cabarets."

What else is Waldo up to these days?

"I'm traveling with Leon Redbone quite a bit. I'm going to be accompanying him to Europe. And I'm writing songs for him, and being music director for his stage shows. And I've got a bunch of new albums of my own that I'm working on. The one we've got coming out now is called *Footlight Varieties*. I've also recorded a forthcoming solo album. Musical Heritage is rereleasing a composite of Susan's things, from her albums. And I'm producing an album of Bob Wright's things and then I'm releasing a bunch of old Gutbucket Syncopaters albums—stuff from '71 and a whole bunch of unissued things. And I'm thinking about doing a New Age album, believe it or not. I'd play piano. I think the roots of the New Age thing come out of Bix Beiderbecke's 'Candlelight Suite' and Eastwood Lane and some of these early players. So I'd like to do 'the pioneers of New Age music' and I'd like to write some stuff myself. I've written some things that are sort of in that vein and I'd like to play with it. And then, next year, I'm supposed to produce a major show for the JVC Festival at a major venue called *Vaudeville Jazz*. And we'll have the Manhattan Rhythm Kings and hopefully I should have Leon Redbone, Doc Cheatham, and Carol Woods. Like that. So it would be stuff that would be popular." Waldo's always got a lot of projects ahead. A lot of dreams he hopes to realize.

"I've been talking to somebody who's trying to get me to CBS International. You know, I think I could be sold the way Harry Connick is," he says. The phenomenal popularity of Connick gives him encouragement. Who could have predicted that this new talent would come up—seemingly out of nowhere—and make a hit in 1990 with a song, "It Had to Be You," that was written in *1924*! Who could have dreamed that rock radio stations would be playing his music, and that young girls would be cheering for his big-band concert appearances? Connick's great commercial success reflected not just his undeniable talent (not to mention his youthful good looks), but also the effectiveness of Columbia Records' high-powered promotional abilities. What Waldo wouldn't give to be hyped so well. He has to wonder: couldn't the young fans who bought Connick's record of "It Had to Be You"—most of whom probably had no idea exactly how old that song was—find some of the old songs Waldo loves just as appealing if they were repeatedly exposed to them?

"I mean, there's a world of material," Waldo notes. "So I'm trying to find some record label that would go along with publicity. And I've got the people who represent the Duke Ellington estate, you know, lawyers and so forth. And they said to me, 'Gee, everybody loves your music. But we don't know what to do with it. Should it be with a jazz label?' And I said, 'I don't think so. Just straight-out pop music is the way to go. Market it like Harry Connick. Just put it out there!'"

1990

Sentimental About the Syndicate

"If you ask me if I would work for the Mafia tomorrow—absolutely. It's the best work I ever had. When I worked for them, they never cared if the cash register rang or not; that wasn't my responsibility. They only cared that I had a good show, a good clean show, that I did things on time," recalls Eddy Davis.

The banjoist/composer/arranger got his first important break at age 20, when a Chicago mob boss took him under his wing and made him a house bandleader at a mob-controlled club. Davis spent most of the '60s working in such clubs. The Chicago Mafia, or Syndicate—Davis uses the terms interchangeably— was grooming him for bigger things in show business. When Davis eventually concluded that they wanted to take excessive control of his career, he parted amicably with them—a decision he sometimes regrets. He is certain he could have attained greater fame and fortune had he let the Mafia control him, but he doubts if he would have had as much artistic satisfaction.

Davis has always relished doing diverse things in music, without necessarily worrying how financially remunerative all of his efforts might be, or how they might advance his career. Although he is very well paid for playing banjo on commercials (like those for "All" and "Wendy's"), Davis gets a bigger kick out of playing and singing old pop songs and novelty numbers—

for next to no money—every week at a New York club called the Cajun. He is happy singing and playing, too, every week in Woody Allen's New Orleans–style jazz band, and periodically puts together shows of his own, celebrating early jazz, ragtime, and Tin Pan Alley numbers. While Davis may be most accomplished as a player of the banjo, he has also played string bass in Las Vegas, sax in Disneyland, and drums for Vince Giordano's Nighthawks. You can hear him playing an old metal guitar on the soundtrack of *Fried Green Tomatoes*. He orchestrated and conducted the theme to the television series *Mr. Belvedere*. He has written a fair number of songs, served as musical director for a few stage musicals, and once put together a successful club act called "Banjos Unlimited," which mixed comedy and music, and in which he and a couple of other versatile banjo players doubled on a mind-boggling total of 28 different instruments. If his career has not exactly been focused, it has been fun. When I called upon Davis at his apartment by Carnegie Hall, he was in the process of tuning a set of cowbells for a Spike Jones–type band he leads from time to time. One question on my mind was where Davis developed such remarkable and unusual versatility. But to Davis, his versatility doesn't seem remarkable. To explain why, he took me back to his Indiana boyhood.

"When I was just a little kid, on my mother's side there was a family band. They would go around to various radio stations—not just in Indiana, but also in Ohio and Illinois—performing on all of the farm reports that they had back then in the '40s. They played tunes like 'Avalon' and 'Darktown Strutters Ball,' but with things like fiddles, saxophones, mandolins, banjos, a piano—it was sort of like a jazz band, but it wasn't," Davis recalls. "And I was always amazed because in that family band, nobody seemed to own any specific instrument. One day I'd see them play and this guy would be on mandolin, but the next time he might be on piano or something else. He'd tell me, 'It doesn't matter what instrument I play.' They'd play anything that was in their hands."

Davis soon was doing likewise. In his youth, he picked up one instrument after another: mandolin, string bass, drums, tuba, sax, and more—all before he picked up the instrument for which he is best known today: the banjo. By his teens, a local music store hired him as its instructor in bass and brass instruments.

Davis' early indoctrination into music came from more than just exposure to that family band. "You see, my folks had records. We had things like the original 78s of 'Hyena Stomp' and 'Billy Goat Stomp,'" he recalls, naming some Jelly Roll Morton jazz sides from 1927. "As a little kid, I used to go around going 'baaaaa,' because of those records. I thought everybody did that; I thought everybody had those records! And my folks had all the Mildred Bailey records and all of that kind of stuff. They also had some of Johnny Bond, who had like a small, country-western swing band, with a trumpet, a clarinet and harmonica player and things like that. He did a lot of things that I do now with Stanley's Washboard Kings at the Cajun, like 'I Like My Chicken Frying Size When I Put It in the Frying Pan.' At age five or six, I used to walk around singing, 'I like my chicken. . . .'

"I was born in 1940, at home—not in a hospital—in a little town called Greenhill, Indiana, that had 26 people in it. The roads going to the town were unpaved; only the mile-long stretch of road through the town itself had been paved. Eventually we moved into Lafayette, Indiana.

"I got to hear all the big bands at a lake just north of Lafayette—a place with a boardwalk, called Ideal Beach when I was a kid; it's called Indiana Beach today. At the end of the boardwalk, they had an open-air bandshell with a dance floor out over the water. What a great sound that was, when the bands would play in there and the music would go across the water! All the bands would come through, because that was a stopover on their way to Chicago. I'd see Ellington twice a year, Louis Armstrong two or three times a year. As kids, we'd stand behind the bandshell—and we'd annoy the musicians, trying to talk to them before or after the gig. As a kid, I remember going back and talking with Ray Nance and Sam Woodyard of the Ellington Band. I noticed Woodyard's white shirt was inside-out. I said, 'Gee, Sam, do you know your shirt's inside-out?' He said, 'Sure, boy. We don't get to the cleaners very often. So some of us buy a white shirt once a week. The first half of the week, we wear it the right way. When it gets dirty, we turn it inside out and wear it the rest of the week that way, then throw it away and buy a new one.' And Ray Nance would talk with us, too. Many years later, when I came to New York, I got to play with Ray Nance at the Copa, which I really enjoyed. I was standing there sort of with my mouth open, you know, thinking: 'what am I doing here, standing alongside this man I remember from when I was a kid?'

"Then when I was in high school, we had a band teacher named R. W. Rowles, who had written 'Burst of Flame' and several famous concert band marches. He decided to offer a music theory class, which was unheard-of in high schools. I wanted it, and found that music theory came natural to me. And by my third week in that course, I was writing arrangements for a little dance band I was playing drums in.

"When I was like 16, I got a job playing second tenor in a tenor band—these were common in the midwest for some reason—which had one trumpet, one trombone, a rhythm section, and three tenor saxophones. No other kinds of saxophone—that's why they called it a tenor band. And we'd go around the region, playing three or four nights a week in the midwest. I was still going to school in the daytime, of course. I was getting like $12.38 a night, playing in this band. And I said, 'This doesn't make it.'

"Lafayette was home to Purdue University, where they had a Dixieland band called the Salty Dogs, and when I heard that band in 1956, I said, 'Boy, I like this music!' The leaders of the band at the time were two guys who had graduated from Jefferson High School: Jim Snyder, who'd later go on to play with Terry Waldo's Gutbacket Syncopaters and the South Frisco Jazz Band, and John Cooper. They told me there was an opening in the band for a banjo player. So I bought a banjo and took lessons from Smilin' Jimmy Wilson. Besides giving music lessons, Smilin' Jimmy worked as a fireman, and—using his banjo, harmonica, mandolin, and guitar—he also would sing and play and do the farm reports on the radio in the morning.

"My senior year in high school, I played with the Salty Dogs;

EDDY DAVIS

the other members were students at Purdue. We'd play at all
different colleges in the midwest, often opening shows for touring acts including the Four Freshmen, the Kingston Trio, George
Shearing, Bob Newhart, Jonathan Winters, and Shelly Berman.
For me, the incentive was that being in the Salty Dogs paid at
least $50—and quite often $100 to $150—for one night's work,
compared to the $12.38 I'd been making with that other band.
We were playing pretty commercial Dixieland—'Mama Don't
Allow' and stuff like that. The Salty Dogs band, back then, was
sort of a crossover between poor Dixieland and Turk Murphy or
the Lu Watters Yerba Buena Band.

"After high school, I enrolled in Purdue so I could keep
playing with the band, but I soon realized I didn't like it and
went to a conservatory instead. I was thinking, 'I don't know
what I'm going to do for life, and I'll do this until I decide.' I'm
still sitting here trying to decide!" Davis adds with a laugh. "I
went first to the Cosmopolitan Conservatory in Chicago, then to
Chicago Conservatory, studying music theory and composition
with the best teachers." One reason Davis continued taking music courses over a span of eight long years was that being a
student saved him from being drafted. His studies did not inter-
fere with his career, which—thanks to his technical excellence as
a banjo player, superior knowledge of old tunes, and gregarious
personality—quickly flourished. And he learned at least as much
from the people he met in the Chicago club world as he did in
any classroom.

"I worked with George Brunis at many places. He didn't
take himself too seriously, didn't think he was making musical
history; he was just out to have fun. Sometimes I think we
need that as a slogan today: 'Put the fun back into jazz.' And I
remember, one night I looked around the band and there were
Al Wynn, Junie Cobb, Darnell Howard, Brunis—God, it was a
whole band like that," Davis recalls, naming jazzmen whose
careers dated back to at least the 1920s, and who had played
with the likes of King Oliver, Jimmie Noone, W. C. Handy, Ma
Rainey, and the New Orleans Rhythm Kings. "I just looked
around and I said, 'Jesus! Look who I'm sitting here with!' It was
the last of those days when the guys were all still around doing

77

their thing. But you know, I also saw that those guys were damned poor. They were trying to find their next meal at that point." Just being able to play traditional jazz well, Davis realized, did not ensure one would make a good living. He didn't want to wind up like so many of the older players he met, scuffling for any jobs he could get. He figured he could expand his options by writing, rather than just playing, music; by establishing himself as an entertainer, not just an instrumentalist; and by staying on the good side of those who were in a position to offer work. In Chicago, to a large extent, that meant the Syndicate.

"The guy that ran the Syndicate was called Joe the Jap. That's what he was known by in the area. His real name was Ken Ito, but very few people knew that. Joe kind of took me under his wing. I was like 20 years old when I first started playing for him," Davis recalls. He was thrilled to be hired to lead a band five nights a week at a club called Bourbon Street, which was the base of the popular Dixieland bandleader/trumpeter Bob Scobey.

"And let me tell you, Chicago really had a lot musically going on in the '60s when I was there. That scene is gone now. The majority of all the nightclubs back then were in a strip four to five blocks long in the Near North Side. They put the Playboy Club and the Gaslight Club in there, too. All the rest of the clubs were basically Mafia clubs with the exception of Mr. Kelly's, which brought in acts like Jack Jones, Barbra Streisand, and Woody Allen; the London House, which brought in Oscar Peterson, among other jazz players; and the Happy Medium.

"They don't seem to have done it here in New York, but in Chicago, every group of the Syndicate, when they put in a new club, tried to outdo every other club that was in town. And they would have the most gorgeous clubs. This one I played in had angling mirrors all the way across the top of the bandstand. The bandstand had four different pyramids on it. They sat me in a little gold-fringed chair up on the top. The drummer was up on a pyramid that was like six feet high. The clubs were unbelievably beautiful. So the Syndicate clubs were really the ones to play.

Because they were the ones that really had the nightclub lifestyle going for you.

"I started playing for the Syndicate because when Bob Scobey got ill, they wanted to bring somebody in to play opposite Bob. So they called me—because I was brash and young and entertaining—and I brought a band in that played opposite his." Scobey (1916–63) had gotten his start in the '40s as the lead horn in Lu Watters' Yerba Buena Jazz Band; he had been, along with Watters and Turk Murphy, one of the key players in the West Coast traditional jazz revivalist movement. To traditional jazz fans in the early '60s, Bourbon Street may have been perceived as Scobey's club. But as Davis got to know Scobey well, he realized the extent to which the Syndicate was actually calling the shots. He saw, for example, the Syndicate wouldn't let Scobey use a particular musician, and later they made him hire another musician he didn't want. "You see, they had told this clarinet player for some reason that if he ever needed a job they'd give him one. So when he came back to Chicago out of nowhere without money, they just put him to work. That's the kind of stuff the Syndicate does."

Of course, Davis also heard stories of *other* kinds of stuff the Syndicate did, which sometimes scared him. He wanted to get along well with the Syndicate—everyone treated him great—without being sucked into it. The better he came to understand Scobey's situation, though, the more concerned he became.

"In the late 1950s, Bob Scobey and his band had been traveling with the Harlem Globetrotters. When they weren't touring, Scobey would either be dropped off in Las Vegas or somewhere—but it was always hooked with the Syndicate. Then Scobey decided he wanted to stay in Chicago because he liked the Chicago mob. All through Scobey's life, he always flirted with the Mafia. He loved to be a part of it. He loved to stand up there and act like he had a gun on his hip and all that kind of stuff. In Chicago, he worked first in a club called Basin Street. Then he told the mob he wanted his own club and they set him up in Bourbon Street. They built up this club called Bourbon Street, around the corner from Basin Street, to be his club.

"Scobey had this love affair with the mob. And there are two different types of people that the Syndicate deals with—that type and the type that keeps their hands clean. They like both types. But they respect people that keep their hands clean. The other type of people they use. This was explained to me because I told Joe the Jap one day, 'I've heard all these stories, you know, and I'm really frightened.' He assured me, 'Listen, Eddy, I like you. I think you have great possibilities. I see a lot that we can do with you. We want to keep you clean. Most of these entertainers and people that we work with, we want to keep clean as long as they keep their noses clean. The other type person we use is like Bob, because Bob really wanted to be a part of what was going on.' So he took me to a room and opened it up, and it was all full of boxes. And the boxes were filled with race-track stubs, because Bob and his band loved to play the horses. So when Bob got ill with stomach cancer, the Mafia let him play the horses all he wanted on their money. It didn't matter, because he was part of the group. That's how the Mafia, that's how the Syndicate, takes care of their own. So they sent him everywhere.

"And Joe told me, 'Bob owed us. Don't get into us, Eddy. If you need $5,000 or $10,000 or $20,000 and you come to us and ask for it, you'll probably get it, Eddy, no questions asked, and you may never hear from us again. But if a year from now, 10 years from now, 20 years from now, we ask you to be at a certain corner and do a certain thing, you'd better be there. Because you've gotten your nose into something. So keep your nose clean and there's no problem. We need entertainment people. We need these full clubs to launder the money out of and to do all this different stuff, so we need legitimate people who work with us. We can use their name because their names are clean. Different things. . . .'"

Joe the Jap also explained to Davis how they had dealt with one well-known entertainer (whose name cannot be used here) who had gotten obligated to the Mafia. "Joe told told me, 'He's come to our table to gamble so often in Vegas and different places that he could never in a million years pay us back all the money he owes us. So what do we do, bump him off? No. We went to him and said, "Do us a favor. From now on, for the rest of your life, you work for our clubs. We'll give you a thousand dollars a week pocket money. You stay at all the places free and sign. You eat and you sign. Gamble all you want, and make a big deal about it, so everybody sees that you're gambling. You don't ever spend one dime of your thousand dollars gambling. You spend our money. What you win, put in your pocket and take home with you. What you lose, forget about it; sign the chit and go on. But you'll work for us the rest of your life." Well, he took that deal, and he has been working in Vegas and other places for us.'

"The Syndicate took care of Scobey. When he got stomach cancer, they sent him to the Mayo Clinic and everywhere else and picked up the tab. Now cornetist Ernie Carson has a theory that the Syndicate killed him. Well, maybe this is true and I'll tell you why. They had sent Scobey everywhere. He was not going to get well; they knew he was dying. Towards the end, he would come in no more than two or three times a week—and even then, he'd be too ill to play, and was just creating problems. His band was falling apart. The Syndicate had taken up all of Scobey's bills and he was now becoming a burden on them, and he was also doing all this silly shit like leaving his wife to run after someone else, and all sorts of other things the Syndicate doesn't like. They're big on family. So perhaps they did kill him, because they had enough of his silliness and he was going to die anyway. All I know is, all of a sudden he was dead.

"If they *did* kill him, that wouldn't have scared me, though," Davis adds. "Because I understand that. I understand the logic behind that. I just didn't want to get involved to the point where the Syndicate had me. I mean, you see all those movies where they slit your throat and stuff—but that situation basically is not there unless you create it. Joe told me, 'Don't worry, Eddy, I'll pay attention to you. You got any problems, you come to me.'"

Davis tested the situation and found Joe the Jap's word to be good. When, for example, the doorman at the club gave Davis some grief for ending a set a couple of minutes early, he merely mentioned he was having a problem; the next day, the doorman was nervously apologetic, saying he didn't know his place. But with most matters, Davis found, the higher-ups simply didn't want to get involved. "The deal was, 'The music department is your department. You take care of it. We don't want to know what's going on.' Like, for example, Jerry Coleman, the drummer, started getting into a row with the doorman that went on night after night. I got called into the office. They told me to take care of my drummer.

"I started to say, 'Well, yeah, but the problem is. . . .' They said, 'Hold it. The music department is your department. Now you're not running your department. If you were, then the discussion between your drummer and this doorman would not be going on. We'll take care of the doorman. You take care of your drummer.' When you went into the office, there was a handwritten thing on the wall listing that for $75 you could get an arm broken, for $150 you could get an arm and a leg broken. Oh, it listed the prices for two arms, two legs . . . all the way down to murder, which cost only a thousand bucks. I was amazed; a thousand bucks was not a lot to get somebody wiped out. This was all right there in plain sight, to test you—to see that you didn't tell anybody—and to keep you in line. So anyway they told me, 'If you're not going to handle your business and you would like to have your drummer's legs broken, then you just let it go on. You want your drummer's legs broken?' I said, 'No, no, no! I'll handle it, I'll handle it.'

"I went back to Jerry and I said, 'I don't care what the problem is. You will stop or I will fire you immediately. Because I've been warned that your legs may be broken and I do not want that to be my responsibility.' Jerry said, 'They won't break my legs.' I said, 'I am not taking the responsibility. If you don't tell me it's over, and you don't go out there in front of the people and shake hands with that doorman right now, then I'm firing you.' He went out and shook hands with the guy. Chicago was as colorful as it could be."

Davis had reason to be concerned about the Mafia because he had a notoriously short fuse. He knows how temperamental he sounded at times because someone taped his outbursts. One night, after some people in the audience popped helium balloons that the club had put up, Davis chewed out the audience for 10 relentless minutes. Afterwards, realizing that he had gone way overboard, he worried that the Syndicate—which demanded that he deliver a professional show *with no problems*—might break his arms to teach him a lesson. However, the only request he got from above was: "Eddy, could you please not say 'bullshit' on the microphone?" Davis gruffly agreed.

Such occasional flare-ups aside, Davis had a good way with an audience. His self-confidence was appealing, his enthusiasm for the old-time music was contagious. And as a singer, he exhibited raw potential. In terms of phrasing, he hadn't developed any real style (he still hasn't), but his voice was pleasingly hearty, his intonation and enunciation were excellent, and his sheer gusto helped put a song across. Joe the Jap told him his personality, rather than his musicianship per se, was his real asset. And that he could be a real star someday.

"The Syndicate also taught me the idea of association," Davis recalls. "They said, 'Davis, you want to get your name bigger? Well, Eddy, association is the answer. In the field you're in, Louis Armstrong and the Dukes of Dixieland are the ones that are popular right now. We'll bring the Dukes of Dixieland in to play opposite your band for six months because they're known.' So they brought them in, and it was continuous music—us for an hour, the Dukes for an hour, us for an hour—from nine o'clock at night until three in the morning. Chicago was a late-night town in those days; it was really something.

"Then there were some test periods. I mean, the Syndicate would test you to see how much you might squeal and so on. For example, when they laundered money from one club through another, sometimes they wouldn't pay off on that first club for a long while. And all the money would be going through the other club. And they wouldn't do anything with the first club for a while. Eventually, after they'd sent all the money out the way they wanted, then the money would funnel back through and come over here. And I knew that. Well, my band was there by the week; the musicians got a weekly salary. But at one point, the Syndicate guys said to me, 'Can you handle payroll next week?' I said, 'Yeah.' But then this went on for six weeks or seven weeks; they were not paying me anything and they were asking me to handle my own payroll, to pay my own people, week after week. So I paid the members of my band even though I was not getting paid in that particular period.

"Well, they were doing the same thing to the Dukes of Dixieland at this time—testing them, too. Frankie Assunto, who ran the Dukes, was saying to me, 'We've got to go to the union, we've got to get a lawyer, we've got to get our money!' I said, 'Leave me out of this.' He was raising all kinds of hell. But, you know, that's what the Syndicate wanted to see, how much hell would be raised—how much you trusted them, how much you were 'in' with them. I finally went to them after about six weeks because I literally couldn't make the payroll anymore. I said, 'Listen, I'll have to take the band out this week because I can't make the payroll this week.' Well, I got all the money I was owed the next day. But the Dukes of Dixieland didn't. The Syndicate put the pressure on Frankie awhile longer because he was yelling and screaming. There were the different tests to see if you would go along with them. Whether you wanted to make trouble, what you wanted to do. But you've got to get hip to all that stuff, and you have to have a bit of trust because that's what they work on," Davis says. The Syndicate liked that Davis cooperated.

"I had a lot going back then. Besides the club work, I was also doing things like producing the jazz series on the West Side of Chicago at a ski lodge. And I wrote a lot of songs. The club Mr. Kelly's was a block up from this Bourbon Street club where my band was. I got to know all the acts who worked at Mr. Kelly's. So I got songs to Jack Jones and all these people, who'd perform them. The Village Stompers recorded a couple of my originals, including 'Penny Candy.' So that's what I was into in Chicago, aside from having this jazz band with the best players that I could find, like drummer Kansas Fields, trumpeter Norman Murphy, bassist Truck Parham."

Meanwhile, the Syndicate was helping build up Davis' name, grooming him for bigger things. "At least two to three times a week my name and picture were in the newspapers," Davis recalls. He was doing well financially, too. There weren't many jazz musicians his age driving an Excaliber automobile like he was. "In Chicago in the '60s, I was the big boy. I was the musician around town. But then the Syndicate told me, 'We don't want you in this field—making music in clubs. We want you to be on television. That's where the money is going to be. We want you to be a talk-show host.' And they wanted to take charge of my whole career. Had I signed with them, they probably would have taken the banjo away from me, too, and have had me sing more. Because they liked my singing better than they liked my banjo playing. They'd say, 'What does this kid want to play the banjo for? He's a good singer. He's this, he's the other thing. . . .' But I was very much into music. So the Syndicate's plan to make me into some kind of a personality for television didn't appeal to me. I'll tell you just how this all happened.

"You know, they liked putting things together, and they used different people for front men. Well, they had a guy named Tony Jacobs,[1] who had a place called the Tony Jacobs Show Lounge. It wasn't his club, actually; he just fronted it for the Mafia. And Tony handled all of their contracts; part of his department was to sign up new artists. So one day he came around with this contract and said to me, 'Sign this, kid.' I said, 'Wait a minute.' He said, 'Sign it, sign it, sign it.' So I started reading it. It was seven years, with two options on their side of seven years, for a total of 21 years. I mean, the option to renew the contract would be theirs, not mine. They would start out by giving me $450 in my pocket, as my spending money. Even if they decided after a week that it wasn't going to work out, I would still get my $450 a week for seven years. And $450 was good money in those days—for pocket money especially. They'd also pick up my apartment, they'd pick up my car, they'd pick up everything else. They'd send me to the tailors that they had, and choose all of the pictures for me and all that. I would just start signing for everything. As I got more famous, they'd give me better apartments and better cars because they want their artists to be seen doing well. I would still get my $450 until I reached the end of the first seven years, and then—if they exercised the option to renew the contract—I would get more pocket money. The contract also stipulated things like: they would then tell me what

[1]The name has been changed for legal reasons.

85

venues I performed at, they would tell me how I dressed, they would tell me what musicians were on my band, they would tell me what kind of music I played—*if* I played music. That was all theirs to decide. It was all laid out to me. And all of that scared me! I mean, at the time, in addition to playing, I was also writing a lot of music—I thought I was going to be greater than Cole Porter—and I really wanted to be in music. So I kept fighting this contract. I kept saying, 'What do I want to be a talk show host for? What do I want to be in TV for?' Little did I know!

"And I said to them, 'How do you know you can make me a star?' They told me, 'Oh kid, you're so stupid. Stars are made, they're not born.' We were having this talk in Chicago, right? Well, he mentioned they could get me into the Copa or the Latin Quarter in New York, or the Copa in L.A., or into other clubs in Puerto Rico, Florida, and Las Vegas. He said, 'There are clubs all over that are associated. They are like a chain. What it is is, different people owe us different favors because we've given them favors. So they give us favors back. So, say the Copa in New York owes us a favor. Now that favor doesn't mean that they'd pay your salary, Eddy. The favor doesn't mean anything other than that they owe us a favor. We will pay *them* to take you.' Yes, the Syndicate would pay the Copa to take *me*—and they would also pay me and my musicians to play the Copa. The deal was that the Copa would give them the space. And say Sinatra was headlining at the Copa at the time; the deal was that my name would go up there on the marquee in small letters. And I'd go out and do my little thing, and Sinatra would have to come out and put his arm around me and say, 'Is that kid great? I think we're going to be seeing a lot more of him. He's going to be the up and coming. . . .' Boom boom boom. Then I'd be booked with another artist and the same thing would happen. Your name gets a little bigger each time. The people get used to seeing your name on the marquee, get used to seeing you around; they know you're the up and coming thing. Pretty soon your name is up there in big letters; you're on top. All of this was explained to me.

"Tony Jacobs, their front man, insisted, 'You've got to sign this contract.' I went to Joe the Jap and I said, 'Joe, I've got a problem. I really want to be a musician.' He warned me, saying, 'Eddy, you may get self-satisfaction out of that, but music is not the direction to go. For you, you're a personality. A personality is the way to go. And I'm really the one behind this. I really want you to sign this contract.' And I said, 'Jeez, I just don't know. Tony is giving me a lot of pressure.' So Joe said, 'All right, I'll tell him to stop pressuring you for a while.'

"But, you know, they were right; I should have stuck with them, and gone into television. Probably I would have been good at it, too, because I love to talk!" Davis says.

"Let me digress for a moment to tell you what became of Joe the Jap. Years later, when I was on tour with Leon Redbone, I was in Johnson City, Tennessee, and I flipped on the TV, and there's some guy with a hood on his head giving government evidence. They explained on the TV that, while sitting in the front seat of his car, this man had been shot by gunmen who had been hiding in the back. Then they had left him for dead—not realizing he had survived the shooting. A couple of weeks after that, those two gunmen were found stuffed in a trunk; he had had *them* killed off for having tried to kill him. And when they said on the TV that this man who had been shot at—*Ken Ito*—was now turning state's evidence, I said, 'Son of a bitch! That's Joe the Jap. He was the head man of all that was going on in Chicago when I was there.' Somebody had put a hit on him, somewhere along the line," Davis recalls.

"Meanwhile, I should mention, I got another interesting offer back while I was in Chicago. I became buddies with trumpeter Don Goldie, and he was being booked then by Joe Glaser—who, of course, managed Louis Armstrong. Well, even though Louis' hit record of 'Hello Dolly' featured banjo playing, Louis had been playing the tune on the road without a banjo. So Goldie told Glaser, 'I've got just the guy for you to put into Louis Armstrong's All-Stars on banjo and guitar: Eddy Davis. . . .'

"Soon Goldie was telling me, 'Davis, I've got it all set up with Joe Glaser now. You're going to go on the road with Louis Armstrong!' But all I could say was, 'Oh shit.' You see, I was draft eligible. The only thing that was keeping me out of the draft then was that I had a student deferment because I was still in music school. If I dropped the student deferment to go with Armstrong, they'd soon draft me. So I talked with Joe the Jap, saying, 'What do I do? I really want to go with Armstrong. This is the thrill of a lifetime.' But Joe only said, 'Well, I don't know, kid. Stay where you are. Don't make waves.' So I said to myself, 'Well, I'd better stay where I am.' Of course Joe the Jap wanted me to stay there. I told Goldie, 'I can't.' Now Joe Muranyi, who played clarinet in the All-Stars, says that Glaser was connected enough that if I would have told Glaser, he could have gotten my draft thing straightened out. I guess Glaser was total Mafia and total connected everywhere.

"You know, the offer by the Syndicate to groom me for television and the offer to become a member of Louis Armstrong's All-Stars are the two things that I'll always look back at and say, 'Jesus, Eddy, you should have just thrown everything to the wind and gone. . . .'" Davis' voice betrays his regret.

"When I finally decided to leave Chicago, the Syndicate guys said, 'Well listen, Eddy, have a good life and enjoy yourself. If you ever get to the point where there's nothing else for you and you need some work, come back and we'll put you somewhere.' And they would do that, you know," Davis says. But it never proved necessary to return to Chicago. He had finished his eight years of music school (four years majoring in theory, four years majoring in composition), and was eager to see more of the world.

After working for a while in California and Las Vegas, Davis made New York his base, often spending his summers in the 1970s in Italy. He initially went to Italy in a band led by Gianpaolo Biaggi, which he remembers chiefly because it included a 19-year-old bass player named Vince Giordano, who became a good friend; in subsequent summers, Davis led his own band there. When Giordano formed his Nighthawks Orchestra, Davis served for several years as drummer and occasional vocalist. He took no money for the work; to help each other out, he and Giordano agreed to play in each other's bands for free whenever possible. "I love singing with Vinnie's band, although he didn't let me sing many songs. But one was 'Stardust,' which I sang in sort of a Jo Stafford style."

There were always new projects to take on. "In 1976, I was involved with Terry Waldo's show *Warren G.*, which Tom O'Horgan directed. We rehearsed it for six weeks and we performed it for four weeks at the Juilliard theater. A lot of money went into it. Waldo's father, who is wealthy from insurance, put up a lot of money himself. I did all the orchestrations and also conducted Waldo's show—and that was a bitch. I'll never again write orchestrations and conduct at the same time. Because when they'd cut the show in the afternoon, I'd have to write the parts and conduct the revised score that night. And oh God, it was really a workhorse thing. After that, I conducted the national company of *Whoopee*."

As much as he liked working on other people's projects, though, he preferred devising his own projects, usually dealing with the roots of American jazz and popular music.

"I did shows at Michael's Pub, leading my own New York Jazz Repertory Ensemble. For example, for our 'Turn of the Century Minstrels' show, which ran for 10 weeks, I got very early pieces from Vinnie Giordano's library—music from before the period his band dealt with. I wanted music from before 1921; Vinnie prefers music from after that. So he had a bin of very early stuff he'd collected, and I picked out things that aren't really jazz and that aren't strictly ragtime—because other musicians, like Terry Waldo, had already put together ragtime orchestras. So I found tangos, waltzes, Indian intermezzos, lyrical ballads like 'Roses of Picardy,' and so on. And then I put together a tea-dance orchestra to play these numbers, with Steve Hanson, who could play string bass, tuba, flute, trombone, and euphonium; J. J. Silva, who played all the saxophones, the flute and piccolo and all the other stuff; and Orange Kellin, my good buddy, got the clarinet chair.' Peter Ecklund said, 'Gee, I'd like to be a part of that,' and I was glad to bring him in on trumpet. Peter had just gotten his start in town.

"Peter really got his start in another band I play with, the Washboard Kings, led by Stan King. Nobody would hire Peter before the Washboard Kings, because he didn't know many of the old tunes; he had been with more modern bands like David Bromberg's. But I told Stan, 'This guy plays great. He's got the potential of being a great horn player.' So he came on that band, and he learned tunes. We'd sing them and then just let him play hot. Up to that point, Vinnie Giordano wouldn't touch him. Vinnie—who's got names for everybody—called him Smokehouse Ecklund. I'd say, 'Man! Come down and listen to the way Peter is playing. He's the hottest horn player in town.' Vinnie would say, 'I won't touch Smokehouse Ecklund.' But eventually he heard how Peter was coming along—and Smokehouse Ecklund became his number-one boy!"

After developing ulcers in the early '70s, Davis slowed down his pace—just slightly. "I took Librax, a stomach relaxer, mellowed out, and wrote a book, *The Theory Behind Chord Symbols*. It's a Bible to a lot of musicians," he declares. Davis also formed a record company, New York Jazz, for which he recorded with great care and affection such veteran jazzmen as trumpeter Doc Cheatham and drummer Freddie Moore (whom he subsequently featured in a show at Michael's Pub that gave Moore the finest showcase he had had in many years). In addition, Davis recorded some of his own originals for the label. He notes, "I keep writing music; I've got all kinds of things. I've got a score written for a show that I'm going to get on the boards one of these days called 'If Beale Street Could Talk.' It could be done in a club like Michael's Pub or—a bigger version—in a theater.

"I really like writing and arranging music. But that's a little tough to do for Dixieland bands because most of them only play the same arrangements that they did 500 years ago—which is why the music's dead. Country/western music is not dead because they always keep writing new songs when they make new records. Modern jazz is not. Bop guys write new songs; the only ones that don't write new songs when they've got new records are traditional jazz players. They're all rehashing the same songs and arrangements. And consequently people would rather go back and listen to the originals. Now Louis Armstrong kept up with pop tunes and he kept popular. So I maintain that the musicians themselves in this business have killed it."

Eddy Davis' Turn of the Century Minstrels included (from left to right): Peter Ecklund, Orange Kellin, Steve Hanson, J. J. Silva, Cynthia Sayer, and Davis (courtesy of Eddy Davis).

Eddy Davis was playing banjo with the Salty Dogs when the top photo was taken, circa 1957. The personnel included John Cooper on piano and Tom Bartlett (who is still a member of the Salty Dogs today) on trombone. In the bottom photo, taken in Chicago in 1967, Davis (who has always loved sporty cars) is surrounded by sidemen Jack "the Bear" Brown, Jug Berger, Wayne Jones, and Jerry Lufstrom (courtesy of Eddy Davis).

The top photo shows a Davis quartet of the early 1970s: Dill Jones, Davis, Bobby Gordon, and Vince Giordano; the bottom photo shows Davis' New York Society for the Preservation of Illegitimate Music: David Grego, Cynthia Sayer, Simon Wettenhall, Joe Muranyi, J. J. Silva, Todd Robbins, and Davis (courtesy of Eddy Davis).

Eddy Davis' New York Banjo Ensemble included (from left to right): Davis, Cynthia Sayer, Frank Vignola, and Howard Alden (courtesy of Eddy Davis).

In addition, Davis notes, audiences often seem to be more supportive of shows re-creating music of the past than they are of original music. In commercial terms, the most successful show Davis has ever put together was one that was strictly a re-creation—and, for that matter, of music far removed from jazz.

"After our success with things like 'The Turn of the Century Minstrels,' Gil Wiest, who owns Michael's Pub, said to me, 'Hey, I'll bet you can't do the music of Spike Jones.' I told Gil, 'I've always wanted to.' That's how our show 'The Best of Spike Jones' came about," Davis recalls. Davis re-created Jones' sharply executed comedy music—punctuated by well-timed gunshots, whistle-blasts, hiccups, birdcalls, screams, and the like. Jones rose to fame in the early 1940s recording for RCA such novelty hits as "Chloe," "Cocktails for Two," and "Der Fuhrer's Face," and also enjoyed some success on television in the 1950s. Following Jones' death in 1964, his son attempted to carry on in his father's footsteps, but without much luck.

The first-rate jazz musicians that Davis hired carried off Jones' music with considerable polish and flair. And enough years had passed to make Jones' brand of musical mayhem new for many people, and quaintly nostalgic for others. The show became a runaway hit, attracting favorable attention even from such publications as *People* magazine and *The Wall Street Journal* (which gave it front-page play). Wiest wanted to book the band out. He knew he would have to work out some arrangement with Jones' son for the continued use of the Spike Jones name; but demand for the music was so surprisingly strong, he was sure there was good money to be made for everyone if Davis were to tour with "The Best of Spike Jones."

Davis recalls, "Spike Jones Jr. came in to see the show when we were at Michael's Pub, and he cried. He said, 'I've never heard an hour of my father's music just played straight.' At that time we were doing nothing but Spike's music. Junior didn't take any money for that first engagement, but we were getting offers to work elsewhere playing Spike Jones' music and so of course we had to talk about that. We signed contracts, giving us the right to use Spike Jones' name. So then we went out and did various shows; playing Boston for George Wein, for example, we sold out three times.

"But Junior, who hadn't had much success when he had tried to do his father's music on his own, wanted to be involved. When our band went into the Showboat in Atlantic City, Junior had to come in with us—at a salary of $1500 a week, plus his room and board—as our 'Creative Director.' The money worked out all right. In selling the show, I found I could ask almost any price. I was amazed. I set a price and then I doubled it—and still the Showboat paid it. It was unbelievable. We did good business. The press loves the name Spike Jones. You can get press at the drop of a hat. And it seems everyone will come to the name of Spike Jones.

"But Junior started switching tunes from one spot to another, until we didn't know what tune we were doing next in the show. It was messing us up. And then he wanted to drop out some musicians and bring in baggy-pants comedians instead. I told him, 'Listen, that's not my conception of your father's music. All I want to do is re-create the sound that was on his original RCA records. I don't want to re-create the Spike Jones TV show.' That corny 1950s TV show certainly would not translate to today. And the band on the TV show was very rough. I wanted the music to be good because that's what had sold me as a kid— that Spike Jones' band back then was really a good band, playing tough charts *and* doing funny stuff. And that's what I wanted to do—not the baggy pants." But even if they got the music just right, Davis could not see himself devoting too much of his life to re-creating it. He had started the project figuring he would be involved with it for only a short while, then move on to other things.

"I told Junior, 'I wouldn't want, 20 years from now, to still be doing what your father did. I don't really like re-creating what people played—and played right—years ago. And your father did it right. I want to play other people's stuff, too.' I love Dorothy Shay, the 'Park Avenue Hillbilly,' and I love Lou Carter, who did the words for Waldo's shows; he's got great stuff. I want to do all of these people's things. And I'd like to write my own arrangements, in the style of Spike or the Korn Kobblers or other bands like that." And so Davis and Spike Jones Jr. split amicably. There is no Spike Jones Band at present. Davis changed the name of the band he had organized to "The New York Society for the Preservation of Illegitimate Music," and works with it sporadically. Promoted as "The People Who Brought You the Best of Spike Jones" or "Formerly the Best of Spike Jones," it plays not just the best-remembered Spike Jones hits but also other bands' comedic numbers, plus Davis' own treatments (in the Spike Jones tradition) of such songs as "New York, New York" and "One."

"This year, various people have been calling me, wanting the 'funny band' as they call it—a lot of festivals and things. George Wein had us play at the JVC Jazz Festival here in New York. We recently played the Sacramento festival, on the same bill with Steve Allen and the Four Freshmen.

"Cynthia Sayer, Andy Stein, and I have transcribed things off the old Spike Jones records, adapting them for our smaller instrumentation; we now use just seven musicians. Dan Barrett's on trombone and Ken Peplowski's on clarinet. Cynthia plays the mallet parts, like the tuned cowbells. We do some Spike Jones numbers—we do 'Chloe' because everybody likes that, we do 'Cocktails for Two' because that's a classic. We've been doing a lot of 'Holiday for Strings' because that's the big cowbell thing and Cynthia loves to play it, and plays it four times faster than it need be. Spike Jones Jr. doesn't get a cut of the money because we're not presenting ourselves as though we're the Spike Jones Band. And I love writing new stuff." Davis is happy to do occasional gigs with the band, in between a myriad of other projects he's got going.

Almost every Monday night, for the past seven years or so, Eddy Davis has played banjo and sung in Woody Allen's New Orleans Funeral and Ragtime Orchestra at Michael's Pub. For Allen, playing clarinet in the band provides a pleasurable change of pace from his filmmaking. Allen first befriended Davis in Chicago in the '60s, and even occasionally sat in on clarinet with Davis' jazz band. Over the years, Allen has grown into a surprisingly sensitive and effective clarinetist in the New Orleans idiom; he actually conveys more feeling than most of the New Orleans revivalists who play clarinet full-time. The other members of Allen's band do not generally match his level of sensitivity, but the house is packed every week, and Allen sees that the customers are satisfied.

Davis comments, "Playing with this band is really Woody's way to get to an audience because he doesn't have a live audience when he makes films. He hated doing stand-up comedy; he used to throw up. But he feels comfortable with this and he loves an audience. And he's really into the, 'Oh, they like that. . . .' He loves doing encores. One night we did five encores!

"Woody asks me to sing with the band. I never ask Woody. I always wait until Woody says on the bandstand, 'Eddy, don't you want to sing one?' Woody now thinks singing sells the band well. So he wants at least every third tune sung. You know, Woody likes the idea of working without a microphone. Well, for a long time, I was singing out to fill the room; I enjoy doing that. But now Woody has started directing me in my singing. He says, 'Here I am, the director.' He wants me to croon now. He's really getting into the thing. He suggests to me, 'Everybody likes the way Frank Sinatra sings.' And he wants me to sing like that. He tells me, 'Give me more head voice.' I explained to him, 'That more intimate style of singing came in when singers started using microphones; then they could push a lot of air—more air than sound, really. I've been singing out in a fairly operatic way because I have no microphone. I learned to project to the second balcony in music school, and I enjoy doing it.' But Woody's tried to take those schooled things out of me and make me just sing with a very slight head voice. He told me, 'I want you to sing as soft as you can with this band—be like Mabel Mercer. Now you're making them fall in the aisle. But I want them to be *crying* when they fall in the aisle. I want that real soft, morbid. . . .'

"I taught Woody the song, 'When Day Is Done.' So now it's like this [Davis sings in real high, thin, delicate, wavery voice]: 'When day is done and shadows fall. . . .' That's what he's got me doing. I told Woody after we tried it that way, 'Man, I could hardly hear myself.' He said, 'Don't worry. It works.' And it does quiet the audience down, although I'm not totally sold that what I'm doing is always right for the band. I go over to Woody's house a couple times a week, and we learn these tunes he wants to learn. And he loves drama. So that's why he likes 'Bilbao Song' and 'Indian Summer' and 'September Song.' You see, he's into emoting.

"With Woody's New Orleans band, sometimes I will intentionally play a chord a little wrong. Because with those bands down in New Orleans, the chords weren't always the same. The banjo player might be banging on a diminished chord instead of the minor chord, where the piano player's banging on the minor. It's sort of a character of the music and makes it not get slick. So if our band starts to sound a little too slick, and I know it's really a minor chord, I might go to the diminished chord intentionally instead. Because there's always something a little wrong with that music. The clarinet player is sharp; the intonation is bad—there's always something. But the damn stuff is infectious. Woody and I talk about it. 'Crude' is a good word for Woody and I; we speak of that often: 'The band is getting a little too slick; we don't sound like a real band from New Orleans. We've got to muddy the air—make the ending fall apart or something.'

"You know, we've recorded some tapes, over a period of a year and a half, with Woody and a hand-picked band of New York musicians who can play in the New Orleans tradition better than the regular Monday night band, including Simon Wettenhall, Peter Ecklund, Dan Barrett, Cynthia Sayer, and Todd Robbins. Woody and I have been discussing what to do with the tapes. He's sure there's enough material for a good album or two, and we'd like to see the music come out. But he said, 'If I used my name, I'd have to go to some big company and get money like I would as a filmmaker, and I don't want to do that. You know what I'd really like, Eddy, is just to be the clarinet player. I'd like the band to be your band. Then on the back of the album, I'll just be listed as Woody Allen, the clarinet player. We won't put a picture of me on the cover or anything like that. But you can use my art department; they can make any kind of a cover you want. And when the record comes out, I'll use my promotional department to promote it.'

"Actually, Woody would like the band to have an identity

of its own and work all different places. And then he could show up for a concert if he wanted to—not having been advertised—and simply play. If he couldn't make a concert, Orange Kellin or Tommy Sancton or Sammy Rimington could play clarinet. Woody would enjoy doing some jazz concerts. The mayor of Vienna recently called his office and said, 'Would you bring a jazz band over and play the Vienna Opera House?' They're discussing possibilities."

A weekly gig with Stanley's Washboard Kings at a club called the Cajun, on Eighth Avenue at 16th Street, gives Davis another outlet for singing and playing banjo on the old-time jazz numbers he likes. And occasionally, Davis turns up at other little clubs around New York City, playing more for fun, he admits, than for money. "They're only paying musicians $50 a night or thereabouts in these type of rooms now. And I suspect it's not going to be long before bandleaders are going to have to buy that position, to get in those clubs. It's not going to be long until the owner of a place like the Cajun is going to say, 'Oh, Stanley, if you want Tuesday night, give me $100 and you can have it.' And then the musicians are going to come in and play for free and Stanley's going to have to pay for the space. I predict that's what's going to happen to those kind of rooms. It's already happened to rock 'n' roll in this town. You pay to be able to go into the club and play. And then quite often they charge at the door, you know, and the band takes whatever the door brings in.

"I love to play in clubs. But if I were just going to go play clubs again, like I did when I was younger, I'd probably go down to New Orleans. I could find my own club down there and build it up. The main reason I stay around New York is because there are special projects that get done only in New York. Like the Paul Whiteman re-creation Maurice Peress put together, which Musicmasters put out on CD; I got to do the Mike Pingatore banjo parts. And we did a thing at Carnegie Hall a couple of years ago, reviving the music of James Reese Europe. I not only played, I contracted all the strings: the mandolins, banjos, guitars, and so on. National Public Radio broadcast the tape of

that concert. Maurice Peress also did concerts playing music of
Ellington and Antheil. I love doing that legit stuff. I stick around
because that sort of thing will only happen here in New York.

"When they announced Lincoln Center was going to inaugu-
rate a jazz program and revive the music of past jazz greats, I
thought that would provide opportunities for me, too. But now,
three years later, it looks like maybe the jazz at Lincoln Center
is going to be almost all black. That's because Wynton Marsalis
is in charge. They're going to bring in their Michael Whites and
all that, and better players around who happen to be white are
not going to get the chance—which is kind of a shame.

"Sometimes I've felt like I've had enough of New York,"
Davis acknowledges. "I've thought, in passing, of moving to
New Orleans. And at times I've thought more seriously of moving to Sydney, Australia, because I could be a king over there.
Australia is like this country was 30, 40 years ago. There's traditional jazz in all kind of pubs, and people are shoulder to shoulder. And then there's a lot of other stuff going on, and a lot of
recording work. Over there, it's not the way it is here; jazz is not
a taboo thing. Over there, jazz is part of everything, like it is in
Europe. They accept jazz. It didn't die, like it did here."

1992

Orphan Newsboy

Holding his cornet at his side, Peter Ecklund steps up to the microphone and, while the other members of the Orphan News-boys quartet provide him with simple yet thoughtful instrumental support, begins breathily whistling "I'll Be a Friend 'With Pleasure.'" It's a welcome surprise to hear that sweetly nostalgic 1930 pop song, associated with the late, legendary cornetist Bix Beiderbecke, thus recast. ("I've always done that," Ecklund will comment to me later, regarding his whistling. "It doesn't seem like anything to me, but people seem to like it so I usually try to fit it in somewhere when I've got a gig.")

His whistling-chorus finished, Ecklund now picks up his cornet, as the audience at the Cornerstone in Metuchen, New Jersey, applauds, and proceeds to play the melody in a seemingly casual manner. He offers few embellishments, but as he lingers in the lower register, he produces sustained, beautifully well-rounded, rich, low tones that almost sound like they're coming from a trombone rather than a cornet. On this number, I'm getting great pleasure simply from the timbre of his horn. Now he and clarinetist Ken Peplowski interweave, responding easily to one another's ideas.

For the next number, he suggests to the other musicians—and they quickly concur—that they play "Once in a While." Not the pop ballad "Once in a While" that was a hit in the late 1930s, but the lesser-known, two-beat jazz stomp "Once in a While" that was recorded by Louis Armstrong in the late 1920s. Ecklund doesn't project quite as searingly passionate and commanding a presence on trumpet as Armstrong did, but—so crucial in playing a number like this—he's got the original rhythmic feel down just right. He soon has me tapping my foot, pulled headlong into the irresistible rhythm—the compelling strength of which is felt more clearly "live" than on a boxy old recording. Hearing him play "Once in a While" now gives me some idea of the impact Armstrong must have originally had, playing a hot stomp like this in a dance hall. As Ecklund and his cohorts dig into the number, I wonder how many of today's younger jazz musicians—most of whom will at least pay lip service to Louis Armstrong, acknowledging him as one of the immortals of jazz—would even know this tune, much less be able to carry it off, impromptu, with such panache. Jazz musicians who, by preference and experience, are primarily into bebop have real trouble playing a number like this convincingly. It simply doesn't come naturally to them, as it does to Ecklund. But Beiderbecke and Armstrong are two of the trumpeters that Ecklund most enjoys listening to in his free time.

Born in 1945, Ecklund revels in the music of the 1920s and '30s. If you see him with the Orphan Newsboys, a group built around Ecklund and Marty Grosz that, depending on the gig, may include anywhere from four to seven musicians in total, you might hear such intriguing and considerably varied old numbers as Jabbo Smith's "Jazz Battle," Duke Ellington's "Jubilee Stomp," Richard Whiting's "Beyond the Blue Horizon," Benny Carter's "Blues in My Heart," Charlie Davis' and Walter Melrose's "Copenhagen," Isham Jones' "Spain," and Al Jolson's "Keep Smiling at Trouble." Almost always, they're offering fresh, new jazz interpretations (in an appropriately old-time style) of such felicitous older tunes, rather than re-creating specific recorded performances. Occasionally, Ecklund *will* pay more direct homage, re-creating a classic recorded solo of, for example, Louis Armstrong. He seems partial both to brisk, upbeat numbers and to melodic ballads; he doesn't seem greatly drawn to deep blues.

Ecklund also works regularly as lead trumpeter in Vince Giordano's 11-man Nighthawks Orchestra. He doesn't do a whole lot of soloing there; mostly he simply leads the brass section, playing the melody on the dance music and orchestral jazz numbers from the 1920s, '30s, and (to a lesser extent) '40s. Because Giordano has such an extensive musical library and is constantly bringing additional vintage arrangements into the band, Ecklund's job requires notably strong skills in sight-reading music with appropriate period inflections. From time to time, Ecklund freelances in other traditional jazz settings (radio's Garrison Keilor is one who appreciates, and periodically makes use of, Ecklund's talents). He also periodically does some nonjazz studio work.

Since graduating from Yale in 1967, Ecklund has actually worked with an unusually diverse assortment of musicians—not just traditional jazz players, but also such pop, rock, and blues musicians (mostly outside of the scope of this book) as Greg Allman, David Bromberg, Maria Muldaur, Paula Lockheart, Leon Redbone, and Paul Butterfield. He's essentially eased out of the pop music field now—he prefers traditional jazz—but he says he has learned a great deal from being exposed to all types of music. His small-band arrangements—listen, for example, to his sextet sides on his Stomp Off album *Peter Ecklund and the Melody Makers*—often sound unusually rich and full; he says he figured out how to produce such rich blends while arranging horn sections for rock recordings. These days, Ecklund would rather lead a small jazz group of his own or play at a jazz festival than play in a pop music horn section. Which is good, because there are plenty of fine technicians who can adequately execute pop charts; but to play the type of old-time jazz Ecklund plays, you have to have a real understanding of the spirit of the music, and of the pre-bebop trumpet tradition, generally. As he clearly does.

Curiously, considering his later professional involvements, Ecklund initially did not have much interest in either rock music or jazz. "When I was growing up [in Woodridge, Connecticut], I only heard classical music and Broadway show music," he recalls. When he began playing trumpet it was with the intention of playing classical trumpet. "I really didn't hear any jazz until I was, I guess, maybe a junior in high school. Then I heard some. Of course, those were sort of the glory years of Blue Note Records, so I heard that modern jazz. And then I heard '20s jazz, too, from my friend Howard Vidal and his father. I first heard Bix when I was in high school; my friend's father had been in Rudy Vallee's band when Vallee was at Yale. I think he had actually heard Bix a couple of times, and he told me about Bix's recordings. Of course, Louis Armstrong was still alive when I was a kid; he was a big star, so everybody knew about him." Ecklund found himself particularly enthralled by Armstrong's vintage recordings, his Hot Five and Hot Seven pure-jazz sides from the 1920s, and his more pop-oriented big-band sides, fronting the Luis Russell Band, from the 1930s.

When Ecklund entered Yale in the fall of 1963, college Dixieland, which had been strong in the 1950s, was in its "death throes," as he puts it, but he got an appealing taste of it. He met and played with other Dixieland musicians at Yale, much as Stan Rubin and Ed Polcer had done at Princeton. "I got to sub in one of the very last versions of Eli's Chosen Six, a group that had started in the '50s. Actually, some of the old Eli's Chosen Six players are still active—like Lee Lorenz, an excellent cornet player, who's now the cartoon editor of The New Yorker magazine, and Roswell Rudd, a trombone player, who's teaching at Bard College. That was when I first started trying to play traditional jazz—when I was still in college. I mean, by that point the Beatles were everywhere, and yet there was still this vestige of another time." And he felt comfortable playing the old-time jazz, so much so that shortly after getting his B.A. from Yale, he and clarinetist Tommy Sancton (a disciple of the George Lewis/New Orleans school of playing) organized a traditional jazz band, which became known as the Galvanized Jazz Band and still flourishes under that name today. "Freddy Vigorito has been running the band for about the last 20 years, but actually Tommy and I started it. The other players in the beginning were Howard Vidal on trombone, Art Hovey on tuba, and Julie Hovey on washboard; originally we called ourselves the Galvanized Washboard Band.

105

I was, I guess, the leader. I mean, I got a lot of the work and so forth." Initially, playing music was but a sideline for Ecklund; to avoid being drafted and sent to Vietnam, he went to graduate school at Yale for a year, and then taught grade school and high school for several years in the Boston area. But in those years he got to meet and play with a wide range of musicians—everyone from Sammy Rimington, a British-born clarinetist who was intent on keeping alive traditional New Orleans jazz sounds, to Maria and Geoff Muldaur, who, singing and playing guitar and violin, were bridging the worlds of American pop and folk music. (Maria Muldaur, perhaps best remembered for singing "Midnight at the Oasis," went on to record four hit albums between 1973 and '78.)

By joining rock bands, Ecklund was able to get into music full-time, living for a while in the early '70s in Woodstock, before finally settling in New York City (where he currently resides) in 1973. Over the next four or five years, he worked part of the time—both touring and recording—in the David Bromberg Band. Bromberg had organized what Ecklund calls a "hippie variety show," mixing in elements of bluegrass, country music, blues, early jazz, and old rock 'n' roll. "I learned a great deal about American music from being in that band, which included string players and horn players from all different backgrounds. I know a lot about country and bluegrass from being around them," he notes. And because the Bromberg Band did not tour full-time, he had plenty of opportunities to work in other musical contexts as well. He recorded, for example, with the Paul But-terfield blues band, and toured with Greg Allman, of Allman Brothers renown. "I learned a lot of music from the guys in Greg's band, actually. They were impressive for a couple of reasons. All of those guys could play maybe two or three instru-ments, and sing. They weren't the kind of instrumental wizards you find in New York, but they had a great understanding of music; I mean, they knew what one another was doing. They had kind of a more basic understanding of the music they were trying to make, rather than a tremendous understanding of one instrument and its possibilities. And they really played that southern R&B very well, and they brought things they liked into it. Even things they didn't assimilate that much, like John

106

Coltrane jazz and so forth—they still allowed it to influence their playing and they really made some good music." While it might be hard for traditional jazz enthusiasts who know Ecklund only from his work in that field to imagine him playing rock, he feels: "All of the other music I've done, it's all American music, and it's all interconnected in one way or another—even the bluegrass and country music. That's very influenced by blues and by jazz." His only complaint about playing in Greg Allman's band: "They were a bit loud for me. But I used to put these styrofoam earplugs in when we played, and then it was bearable. Oh, whenever you go to hear a big rock show, you know, you've just got to stuff your ears up, because otherwise it's unbearable. That's how people are used to hearing music these days."

Ecklund recorded and toured with singer Paula Lockheart, who was into blues and early jazz. And in the late '70s, during the disco boom, he did a lot of recording, since disco music generally used horn parts. Aside from Gloria Gaynor, he doesn't even recall the names of the disco artists on whose recordings he played; his studio work he did simply for money. "I did a fair amount of work arranging horns on some very forgettable music—but at the time it was some good employment," he says. Beginning in 1980, he worked a good deal—both touring and recording—with Leon Redbone, who mixed old-time pop and jazz sounds. He played note-for-note re-creations of Swing Era classics in Stan Rubin's big band at places like Roseland dancehall. He toured with Sandra Reaves-Phillips' *Late, Great Ladies of Jazz and Blues* show, which he considered both entertaining and educational. (Traveling in the south with an otherwise all-black group, he experienced a bit, he says, of the indignities due to racial prejudice that blacks may often encounter. He can recall with discomfort, for example, the suspicious, critical looks they received from whites upon walking into a diner.) And all through these years, as opportunities arose, he did occasional, freelance Dixieland work. Gradually, he increased his involvement in the world of traditional jazz and moved away from rock and pop. "It's really music that I've always liked better," he notes. "And in jazz, the role of my instrument is central. In rock horn sections, you're an accessory, peripheral."

Occasionally, he used to sub in Vince Giordano's Nighthawks, which brought him heightened visibility to fans of old-
time music. He very much liked that band, even if he was rarely
given opportunities to improvise freely; more often he was reading section parts or being asked to re-create, note for note, a
solo of some famed past artist, such as Bix Beiderbecke, Louis
Armstrong, or Bunny Berigan; he didn't mind playing their music at all. By 1984, he was subbing frequently in Giordano's band,
and in 1986, following a major reorganization of the band, he
became its lead trumpeter. He's chosen to stay with the band
ever since (taking time off, of course, when he gets gigs of his
own or other enticing opportunities). "I keep working with Vince
because a lot of the music is technically difficult and because
Vince is so dedicated. I mean, his knowledge is so tremendous
and he's really a good musician. I can't say that about other
bandleaders, but—particularly on the bass saxophone—Vince is
really great. Mainly, though, it's that he's just so fanatical and
he knows so much, and he's always bringing in new material. A
lot of jobs get boring if you do them for a long time, but he's
always finding new stuff and writing new transcriptions. And
the music is so damned difficult that if I play with that band at
least once a week, I'm pretty much ready for anything. Playing
in Vince's band requires precision, and getting styles—which can
change from tune to tune—just right. Actually, a good number of
the tunes that Marty Grosz and I have been playing with the
Orphan Newsboys, I've discovered playing in Vince's band.
Vince's repertoire is huge; he has thousands of stock arrangements of obscure pop tunes from the '20s and '30s, and when we
play these stock arrangements, you hear, of course, the original
melody and also the original chords. And I'm always keeping
lists of songs that I like, of the many that we play, for future
reference and use. For example, 'Little by Little' is a song I
discovered playing in Vince's band, and Marty and I both liked
it, so we just recorded it on an album Marty's doing for Jazzology.
    "I don't play very much jazz in Vince's band, really—I'm
the lead trumpeter—but I'd just as soon play lead trumpet as be
a jazz soloist because it's better practice from the standpoint of

staying in shape as a trumpeter, and, of course, playing the melodies of these old numbers helps me to learn the melodies. In that band, I'm playing a trumpet, rather than a cornet, which I use in small groups. I use a trumpet when I'm playing in big bands because it projects a little better, and it's good for playing with other trumpets in a brass section. But you don't get quite the variety of sounds that you get out of a cornet. With the cornet, the low register really sounds good. The upper register doesn't sound quite as piercing as a trumpet—especially if you use the right mouthpiece. A lot of cornet players, particularly on the West Coast, use fairly small instruments with shallow mouthpieces, which gives the other cornet sound—like in the Lu Watters band—a very percussive, bright sound. But the sound I favor is more like the traditional, legit cornet sound that you found at the turn of the century. And then you can add all sorts of things to it."

Besides Giordano, the one other musician Ecklund has chosen to particularly ally himself with is Marty Grosz, coleader with him of the Orphan Newsboys. In that band, Ecklund gets to express himself rather freely as a jazz soloist (rather than re-create someone else's solo as he does in Giordano's band), playing music mostly from the 1920s and '30s. He notes: "The band started at the Conneaut Lake Jazz Festival—Joe Boughton's annual festival in western Pennsylvania—in '88. And we played a festival in Toronto, and one in Los Angeles, and several others around the country. Marty and I are the coleaders. Although he is the main onstage presence, he and I basically share the business and the making of phone calls and the booking of engagements, and also the production of the records. His orientation is more towards performing live, and he tends to get impatient with the tedium of recording—although he makes wonderful records.

"I choose to work with Marty because he's such a wonderful rhythm guitar player; it's really very comfortable to play with him. He makes you sound good, and he plays the right chords. Marty's rhythm guitar—that's just a very infectious sound! And he's also a very funny guy to be around. I mean, in music, you spend a lot of time basically doing nothing on the road and so he always keeps you entertained. Vince and Marty are the two musicians I work with the most.

"Marty and I probably talk on the phone maybe four times a week. And we work together maybe three or four times a month. A difficulty connected with the Orphan Newsboys is that one of the principals, clarinetist Bobby Gordon, lives in San Diego, while the rest of us live in New York, so really we only do some of the jazz parties and jazz festivals with him. Several clarinet players who live on the East Coast often play with us: Ken Peplowski, Billy Novick, Joe Muranyi. Greg Cohen is our regular bass player, but Murray Wall and Vince Giordano play bass with us sometimes. On our first album, *Extra! The Orphan Newsboys* [Jazzology JCD-190], Ken Peplowski and Murray Wall played on some cuts. Lately it's been more like the Orphan Newsboys consist of Marty and I—and whoever we choose to invite that evening! Sometimes we have a slightly larger band than the quartet we started with. Sometimes Dan Barrett plays trombone with us. At a concert we did recently for Planned Parenthood of Pennsylvania, we had Vince Giordano on bass and tuba and bass sax, and Keith Ingham on piano. Sometimes Arnie Kinsella—the drummer from Vince's band—will play with us. And on our album *Laughing at Life* [Stomp Off CD1225], a friend of mine, Dick Feigy, who had been in the David Bromberg Band with me in the '70s, played mandolin. He's a wonderful jazz mandolin player and jazz guitarist. He now makes his living playing country music in recording studios in L.A., and he also works for a company that researches music, like if someone wants to find a song to use in a movie, or wants to find out who owns the rights to a song. I love his playing! Even though he doesn't play with us regularly—he lives in L.A.—he was able to step in and really give the band a different sound. I really like that string band sound. The David Bromberg Band, although it wasn't particularly a jazz group, had that sound a lot of the time. There were three horn players and three strings players, so you'd have all these combinations like mandolin and two guitars, or two mandolins and violin, or three violins, or banjo, mandolin, and guitar. I liked the different combinations of sounds."

Peter Ecklund, cornet, and Ken Peplowski, tenor sax (photo by Chip Deffaa).

Ecklund leads a front line including clarinetist Bobby Gordon and trombonist Bob Havens at a jazz party (top photo, by Al White, courtesy of Peter Ecklund), and solos in Vince Giordano's Nighthawks at the Red Blazer Too (bottom photo, by Chip Deffaa).

Marty Grosz, guitar, Peter Ecklund, cornet, and Bob Haggart, bass, at the 1988 Conneaut Lake Jazz Festival (photo by John Bitter, courtesy of Peter Ecklund).

Peter Ecklund (photo by Chip Deffaa).

The sound of the Orphan Newsboys group can vary from number to number, sometimes taking on a spritely, somewhat ricky-ticky 1920s feel, sometimes opting for a smoother, late '30s, riffing small-band feel. Ecklund's own playing varies as well. "I don't play exactly out of one period," he notes. "I mean, I don't play with much bebop influence, but I just sort of play what seems appropriate, rather than trying to sound exactly like Bix in the '20s or Roy Eldridge in the late '30s or whatever." Playing what seems appropriate, he notes, is basically all he's ever done, whether playing with David Bromberg, Greg Allman, or a traditional jazz group.

"The Orphan Newsboys play in all different venues—some clubs, some private parties, and some of the jazz parties, although the problem with jazz parties is that they're always looking for individual musicians. So Marty has to sell them on the idea of hiring a band, rather than individuals. And—if I can put in my two cents' worth—they're really mistaken in always wanting to hire individuals! It's much better to have a band, or at least people who are used to playing together all the time. Otherwise you just get numbers that everyone knows, like 'Take the A Train' and so forth, over and over again. But a lot of the impresarios who put on these jazz parties primarily hire individuals and then put them together in bands—bands composed of people who may or may not actually want to play together or even like each other! But where our band has been able to play, we've gone over very well. And I had great fun playing with Marty on a tour in Germany last October. It wasn't exactly the Orphan Newsboys; it was more like a little swing band, including a full rhythm section with Chuck Riggs on drums and Bob Haggart on bass.

"We'll be making a new Orphan Newsboys record in September. We're playing the Los Angeles Classic Jazz Festival, and right after that we're going to make a new Orphan Newsboys record. I'm looking for material for that now. Actually, with this one we want to have some kind of concept that will capture people's imaginations, rather than just have a bunch of tunes. Maybe the old songs of Broadway or something like that."

Ecklund is also pianist/bandleader Terry Waldo's cornetist

of choice when Waldo gets a small-group jazz gig. "Well, for example, last night I played with Terry Waldo at Michael's Pub. We're doing a show there for a few weeks, about American political songs. We play for about half the show—some rousing political Dixieland and some funny and curious songs from the early part of this century—then a comedian does about half the show, and then we go back and parade him off the stage in the manner of political conventions of long ago. It's a good concept.

"The night before last, I took off from Michael's Pub and played with the Black Eagle Jazz Band up near Framingham, Massachusetts, where they play every Wednesday—filling in for their regular cornet player, Tony Pringle, who was away on business. I play with them maybe once a month or once every two months. They are one of the few bands that plays really a lot of New Orleans–style ensemble playing—in other words, all three horns improvising polyphonically at once. And they really do it well. They're an interesting example of a band that has a really distinctive sound. Although some of them aren't terribly accomplished musicians technically, they're very expressive and they have a wonderful group sound. They play a New Orleans kind of repertoire—New Orleans revival-style jazz, like the George Lewis band or the Preservation Hall Band. Two of the band members are European. Tony Pringle is from England and Pam Pameijer is from Holland. I know Billy Novick, the band's clarinet player, from the David Bromberg Band in the '70s. That's where we first worked together. So it's fun to work with him. Occasionally I do other projects with him in the Boston area, too—some film scores and television music. And he recently played with me at one of my gigs at the Cornerstone in Metuchen."

Ecklund must really be strongly motivated to play with the Black Eagle Jazz Band, I suggest, since Framingham, Massachusetts, is almost a three-and-a-half-hour drive from New York City.

"I enjoy playing with them," he acknowledges. "I mean, I've been doing this kind of work for a long time, and I've finally gotten to the point where there's usually enough work for me.

So it's really more a matter of two things: whether I really want to do it, or how much money I need to make that week or that month. Whether I want to do it seems to have more to do with what work I take, as time goes on. Which is one of the nice things about being a free-lancer. On the one hand, you have total insecurity; but on the other hand, if you don't want to work for someone or do something—no matter what it is, or for the most absurd reason—you can just say no.

"You know, I also play some things that really aren't jazz at all. Some contemporary music that's kind of a mixture of maybe jazz and classical music or whatever. Like one group led by a wonderful saxophone player, Lenny Pickett, who plays regularly in the *Saturday Night Live* band. He's composing an opera that's going to be presented in Philadelphia this June, based on, I believe, a *cinéma vérité* film by Fred Wiseman, called *Welfare*— scenes that actually happened in welfare offices. We've rehearsed some of the music, but I don't know exactly how it's going to be staged. I work with him maybe three times a year. And I also do some recording dates with him and other friends of mine.

"I don't do a lot of commercial recording. I do probably one recording date a week—all different types of music. The work that tends to come my way are things that require authentic American whatever—whether it's jazz or just sort of old music. The people who do television commercials and movie scores and so forth tend to call me for those things. For example, I played in the public television production *The Civil War*. And I also played in the score of the film *Fried Green Tomatoes* in a few places; Greg Cohen, the bass player in the Orphan Newsboys, produced some of that music. And in many, many movies that hardly ever saw the light of day. It seems for every recording you do for a movie that actually comes out, you play on five that disappear the same day they're released; that's the nature of the movie business. I do music for TV commercials maybe once a month or once every two months. But actually that's a fair part of my income, just because it pays well. I recently did a date for an old friend of mine, Geoff Muldaur, who used to be in the Jim

Kweskin Jug Band, and Paul Butterfield's band and so forth. He was in town recording some music for Raytheon; so we were honoring Raytheon in music, in the recording studio!

"Playing traditional jazz probably accounts for about half of my income. Playing in clubs doesn't pay very well, but some of the jazz parties and tours pay well. The music I prefer playing is jazz, certainly." Yet he occasionally feels restrained in the jazz world. "Sometimes I get impatient with traditional jazz because its orientation is very conservative, since it's basically re-creating an old kind of music. When I was first playing professionally in bands, in the '70s—in David Bromberg's Band, or various other rock bands I was with, or whatever—we didn't really have that point of view. It was like you could do anything if it worked; if it sort of made sense musically, then it was all right. But now, much of what you find in traditional jazz is a repertory approach. It's either like the Vince Giordano band attempting to do an accurate re-creation of something that existed long ago, which I think is a perfectly worthwhile enterprise, or, in the case of the Orphan Newsboys, getting sort of an authentic feeling from another time and translating it into our time, which is also perfectly valid. But I don't feel that such playing really sums up everything I do.

"I've been working on another project, writing original music that's sort of in a swing jazz style and sort of not, actually. What I've been trying to do is write little pieces that have enough harmonic structure of the sort that I'm used to, so that you can improvise jazz to them, but they aren't necessarily identifiably the old-style jazz that I usually play. The music I've been writing is sort of hard to categorize. It's all very melodic. So it's traditional to a certain extent. It has major and minor chords. It has harmonic lines that move sort of like old songs. But it doesn't sound exactly like old songs; it has other elements in it, too." But there are no radical descents into dissonance, or anything like that in his music, he notes. "No, I've been trying to write music that's really pretty simple, harmonically—but is still pretty strong."

He has just begun giving public try-outs of some of his new music in New York. "I did a performance of my originals recently with Frank Vignola on guitar and Greg Cohen on bass, at the

Cornelia Street Cafe, which is a wonderful little room—the kind of place where you'd expect Allen Ginsberg to get up at any moment and start improvising poetry while someone else plays bongo drums. I play some guitar, also. Since Frank is a fine guitar soloist, I'll play some rhythm guitar, and then pick up the horn at other times. And I'm doing some recording of this music, on my own, with Frank and Greg. I don't have a contract with a record company at this point. I am just going to record it and see what direction to take with it. Because it's all original music, it won't compete with the Orphan Newsboys band, which is very close to my heart. Having a group that does all original music in semitraditional jazz style—I mean, it's really quite different from traditional jazz—may create no interest at all, or it may create a lot of interest; you never know."

I'm glad Ecklund is striving to create new music, as well as to re-create and rework older types of music, for exploration is always to be encouraged in the arts. And Ecklund will be able to express aspects of his musicality he has felt unable to express in traditional contexts.

Ecklund worries sometimes that jazz has gained respectability in our culture over the years, but at a certain price; risk-taking generally seems less common these days than it was when jazz was new. "Jazz is becoming almost like classical music, in that it's a repertory music and it's a concert music, and people who play it are expected to have tremendous technical facility and not make any mistakes. And, as has happened in traditional classical music, the range of what is permissible, in terms of playing, has become more and more restrictive than it used to be. Listen to very old classical recordings and you'll hear how things have changed there. I remember hearing Rachmaninoff—well, that was maybe the late '20s—playing his own piano concerto. The way the violinists were playing was almost like salon and cabaret music of the turn of the century, or like old film score music. Just very soupy, and with lots of expression, and basically no-holds-barred—a style that would be considered almost in bad taste, now. Well, I think maybe this is happening in jazz now. That it's becoming a concert music, and something in which everybody knows all the rules and it's all defined. And the repertory is set.

And in terms of expression, the limits are very well defined. Everyone plays in tune and has a good sound and so forth." But the individual player's self-expression, he suggests, is limited.

"And although jazz has been making a big resurgence of late, its place in society is really very different from what it was before." Ecklund mentions, for example, having attended a recent film opening, where "they had a wonderful jazz group. But it was very polite and refined and well-played music. It probably bore the same relation to its society that maybe a string quartet in Mozart's time would bear. I mean, it was background music designed to create a lofty atmosphere.

"That is in fact the way most people experience music now, in the background—it's like decoration, or to create a mood. People buy these Wynton Marsalis records of standards and play them at very low volume. It's not terribly involving. But it has a kind of subliminal and decorative effect. People probably like New Age music for the same reason.

"Whereas in old New Orleans, as they were marching or dancing to early jazz, that was functional music. And it was very immediately and emotionally involving. And Marty talks about this a lot; he says he wants to bring back the effect of a saloon with the Orphan Newsboys. I mean, we've really gotten very far away from that in music."

While Ecklund acknowledges that rock music also has a lot of energy and emotionalism, there is simply not enough substance in most rock to hold his interest for very long. The carefully crafted, often harmonically sophisticated, popular songs of the 1920s, '30s, '40s, and prerock '50s generally have much more to offer a jazz musician, Ecklund believes. His well-thought-out and articulated comments are worth taking notice of, particularly since his background includes work in both the rock and jazz fields.

"Most rock music is simple harmonically," he points out. "There's not a great deal of harmonic tension or harmonic movement in it. It's all little discrete bits and rhythms and things; that's what gives it its power. It's really not very good music to improvise to, because you can't sort of twist it and turn it—if you change it at all, it sort of loses what it is. I mean, rock is

PETER ECKLUND

based on little bits put together in a certain way. Like rhythms
and little melodic bits called hooks and maybe little drum parts
and bass parts that all fit together. And you can't really change
them without losing what you have and having something else.
But something like 'All the Things You Are,' which has very
powerful harmonies—you can do all kinds of things to it and it
will still sound a bit like 'All the Things You Are.'
   "That's been the problem, I think, with things like the jazz-
rock fusion. A lot of the improvising of the people who started
improvising in jazz-rock fusion would just be a salad of notes
because there isn't the thing that you find in traditional jazz. In
traditional jazz, you play the melody of the song and at the same
time you have the harmony; and then as you improvise, you
continue the harmony of the song through the whole piece.
And that gives the improvising a certain character—say you're
playing 'Limehouse Blues,' which has a very distinctive and
powerful chord progression that you repeat all the way through
the song; no matter what somebody's improvising, it's still going
to sound a little like 'Limehouse Blues.' That's a very powerful
thing about traditional jazz and swing, and you don't really find
it in things that happened later, like rock 'n' roll.
   "Harmony in popular songs was becoming more complicated going into the '50s—I mean, you had all these pop tunes
like 'Laura.' But much of the public moved away from that type
of music towards rock 'n' roll. I mean, pop music also got very
slick in the '50s and kind of insincere, and that's what made rock
'n' roll possible. People—young people especially—just didn't
want to hear that kind of stuff anymore. Now, early rock 'n'
roll—a lot of it is just blues or it's just one or two or three chords.
What gives most popular music since the advent of rock 'n' roll
its power is not having a particular harmonic structure, but just
having a certain structure based on rhythms and based on little
melodic ideas. But you can't really improvise over that and have
it sound like very much. Or sound very different from improvising over another rock song.
   "Interestingly, some of the most successful music after the
'50s, as far as jazz improvisation, was bossa nova music. And
those songs have a great deal of harmonic structure. It's very

121

strong. So they really lend themselves to improvising, even though they're not based on a swing beat at all."

Ecklund scoffs at the notion—popular in some quarters—that music is continually progressing, becoming ever more sophisticated. "You know, music doesn't really evolve. It just changes. And generally, when you add something in one department, you subtract it in the other. For example, a lot of people thought the Stan Kenton Band was absolutely the most developed, complex music the world had ever seen. But if you take away all those horns and all those harmonies, what you have is sort of a tea-dance orchestra playing fox-trots. I mean, it's really very simple music *rhythmically*. It's actually much simpler and less sophisticated rhythmically than, for example, the Luis Russell Band in the early '30s, which had a very hard-driving, and really very sophisticated sort of rhythm section."

Ecklund listens to a great deal of jazz and old popular music, generally—as well, of course, as to music wholly unrelated to jazz. Just out of curiosity, I ask him what trumpeters he listens to the most.

"Probably Louis and Red Allen and Bix and Miles Davis," he responds. "Well, Louis, it's because he does such great things with the melody, and he gets such a wonderful sound, and his rhythm is so incredibly creative. I mean, the same thing is true of Red Allen. Those New Orleans guys in particular—they've got their own time. When Louis started playing ballads, he found that way of playing the melody, or playing melodically, but with extremely sophisticated phrasing. I say sophisticated just because it's really very complex. It's not intellectual at all; he just felt it. But he found a way to make the simplest things interesting and really grab your attention by little things having to do with the timing and the phrasing.

"Red Allen I discovered later than the other trumpeters I mentioned. Actually, this wonderful lady who's a great jazz collector, Molly Kikuchi, who lives in Brooklyn—she has a wonderful Red Allen collection and she's given me many tapes with all of his best work. I particularly love the Rhythmmakers things that Henry Allen did.

"Bix, I guess, is inspiring partly because—although obviously I'm in a much later time than he was—I kind of come out of that same tradition, or approach to music that he did. I mean, he basically came out of light classical and concert band music and so forth, and then from there went into jazz; that was the music he came up with and listened to. And he plays with a very precise attack and kind of almost a legit tone, although he wasn't a legit player. And his rhythm was always very good—not as creative as the black guys, the New Orleans guys, but he still was very accurate."

And certainly there are other trumpeters he appreciates. He notes, for example: "Bill Coleman was a wonderful melodic player, who probably would have been more famous if he'd stayed in the United States instead of living most of his life in France. He's got a great sound. He sounds a little bit like Bix, sometimes." And he has shown his admiration for the late Jabbo Smith by keeping alive a bit of Smith's rarely revived music. "Jabbo would play brilliantly, but carelessly. Very exciting— frequently right on the edge of being out of control," he notes.

Ecklund's appreciation of players like Louis Armstrong, Henry "Red" Allen, Bix Beiderbecke, Bill Coleman, and Jabbo Smith—all of whom emerged in the 1920s or '30s—should come as no surprise to anyone familiar with his playing. He clearly draws upon their heritage. But his naming of a bebop-and-beyond stylist like Miles Davis *does* come as something of a surprise.

"I like Miles Davis for the same reason I like Louis Armstrong," he responds. "It's just the economy of notes. Particularly in certain periods. Just where he places the notes is wonderful. A lot of people who like traditional jazz don't like the sensibility of his music. I can understand that; either you like it or you don't. But as music it really holds up on its own terms. I don't listen to a lot of bebop other than Miles Davis. But I've always loved Miles' playing of ballads. Not so much for what he played but for his approach to the whole thing. He has such a terrific understanding of space and how small, rhythmic variations can be very powerful. And there's a lot of drama in his playing that I've always admired. I don't aspire to play in the bebop way at all. But I've always admired his approach to jazz. I think it's really wonderful."

Are there any Miles Davis records that Ecklund particularly likes? *"Kind of Blue* is one of my favorites. I mean, it's a simple Miles record. And I also like the records he made with Prestige right before he went to Columbia, when he was recording all those standards. I've always greatly admired Lester Young, too, and I think in that period of Miles' career, he was particularly influenced by a Lester Young concept of melody and a spacing of rhythm and so forth." Not surprisingly, Davis' later work—when he got deep into jazz-rock fusion—holds little interest for Ecklund. "I don't think any of that was really as successful," he says. "I don't think it was his fault. It's just the problem with that kind of music. A lot of times when you hear the great players of bop doing a jazz-rock thing, you sort of hear them trying to play off changes that aren't there. Because if you're playing basically one-chord music or free-form music, you just don't have the harmonic tensions that you find if you're playing on either standard tunes or jazz standards.

"If you hear Miles playing a standard like 'Stella by Starlight,' for example, that's a quite complicated, chromatic melody. It's one of the songs the kids in the '50s hated when they embraced rock, but it's a very well-constructed song, and there are all these opportunities for sort of harmonic tension and release that a great player like Miles uses for expressive effect. And you just can't do that if you're playing, say, on a Jimi Hendrix song or something, because there's a great deal of rhythm but not really a lot of harmony.

"Miles was trying to stay current. See, jazz has always been influenced by the pop music of the time, right from the very beginning. It's like improvisation based on whatever was currently popular. And for Miles it was very logical to continue in that way. He wasn't terrified of these rock musicians who took drugs and had long hair and so forth. So he was just trying to continue the direction that jazz always took, taking popular music and making improvisations on it. But that really didn't work so well after rock came in. It's not the fault of the musicians; rock is music that's inherently not so great to make improvisations with. It doesn't have the internal structure that you need."

Davis may well have moved into jazz-rock fusion primarily for commercial reasons—there were obviously big bucks to be made by wooing the mass, rock-oriented audience—but he maintained that he made the move for artistic reasons; he suggested that continuing to play the old songs, in the established manner, would constitute an artistic dead end. And some jazz critics, I mention to Ecklund, seem to feel that traditionalism and revivalism in jazz fall generally into the "artistic dead-end" category.

Ecklund doesn't buy their argument. He notes that he sometimes plays Renaissance music, written hundreds of years ago, using the type of old-style, valveless trumpet used when that music was new. No one complains of artistic dead ends when music from the Renaissance is played. How can anyone argue it is wrong to play jazz in a general style that flourished earlier in this century? Or even to re-create, note for note, classic older recordings?

"Even the recorded jazz of the '20s and '30s—people will never get the opportunity to hear it played live unless there *are* groups that play it. And it's music that deserves to be heard," Ecklund says. "Particularly now, when there's no one musical movement that's capturing everybody's imagination. In the late '60s and '70s, when rock was new, that was really music that captured the imagination of a generation, and there was a great deal of creation in that. But there isn't anything like that happening now. Many different things are going on at the same time in music now. And I think jazz repertory is certainly valid as a part of all that—if only because this music is perfectly valid music and isn't heard that much."

1992

125

Listen to the Rhythm King

Marty Grosz is unsurpassed at what he does. He's also damned near the only one left doing what he does.

Marty Grosz plays acoustic rhythm guitar. The guitarists that he idolized and took inspiration from in his youth are mostly gone now. Carl Kress, Dick McDonough, Eddie Condon, and Django Reinhardt have all died. Bernard Addison went into retirement years ago. George Van Eps is still playing—but now uses an electric guitar, which Grosz feels is another instrument altogether in terms of sound and technique.

Grosz plays a 1929 Gibson L-5 guitar, a recent replacement for a 1933 Epiphone that he had long owned. He insists he hasn't heard any new guitars that are nearly as good as the old ones. And using such vintage instruments certainly seems appropriate for Grosz, considering that the musical phrasings of the late 1920s and early '30s come so naturally to him. Grosz also occasionally sings, specializing in spritely material from the 1920s and '30s, usually delivered in a tongue-in-cheek style. He's a popular figure on the jazz party and festival circuit, whether working in pickup groups or with his own Orphan Newsboys. At his spacious hilltop home in Piermont, New York, overlooking the Tappan Zee Bridge, we spent an afternoon talking about the old-time hot jazz he loves, and the life he has made for himself playing it.

"I've often thought I was born 20 years too late or something," declares Grosz, who was born in Berlin on February 28, 1930. It's not just that he likes playing jazz of the 1920s and '30s, he likes to listen to recordings from that period as well. And sometimes, he adds, "I wish I could be back there."

Well, if he *could* travel anywhere in time, what would he most want to witness in jazz history?

He warms to the idea. "I'd like to go and see something like King Oliver's Band, with Louis Armstrong, at the Lincoln Gardens in Chicago in the '20s. I'd like to see what that was like, before jazz became such a self-conscious thing. When you had to play for dancing; your solos—the feeling of the music—had to make people want to dance. And then, let's advance 10 years and go to Harlem and see Red Allen and Coleman Hawkins playing someplace. That would be something, you know. I'd like to see the Summa Cum Laude Band [which Bud Freeman organized in 1939] at Nick's; I've got a picture of them upstairs. There are a lot of things I'd like to see," he says.

His choices, I note, all predate the advent of bebop in the '40s. "I was never a champion of bebop," he acknowledges. "Hearing the bebop records now, I like the energy in certain things, especially things that Dizzy Gillespie and Charlie Parker and guys like that did. Some of the bebop records are nice, of course, and most of the guys can surely play their instruments. But generally, the attitude is too academic for me. And most of the bebop musicians, their attitude of disdain for the audience— well, I just can't buy that."

Most modern jazz holds little interest for him, he notes. Too often, he feels, the gutsy vitality that was found in early jazz has been squeezed out of the music. "I've always thought jazz should have one foot in the cotton field and one foot in the saloon. And to me it was dance music that informed jazz—certainly the first 50 years of jazz was all informed by dance music. Even when they were playing concerts, it was still a dance beat. Now, it's a totally different thing. Now it starts in a school, like the Berklee School. I went there and saw a guy copying down—transcribing—a Coltrane solo and stuff. And I think, 'Why is he doing this? Why isn't he playing someplace for somebody?' And they come out very educated, but it's not necessarily where you make jazz. Most music schools raise music teachers; they don't train musicians. It's a different emphasis."

Where did Grosz get his passion for hot jazz?

"I don't know. I think developing a big interest in jazz—or kids today developing a big interest in rock—has to do with puberty. Around 12 or 13, all of a sudden, out of the cocoon comes this latent interest," Grosz says, struggling to find an adequate explanation. Looking back, he notes he can see inklings of his own preferences emerging even before puberty. "I can remember, my older brother would have the radio on to the top station, and you would hear 'In the Mood' and the Andrews Sisters and this type of pop music, endlessly. By the age of 10 I was already saying, 'Uuuh, gasp, not again!' One time, my brother and I were eating something in the kitchen, and he turned on the radio and they had 'In the Mood' on three different stations. And I said, 'Geez, that's boring.' Which it kind of is. It's very repetitive. And enough already. They were saturating us with it. And I think I just had a yen to do everything a little bit different from most people, a little bit off-beat. So jazz was naturally attractive to me.

"I started reading a few books about jazz and hearing a little bit about it from friends, and there was a lot of romantic stuff about it. I developed romantic notions about jazz. That, you know, there are these guys in little dens—neglected—geniuses who play in saloons. They don't want to follow Mammon. They don't want to be in the phalanxes of the big orchestras. They've eschewed the glory and the spotlight to ply their lonesome craft in art! That gets you when you're 13. And there was a little bit of truth to those notions. There *were* guys like that. Certainly Pee Wee Russell, one of the greatest jazz musicians of all time, felt better in an uninhibited, small context; he knew it would have been a waste of his talents to sit in some section, playing third alto on 'In the Mood.' It would have been a waste of Eddie

Condon's talents, a waste of a lot of guys' talents." For young Marty Grosz, then, jazz was the music of the outsider, living solely for his art. And his own family background, as he made clear, helped give him a fundamental sympathy for the outsider, for the artist.

His father, George Grosz, was a well-known member of the expressionist group of artists in Germany—a man who, in the 1920s and early '30s, felt increasingly set apart from the society around him. "My father was aware of where the Nazis were headed, very early. He had caricatured the Nazis at the time of the Munich putsch, and was generally against the military. He was tried twice by the German government in the 1920s for sedition. He drew Christ with a gas mask and Army boots on, and this offended people, and they said it's against the state religion and so forth. Each time he was tried he got off, but he knew which way the wind was blowing. His studio was raided by Brownshirts, even before Hitler came into power. They had sort of a paramilitary organization, and they got away with things that were illegal; the police often made believe that they didn't see what was going on. My father was a target of the Nazis for political reasons. He had been a Communist, although he quit in in 1930; he couldn't really get into the Communist ideology of worshiping the workers. But he remained left of center; he believed the fat cats should be toppled."

His father, Grosz adds, was also generally fascinated by American culture. And, while still in Germany, he was exposed to—and intrigued by—American jazz. "He saw dance bands. In fact, he reviewed Paul Whiteman when Whiteman came to Germany in the mid '20s. And he saw *The Chocolate Kiddies* [a trailblazing all-black show with Sam Wooding's Orchestra that helped open up Europe to American big band jazz], when it came through in 1925. So he decided he wanted to play the banjo—*hot*—but he didn't know how to go about it. I mean, how do you go about it, in Germany in the 1920s? He bought a banjo, and he got an Italian music teacher with a big black cape, which was all wrong. But he was crazy about jazz."

In 1932, George Grosz accepted a post at New York's Art

Students' League. His family remained in Germany while he checked out the scene in America. Among his students was E. Simms Campbell, a cartoonist who happened to be black. "Campbell would take my father up to Harlem, where he saw whatever was going on there in terms of music. Other friends took him other places, you know. One time, he went to a party where, he told me years later, he saw George Gershwin pass out from too much liquor; Gershwin was then carried out of the room—chair and all—so the rug could be rolled up for dancing." Grosz remembers his mother saying that the American popular composers—people like Gershwin, Porter, and Kern—were musically far ahead of those in Germany.

"Then when Hitler seized power in Germany and the Reichstag was burned down, my father returned to Germany and got us—my mother, my older brother, and me. We all moved to the U.S. in '33." The family settled in Douglaston, Long Island, glad to have escaped the Nazis; not all of their friends were so fortunate.

The Grosz family was not religious, Grosz notes. "But my father once told me, if he had become anything—converted or anything—he would have become a Jew, because they were all the people who helped him. And during the '30s, our house in Douglaston was never without a guest. We were like a way-station. My father got a job illustrating for *Esquire* magazine, and he got other commissions, so there was some money coming in. And so he could afford to vouch for people coming into the United States from Germany. We were never without one or two or three people, who were Communists usually—political refugees, whatever the categories were. Some were Communists and Jews at the same time—there was a lot of that in Berlin especially; Communist, Jewish, homosexual—that was there, too: all three. I mean, being in any one of those categories could have gotten you in trouble in Germany. And they would be staying at our house all the time, which made it very colorful. We had one guy, I remember, who had lost a finger in a concentration camp due to an infection or something. He happened to be a Communist and a Jew and he was also a leading philosophy teacher at Berlin University. He spent about a year in a concentration camp and managed to get out of the country. He stayed with us quite a while. So it was a colorful atmosphere." The refugees whom his father sheltered—all outsiders of one sort or another—impressed young Grosz as witty, urbane, and stimulating. A lot more so, he felt, than the average, far more conventional resident of Douglaston.

Douglaston had produced one local celebrity, however, to whom young Grosz could and did look up. Bassist/composer ("What's New," "South Rampart Street Parade," etc.) Bob Haggart, a star of the popular Bob Crosby Band, had come from Douglaston. And it was via a Bob Crosby Band recording that Grosz first really became aware of jazz. From the Crosby Band's brand of Dixieland he went on to explore other styles. He soon was spending his allowance and lunch money on jazz records. The first record he remembers buying was the Kansas City Six's "Pagin' the Devil"—which he selected because of the title. He got books about jazz from the library, too, like Ramsey and Smith's *Jazzmen* (which, incidentally, included a chapter by his father's old friend E. Simms Campbell), Goffin's *Jazz: From the Congo to the Metropolitan*, and Panassie's *Hot Jazz*. He was 13 when he bought himself a guitar (he soon acquired a banjo, as well) and taught himself to play it. He deliberately opted *not* to take lessons because the jazzmen he most admired had all been self-taught. (Today, he has mixed feelings about having been self-taught. He acknowledges it might have been an asset for him to have learned to sight-read with facility, but he still has a hunch that formal training can give a musician an academic quality antithetical to the real jazz spirit.)

Exactly why he opted to play guitar and banjo, rather than any other instruments, he isn't entirely sure. But the first musician he ever saw "live" that made an impact upon him, he notes, was a banjo player named Gene Sheldon, whom he remembers playing "Margie" wonderfully in a stage show at the Roxy Theater. He remembers, too, being impressed by an unknown guitarist's playing on the soundtrack of an abstract cartoon shown in the British building at the 1939–40 New York World's Fair. And he often found himself noticing the contributions of guitarists, while listening to bands on the radio, or sitting in movie theaters waiting for films to begin.

When Grosz formed a trio with friends, the first tune that they learned was Hoagy Carmichael's old favorite from 1931, "Up a Lazy River." Grosz felt no need to follow the latest trends in modern jazz. About the only explanation he can offer is: "I have always had a wanting to be different and to go the other way." He *was* aware of new developments in music that came along, he says. "Guitarists Oscar Moore and Charlie Christian were all that any aspiring musicians were talking about in those days. And Les Paul was coming up, too. I mean, electric guitar was all the thing. But I wasn't interested; I didn't think it was a romantic notion."

In 1942, just around the time that Grosz was really getting into jazz, a recording strike got under way. Until the strike was settled (in 1944 for most companies; in 1943 for Decca), companies were unable to make new records with any musicians. To try to fill some of the void, companies reissued many older sides, thus exposing members of Grosz' generation to classic jazz recordings of the 1920s and '30s they might not otherwise have heard. "The record companies all started reissuing. I don't think they would have reissued Jelly Roll Morton otherwise. All of a sudden the companies hired guys like George Avakian, who wrote about jazz, and said to them, 'Help us with this reissue program.' The exposure to reissues—for a while they were all you could buy—had a big influence on me. When I was 15, I worked at Cape Cod as a kitchen boy, and I used practically all my summer earnings to buy Brunswick reissues: Red Nichols, Jimmie Noone . . . and I've never regretted that. They were beautiful sides. If there's anything more optimistic than 'I Know That You Know' by Jimmie Noone, I'd like to know what it is. That's a wonderful record to start the day with. And that reissue program, I think, influenced a lot of us. They also had an Ellington album on Victor—these were all 78 r.p.m. albums, of course—that I bought which had an old record of 'East St. Louis Toodle-Oo,' and it had 'Stompy Jones' in it. And it went right up through 'Dusk'—1940. So it had a broad spectrum. And for the first time I heard The Quintet of the Hot Club of France—

132

which I thought sounded like western swing. And then there was a *Hot Trumpets and Hot Trombones* album. These reissues introduced me to a lot of guys that I wouldn't otherwise have heard—like Floyd O'Brien and Benny Morton and Miff Mole, who had sort of had an eclipse. I can hear Miff's wonderful record of 'Dixieland One-Step' to this day. And of course Teagarden's 'Making Friends.' And then there was the Bix album. And the Louis Armstrong Hot Fives came out, and I got all those.

"Of course, all the kids at school back then knew who Glenn Miller, Benny Goodman, Duke Ellington, Count Basie, Kay Kyser, and other big band leaders were. But they weren't really into Bessie Smith and Bix and Jimmie Noone, Bechet, and so on, like I was. Only about 5% of the kids were really into jazz. We were a little elite. I remember, I ran into a guy in the school library and I saw 'Bunny Berigan and His Blue Boys' written on his notebook cover, the way other kids might write the name of a football team. And we got to talking: 'Yeah, I like jazz. . . .' And then a few of us would get together and it was very much an 'in' group; we knew things that *they* didn't know. We'd make up all-star bands. One of the kids said, 'Who do you like on guitar?' I said Allan Reuss or George Van Eps or Carl Kress or something. And he said, 'No, the *real* guy is Eddie Condon. *He* doesn't take solos; *he* plays for the guys in the band.' And there was romance in that." Thus Grosz' own adolescent goal was not to become a guitar soloist, he notes, but rather a rhythm player, contributing to the overall success of a band. And even though, in time, he would naturally be forced to take more and more solos, he still proudly refers to himself as a rhythm guitar player today.

"Our group was very clannish," he says. "Because when you're young, there's safety in numbers. You have to buttress your identity up. And you have to have cohorts that'll help you out over the rough spots because the rest of the people are sort of laughing at you, or saying, 'Oh, you're playing that goofy stuff. Why don't you play so-and-so.' I mean, at a typical party, they would play Perry Como and Frank Sinatra and Bing Crosby records—the latter-day ones that are real drippy and goopy. And I'd try to go sneak on 'Sweetie Pie' by Fats Waller or something.

And have everybody say, 'Oh Gawd, what's that? Take that off!'"

At thirteen, Grosz was sent away to the prestigious prep school Phillips Academy, Andover. He views his mother as misguided for sending him there; her idea was for him to receive a solid, traditional New England education, preparing him for an eventual respectable career as perhaps an insurance underwriter or mortgage consultant—which held no interest whatsoever for him. What did interest him was jazz. Since Andover was not too far from Boston, Grosz managed to see a lot of touring big bands in his student days: Count Basie, Benny Goodman, Duke Ellington, Glen Gray and the Casa Loma Band, Charlie Spivak, Bobby Sherwood, and more. He would especially watch the guitar players. After three years at Andover, though, Grosz was kicked out. He had been caught sneaking off to Boston to hear a band when he was supposed to be confined to campus. He finished high school in Long Island.

After graduating in 1948, Grosz and a friend hitchhiked west, settling in Chicago. Grosz still imagined the Windy City was a center for jazz as it had been in the 1920s, when brash young members of the Austin High Gang and others had made music crackling with vitality. "I always thought those Chicago guys were wonderful; I still do," he comments. "But my going to Chicago was like going back to New Orleans, you know—long before I got there, the city's best jazz players had all left. I mean, by then Joe Sullivan was on the West Coast. Jess Stacy was gone. Art Hodes was in New York. Bud Freeman was basically based in New York. About the only guys left in Chicago in 1948 were Floyd O'Brien, who had come back from playing on the West Coast; Bud Jacobson, who was never a major luminary; and Baby Dodds, who had come back after working with Bunk Johnson—but he was not very active in Chicago then.

"When I went to Chicago that first time, I worked as a soda jerk and short order cook and in a music store, and unloaded boxcars—and played wherever I could. Trumpeter Lee Collins had a trio in a saloon, working from like seven o'clock at night to three in the morning; almost anybody could sit in, just to give him a break, and I did. That was a wonderful experience for me. I met people down there, all kinds. But it was a fleabag. And then next door was a place called the Glass Pub that had male strippers. That was where a guy who was living in the same rooming house as I was got a broken bottle pushed in his face. And I went to rent parties at Jimmy Yancey's house, with Albert Ammons, Don Ewell, George Zack—all those guys. Anybody who was in town might fall by and play. And I was just a kid with my eyes open.

"I met one guy in Chicago who was my buddy for the longest time; we were very close. That was Frank Chace, the clarinet player, who lives out there. And he really hipped me onto Tesch and Pee Wee. He was crazy about them. I met him when I was looking for jazz records in a music store. I asked a clerk, 'Do you have such-and-such?' and this guy turns around and says, 'Oh, do you like so-and-so?' We started talking, and we went to his house. We listened to all kinds of things: Ellington, King Oliver, everything. He was nuts about Pee Wee Russell." With the ardor of youth, Grosz and Chace were fierce champions of musicians like Russell, Teschemacher, Joe Sullivan, Muggsy Spanier, Davey Tough, and Bud Freeman. As Grosz puts it: "It was our guys or nobody."

He reflects: "Andre Previn once said that with jazz music, it's the stuff you start with that stays with you. The way you came into it sort of determines your life in the music. He was using that to explain his liking for Art Tatum; despite all the things that have come along since in music, that groove is really where his heart's at. And I suppose that's true." To a large extent, he acknowledges, his own musical tastes were shaped in puberty. And although he has broadened his musical interests somewhat since those days—becoming, he feels, less parochial—the hot jazz he first loved still holds a special place in his affections.

After about a year in Chicago, Grosz returned to New York and started playing around wherever he could. He landed a steady job on weekends at a place called the Rathskeller, on Fordham Road in the Bronx. "And I'd also go and jam at Nola's Studio, where I met guys like Dick Wellstood and Bob Wilber.

We would chip in, like 50 cents or a dollar apiece, to rent the studio to rehearse. And we would go and sit in at various clubs. I remember I used to sit in at a place called the Riviera Lounge, on Sheridan Square, where Willie the Lion Smith and Art Hodes played. And Willie the Lion was tough! He took no prisoners. Before you'd even gotten your instrument out of the case, he'd be telling you, 'Come on! Let's go!' And then he'd say, 'You ain't even tuned up yet!' And he'd keep changing keys and stuff to try to throw you off—which he often did."

Grosz found other young traditionalists with whom he could work, like multi-instrumentalist Johnny Dengler, just a couple of years out of Princeton (where he had led a highly popular Dixieland band), who hired Grosz for a summer in the Poconos. Among the special guests who sat in with Dengler's band were Bud Freeman, on tenor sax, and actor Jackie Cooper, on drums. In 1951, Grosz made his recording debut on the Jolly Roger label, leading an eight-piece group: Marty Grosz and his Cellar Boys, including young Dick Wellstood on piano and veteran Pops Foster on bass.

To placate his mother, who thought music was fine as a hobby but hardly suitable as a career, Grosz enrolled in Columbia University; within a couple of months, however, he was drafted into the Army. Throughout his two-year hitch, he practiced guitar in his spare time.

"When I got out of the Army, I went to visit a friend of mine in Chicago—and I wound up staying in Chicago for 20 years! I should have gone right back to New York, but I didn't feel I had roots in New York anymore. My mother was still saying, 'You've got to find something to do. You mean you want to just sit in a band and go ching-ching-ching?' I said, 'Yeah, Mom. That's what I want to do.'

"Back in Chicago in '54, I resumed where I'd started off, playing around with other people. And playing a lot with my buddy Frank Chace—who wanted to be the second Pee Wee Russell, which was impossible. You can't be anybody else. We all start out that way but eventually, hopefully, find our own styles. You know, I wanted to be Eddie Condon. And I knew lots of guys who wanted to be Louis Armstrong. I always feel

Marty Grosz (photo by Chip Deffaa).

Grosz, on guitar, is flanked by Bob Lovett, on clarinet, and Hugh McKay, on trumpet, at the Rathskeller in the Bronx, 1950. Lovett later became a film editor, nominated for an Academy Award for his work on The Cotton Club *(courtesy of Marty Grosz).*

The top photo (courtesy of Marty Grosz) depicts a 1951 recording session: Johnny Dengler, bass sax; Pops Foster, bass; Hugh McKay, trumpet; Grosz, guitar/leader; Frank Chace, clarinet; Tommy Benford, drums; Dick Wellstood, piano; and Ephie Resnick, trombone. The bottom photo (by Chip Deffaa) depicts a 1992 Orphan Newsboys gig at the Cornerstone in Metuchen, New Jersey: Peter Ecklund, cornet; Marty Grosz, guitar; Ken Peplowski, tenor sax; and Bill Holoday, bass.

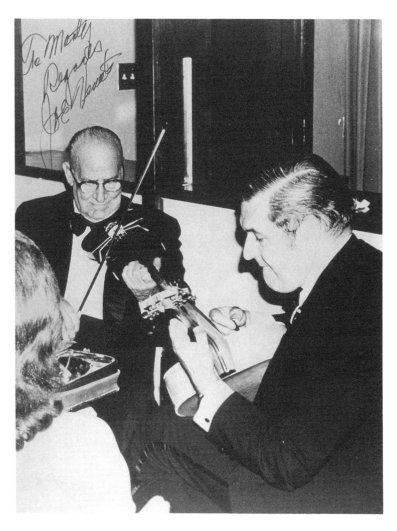

Violinist Joe Venuti and Grosz (courtesy of Marty Grosz).

slightly sorry for the guys who are still doing other people, like all the clarinet players who want to be Benny Goodman."

Grosz made one final stab at higher education, enrolling in the University of Chicago, but he only lasted a few months; jazz simply held a greater attraction for him. "I got chances to go on the road," he recalls. The music business proved less glamorous than he had originally anticipated, but he figured he had to pay his dues. "They were pretty mediocre bands I played with—just minor Dixieland groups that were around then. When I was on the road and had a free afternoon, I used to go around to Salvation Army places and used book stores and junk shops in small towns, and they'd have piles of old sheet music—a nickel a copy, or two for a nickel. I'd get these things, sometimes just because they had amusing covers. If I saw, 'I Wonder Where My Baby Is Tonight,' maybe I'd say, 'That looks pretty good; I'll pick it up, in case I get a request for it.'" He never *did* get a request for that particular tune, he adds, but he did eventually record it.

"Then finally in 1957, Frank Chace and I got a job playing in a trio led by a pianist, Jess Sutton, at the Gaslight Club in Chicago. I played there for five years, off and on. People would come in and get smashed. And the place was packed! I worked in a room called the Speakeasy; you had to go through a telephone booth and say, 'Joe sent me.' Ha ha ha ha. And everything was like that. We were dressed up in the stupid striped shirts. And this little piano player was dressed up as a Keystone Kop. The club's motto was, 'Every night is New Year's Eve.' And they've got to keep the excitement going. So they had little wooden mallets and ceramic popcorn bowls on every table. With the mallets, the customers would bang time. You can imagine what that sounded like. Like when everyone is drunk at Santa's workshop!" Not only the customers drank heavily there, he notes; the musicians did, too. "We drank out of cups, and when we finished the bartender would just take the cup and fill it up again. So all of us were alcoholics at that time.[1] And then we'd take bennies or dexies [benzedrine or dexedrine] so we could make it through the night. And when a day off came, then I'd be home. I had a

---

[1]Grosz does not drink at all, today.

wife and a little kid. And I'd be like this [Grosz gives a look of utter exhaustion], and my wife would be saying, 'I want to go places and do things!' When you're young, you can take that.

"But working at that club was good for learning a bunch of tunes and good for the chops," he says. Tired of playing familiar numbers like "Five Foot Two, Eyes of Blue," "Charleston," and "Bye Bye Blackbird" night after night, he started bringing in music of Bix Beiderbecke, Jelly Roll Morton, and Duke Ellington. Besides the tunes he learned from sheet music, he began jotting down others he heard on old records. "I taught myself how to sort of half-ass read music and write music and I'd write out different tunes to play." Grosz gradually developed an enormous repertoire of vintage numbers, both famous and obscure. When old-time songwriter Ted Fiorito came into the club one night, Grosz swung into a long-forgotten Fiorito ditty called "I Need Some Pettin'." Fiorito said he hadn't heard it played in 30 years.

"Oh, we made some money at the Gaslight," Grosz acknowledges. "We got tips. They had a clothesline with dollar bills hanging from it. And every time a guy put a buck tip on the line, a bell went off. But finally, after five years I'd had enough of the place." He resented the noise, the smoke, the less-than-inspiring playing of the pianist. He believed a life in jazz should offer more. But finding what he wanted was far from easy.

"For a while, I went on the road with the Village Stompers, an eight-piece band playing a mishmash called 'folk-Dixie.' Their big hit was 'Washington Square.' But I didn't like the Village Stompers. I mean, what was there to like? It was an idea that was born in some agent's office. It was totally hokey. And one arrangement was just like the next. It was a show biz act, not jazz.

"Then I got an offer to go into a place in Chicago called the Velvet Swing; it actually had a girl on a velvet swing. Between sets by a band, I played banjo as an intermission act—doing 'Alabama Jubilee' and stuff like that. Once in a blue moon, I used to fool around, singing, back in the band room. And the guy told me to do that out in the club. I found out that singing was an asset. You make more money—a little shtick, you know. Hokey. So I started singing every night. Before that, I hadn't really sung," he notes. "But that club was a terrible dump. They were all dumps.

"And then from the Velvet Swing, I started playing in and around Chicago and Canada and the midwest. I toured in a little roadshow with four girls who danced and a five-piece band, and we'd travel all over, like to conventions. But I was stagnating in those years, eating my heart out. Oh, there were occasional good jobs. At one point, I had an eight-piece band called the Sounds of Swing, with trumpeter Norman Murphy, and we even got on nationwide TV in a series called *Just Jazz* that Dan Morgenstern put together. And for a year, Murphy and I had a band at the Blackstone Hotel, including Kansas Fields, Truck Parham, and Harry Field; that wasn't too bad. But basically, you're dying out there. It ain't happening. For 20 years I stayed in Chicago. I did everything you can do there. It just doesn't work. It works better here in New York.

"Some of the jobs I had to take were terrible. I was working with guys opening up at the Wisconsin Cheese Shop. More marching around with the vests, and playing on boats and on horse carts, and all kinds of crap. And then I remember Murphy and I were playing for Riverside Savings and Loan on the Chicago River, and every time the guy who was in charge of the promotion stuck his head out, we had to play 'Down by the Riverside.' They had girls dressed up like Scarlett O'Hara handing out brochures; you know the kind of ballyhoo people think up. And we were dressed up—for some reason, we had to wear propeller beanies. And they actually wanted us to wear shorts. And big bow ties. I drew the line. Here we are, Murphy and I and a tuba player. And I said, 'That's it! Death, where is thy sting? There's got to be a better way.' I was really thinking of something else to do, outside of music. I got a U.S. government list of job positions and was studying that," he recalls.

"It was right at that time, when I was thinking about getting out of the business, that Bob Wilber called and asked me if I would like to join Soprano Summit. I said, 'Of course!' I saw it as a chance to get out of the doldrums. I don't care what anyone says; Chicago's great days were in the '20s. Trying to make an impact in jazz while living in Chicago is like trying to make an impact in ballet dancing in Tucson, Arizona," says Grosz.

Soprano Summit was one the finest new mainstream jazz groups to emerge in years, and becoming a part of it gave Grosz terrific exposure. Its coleaders were Wilber and Kenny Davern, playing soprano saxes and clarinets; George Duvivier was on bass; Bobby Rosengarden on drums. For some dates, the group also used a pianist (generally Dick Hyman). Grosz was brought in to play guitar (succeeding Bucky Pizzarelli, who had played on the group's debut album), and also to help arrange. "What a change in my life joining that group made! One week I was playing banjo for the opening of a cheese shop in Chicago's Union Station; two weeks later, I was with Soprano Summit at Carnegie Hall!

"But backstage at Carnegie Hall for that first big concert, my knees sounded like castanets, I was so nervous. All those people out there! And there was Dick Hyman, you know, and all this heavy artillery. And this break was happening late in my career; I was like 46. But it worked out OK." In between dates with Soprano Summit, Grosz free-lanced. Being with them opened the door to assorted other jazz party and concert bookings, record dates, and gigs with leaders like Dick Wellstood and Dick Sudhalter. Grosz comments: "Coming back to New York from the boondocks concentrates the mind. You start practicing and thinking, 'Hey, this is for real.' You know, you get into sloppy habits when you're playing with sloppy players in less than challenging situations. And now all of a sudden, here you are, playing in the same band or on the same record date with guys you've been in awe of all your life. You're saying, 'Oh my God, that's Milt Hinton, that's Cootie Williams.' There's nothing like that to make you serious about playing again if you've been coasting."

Grosz got opportunities as a leader which he could never have gotten had he remained in Chicago, no matter how well he had played. "For example, I led a band that did the opening credits soundtrack for a 1976 Sean Connery film called *The Next Man*. They wanted a '20s thing. So I got Davern, Wilber, Hyman, Warren Vaché Jr., and Jack Gale. And I did a commercial for Owen-Corning's Chameleon eyeglasses. They had a little cartoon chameleon and I had to sing and I had to say: 'They'll change your whole outlook.' I had to stand there and do that like 80 times. They'd say, 'Marty, I've lost that a little bit; could you give us a little more. . . .' And you finally wind up [and now he goes into an exaggerated voice reminiscent of the Kingfish from the *Amos 'n' Andy* show]: 'They'll *change* your whole outlook.'

"Soprano Summit lasted, off and on, for a couple of years, and then broke up [in 1979]. That was inevitable. You can't take guys of that caliber and expect them to hang in there saying 'all for one and one for all,' forever. I mean, guys have to pursue their own things.

"We formed the Classic Jazz Quartet in 1984—Dick Wellstood, Joe Muranyi, Dick Sudhalter, and myself—and did that for a few years. But after Wellstood died in 1987, I had no interest in trying to keep the group going with anybody else. Sudhalter did. But I wouldn't have any part of it. To me, Wellstood was really the guts of that group. He was *it*. And nobody could take his place. In fact, I told him when we formed it, 'This should be Dick Wellstood and his things. You should play the first half of every one of our programs as a solo pianist, and then later bring us on to help you, as a little change of scene.' So I said 'no' to going on with the group after he died."

Grosz got more offers to record under his own name, and put together various little groups, finally hitting upon a combination he hopes to be able to stay with, the Orphan Newsboys with Peter Ecklund. Grosz is a firm believer in the value of maintaining organized groups. Because there are few organized groups anymore and because many musicians don't make the necessary efforts to keep the music fresh, he gets pessimistic concerning the future of traditional jazz. Over the years, he has given a great deal of thought to such matters; his opinions merit careful consideration.

"We can all forget talking about the kind of jazz I like until you have a chance to play it more," Grosz offers as an opening salvo. "I love ensemble playing. I like to hear horns—if they're good—play lots of ensemble. That's almost a lost art these days.

You have to be together a lot, and come from the same tradition, to do it. Almost every time I play, it seems I'm thrown together with guys that I never play with or maybe I don't want to play with.

"Unless you can have permanent groups that work together and rehearse, I don't think we're ever going to hear the kinds of sounds that the King Oliver Band or the Chicago guys got. I mean, when you hear the ensembles of the Summa Cum Laude Band and stuff, those guys are all on the same wavelength. But how are you going to get on the same wavelength if you don't play together regularly? And there's just not enough work today. There's not even a place in New York where you can play steadily five nights a week to get that feeling—to learn some stuff together, and work out your parts, and really do it. If you could, then your band would be a killer. You could do jazz concerts and wipe everybody away.'

"But nowadays it's always a jam session. The thing that was designed to give you freedom was the jam session. In the old days, guys were all sitting in sections of bands saying, 'Oh, I can't wait to go down someplace to jam and do my own thing.' Well, OK, now everybody is doing his own thing all the time and it's no fun. Musicians need some discipline. People forget that King Oliver rehearsed that band—that they worked out their parts, that they had a sense of form. Same with the Louis Armstrong Hot Fives and the Jelly Roll Mortons. It wasn't just guys blowing.

"There's too much freedom today. You don't have the pleasure of saying, 'I've been sitting in this band for half an hour. Now I'm finally going to get my chance to wail.' You wail all the time. And good jazz soloists who can really sustain interest for three, four, five choruses aren't that readily available. Maybe the old records were kind to a lot of players. They'd only get to solo for eight or sixteen bars on a record, but they're remembered very well. That's not so bad. To be remembered for sixteen good bars is better than being remembered for eight mediocre choruses. Nowadays I hear these records and they're all the same. I mean, it's a tenor sax and a rhythm section. The sax plays until he gets tired. Then the piano player plays until *he* gets tired. Then they pass it around with the bass and the drums or something. And then they play the head again. They have thousands of records like that. And that doesn't strike me as very creative."

Experimenting on gigs is important to Grosz. "I try to find numbers to play that not everybody is playing, and I'm always trying to think of different ways of doing things. Almost anything is better than a rhythm section and a bunch of guys standing up there. A band is not a rhythm section with five or six horns playing solos against it. A band is when horns interact. And I encourage musicians to do anything. *Anything*. I don't care if the bass player tap dances, if he wants to. It's jazz. It's free. My own tendency is to get more and more into the theater of the absurd, because the other thing is stagnating." I think of having seen Grosz, with the Classic Jazz Quartet, lead a whimsical group vocal on "Mississippi Mud"—*in German*. Or of having seen him, with the Orphan Newsboys Quartet, suddenly start chanting "Fe-Fi-Fo-Fum, Fe-Fi-Fo Fum" in the middle of one old chestnut; his fellow band members were clearly surprised but they took up the vocal chant, effectively building tension, which Ecklund finally used as a springboard for a cornet solo. Grosz comments: "When the guys were first playing jazz, they weren't always thinking: 'What is it I'm doing? Is it right or is it wrong? Or does it make sense?' And I would like to leave all the avenues open. Ideally, it should happen naturally and spontaneously.

"Greg Cohen, the bassist of the Orphan Newsboys, and I talk about this. He's more than just a bass player, you know. He does theater work. He produces records. He does avant-garde stuff. He's done the music of Charles Mingus. He did a session with guys from the Rolling Stones. Crazy things—not necessarily related to jazz. Anyway, so Greg said, 'I think they should release some pigeons while the drummer is soloing.' And I said, 'Why not? It would be an excellent idea. If I have to sit through another five-minute drum solo. . . . I mean, it *needs* something like that.'

"And I think about the bands I saw when I was a kid. I saw Ellington around 1946, and it was a stage presentation; it was not just guys playing hot choruses. Ray Nance came out and did his bit. The three singers he had at that time—Joya Sherill, Kay

Davis, and Marie Ellington—they did 'It Don't Mean a Thing' and stuff. Ellington himself did a monologue, about a guy standing on the street corner of Harlem, with woodwind things playing behind him. He had a cat standing, with a big key chain down to here. Oh, yeah! I mean, he did theater. That was all well produced. And they had a pit band, too. It plays a bit and the announcer says, 'Ladies and gentlemen, we present the music of Duke Ellington and his Famous Orchestra.' The curtain parts and there's a blue scrim. You don't see anything but the outlines of the players in the Ellington Band. The band starts playing and they get a hand. Then the scrim parts and you see the band itself; another hand. Now Ellington himself walks onstage to stand in front of the band. Another hand. So he's had four hands before he's really started the program. He's already got the audience in that gung-ho mood. Why not do those kinds of things now?

"At some of these jazz parties whose names I won't mention, all the musicians line up onstage and everybody plays the head. And it's always the same old head that they played the last time you heard them—'Undecided' or 'A Train' or, you know. . . . You could puke already! A jam session is supposed to be for imagination, not to trammel it. And it turns out, guys are playing by rote."

Most professional jazzmen today, Grosz feels, don't experiment enough. Sometimes, due to economic realities, they simply don't get many chances to. "They're grinding away their lives, going on little concert tours and to jazz parties where they're playing with some of the musicians for the first time in their life. They turn around and say, 'Listen, does everybody know "When I Take My Sugar to Tea"?' And they hear, 'No, I've never played it actually. How's the bridge go?' 'Oh well, then we better do "Honeysuckle Rose."' They have to settle for tunes everybody knows. And that's how they're spending their lives.

"I believe that you have to form groups; that's the only solution. But the problems of keeping a group together and working regularly are huge. I mean, I've got the Orphan Newsboys working the L.A. Classic, and the Atlanta Jazz Festival next year. I don't think that will start a trend. I'm *sure* of it! But we *try* to get together."

One reason Grosz opts to work as often as he can with Peter Ecklund, who is 15 years his junior, rather than some more seasoned veteran, is that he finds Ecklund so open to new ideas. And Ecklund does not copy any one jazz musician's style when he plays; unlike some trumpeters, he does not try to be a clone of Bix or Louis or Dizzy or anybody else. Grosz observes, "Peter has an interesting style. When I first heard him, I liked the fact that he didn't particularly sound like anybody I knew. I mean, I could hear influences—I heard Jack Purvis, and a little bit of Bill Coleman and a little of this and a little of that, and there's sort of a Bixian influence sometimes, and stuff—but it sounded eclectic. And I think that should be encouraged.

"And younger guys like Peter Ecklund and Greg Cohen, and Ken Peplowski and so on—they'll do things that other people won't do. An older guy might say, 'What are you doing that for? Nah, that's no good.' Because guys get very set in their ways: *There's this way to do this, the way I've always done it.* But these guys aren't afraid to do some crazy things or to go at a tune a different way. The way some older guys play, you're not going to get stimulated. There's nothing new and exciting and different. And there *is* new and exciting and different stuff that can come out of traditional music or mainstream music—just as much as can come out of bebop.

"It amuses me when bebop musicians sneer at trad, or trad guys sneer at bebop. I mean, it's all historical now! One's not any better than the other. Most of us have a mistaken notion about progress: if it's newer, it's better. But even in traditional and mainstream music, there are things to be brought out of it. There are things that can be done with improvisation. That doesn't mean you can't have a band that plays in the King Oliver mode or in the Jelly Roll Morton mode or in the John Kirby mode. But I think you should try to adapt the music, not simply re-create it. Because when King Oliver's Band was playing, they didn't think of themselves as 'traditionalists.' They were playing what was hip to the day. And they played any tune that they were given to record. I think there's too much repertory stuff around—guys doing Jelly Roll Morton, guys doing Beiderbecke, guys doing Glenn Miller. And my God, we've got the records! Well, I can justify it in one way. A live performance of a Fletcher Henderson chart or something—young people will have no chance to encounter that again in their lives. So for that reason, it has a limited worth. But to play it, and to have to do other people's solos, and to forever be locked into doing what someone else did on a record—that's a bit stultifying for a musician.

"I think the worst trend that's happening in music now is guys' having to play all different styles. One day they're playing in a big band and they've got to *be* so-and-so. It's like the typical studio thing, where musicians are ordered: 'Give me like a little Bobby Hackett ballad fill here.' Or, 'Hey, now I want you to growl; give me that Duke Ellington–Cootie Williams–type stuff.' Or, 'Can you give me a Harry James sound?' That makes for chameleons. But any real great jazz musician has his own identity. You listen to almost any record that Coleman Hawkins is on, and you know within a measure or two: 'Hawk is on that date.' And the same thing goes for Louis Armstrong or Pee Wee Russell or Joe Sullivan.

"The worst thing for jazz is the studio kind of influence. I play with studio guys who'll say, 'What kind do you want? You want a bossa nova kind of groove? You want a little bottleneck blues? You want this—' They can do a reasonable job of reproducing all different styles. Some guys will come to a record date and say to me, 'How do you want me to play?' And I say, 'If I make any suggestions about how to play a thing, please kick me! You just do whatever *you* feel is appropriate to the tune, to your mood. If you had a fight with your old lady, so, get mad! It'd probably make the tune better.'"

He likes variety in his recordings. He doesn't hog solo space. Solos may be taken in turn by the likes of Paul Bacon on comb ("He really plays the damned thing; he's right on the money," says Grosz of Bacon), Ecklund on cornet, Joe Muranyi on clarinet, Andy Stein on violin, and so on, while Grosz concentrates on holding the band together.

"I don't like copying old records. I try to get the sheet music to an older song, if possible, and just play through it, and approach it totally as if I'd never heard a record of it—as fresh material, the way the guys who first recorded it did." Learning numbers from original sheet music rather than from other performers' recordings has its advantages, he notes. Even a frequently re-corded old song that "everybody knows" is often remembered only for its first chorus. However, the sheet music that vaudeville performers originally used may have included, besides the famil-iar chorus, an intriguing verse, seldom-heard patter, and an encore chorus. In vaudeville, Grosz says, "you had to have a lot of different words to keep people entertained. So verse-chorus-and-patter was a very common form in the 1920s—created for the stage. A song like 'I Left My Sugar Standing in the Rain' has a verse. It goes: 'Somewhere the sun is shining, but here it only rains. . . .' After the verse, you get into the chorus: 'Oh, I left my sugar standing in the rain. . . .' Then after that chorus, there was patter, with lines going 'You don't miss your da-da till the da-da-dee.' Like: 'You don't miss your money till the market drops. / You don't miss your butcher till you're out of chops. / I didn't miss my sugar till the other day. / I bought her shoes, she put 'em on, and walked away.'" Grosz liked the feel of the patter, but when he decided to record the song (on the Stomp Off album *Marty Grosz and the Keepers of the Flame*) he felt it necessary to change a couple of lines because they reinforced outdated ethnic stereotypes. "I couldn't sing some of the original lines. They had some words like, 'You don't miss the Chinese till your shirt needs pressing' and, 'You don't miss the Greeks till you're hungry' or something. I said no, no, no, no."

And while Grosz liked the melody of "Oh! Miss Hanna," he was not comfortable singing the Negro dialect lines that white performers were expected to sing in 1929: "Oh, Miss Hanna, ain't you comin' out tonight? / De mockingbirds am singing and de moon am shining bright. / De roses am a-noddin' and a-swaying in de breeze. / Put on your Sunday go-to-meetin' clothes and come along please." Grosz decided to update the song, devising these replacement lyrics: "Oh Miss Hanna, ain't you truckin' down tonight? / The Nighthawks are a-swingin' and the neon's shining bright. / The old folks are a-stompin', just listen to them wheeze. / Put on your rhinestone-studded jumpsuit and come along please." If he can get an occasional laugh out of the audience with a vocal, he's happy. He feels it is wearying to subject audiences to seemingly endless, sometimes narcissistic, bouts of instrumental jazz improvisation. He believes jazz lost a large audience to other styles of music, such as rock and country/western, because it became too introspective and "artsy." His instrumental solos are generally brief but intriguing. His playing is more emotionally expressive than his singing, which tends towards a cheery, Fats Waller–inspired vein. I find his vocals entertaining when offered sparingly, for variety, but think that those festival and record producers who insist he sing one number after another are unwise. His forte is clearly as a player and bandleader, not vocalist.

His occasional humorous quips and comments between numbers have become no less a part of his act than his singing and playing and, he believes, have contributed to his popularity. "The shtick is what gets me over," he says. "That's why they want me in England and stuff. Because I get up and talk and clown around with them and everything. When I was in Germany recently, I talked a lot about George Bush. I told them, 'You know who we've got for a president? You know what Skull and Bones is? It's that exclusive club at Yale—like a little finishing club for the big men on campus. Do you realize that, as part of the Skull and Bones initiation rites, the president of the United States once had to lie naked in a coffin and describe his sexual exploits? That's the beginning of politics. Because obviously they have to lie, you know, to make themselves sound more adept than they really were.'" When Grosz tells such stories, one might almost infer that he would rather be a stand-up comic than a musician. But he insists: "My happiest moments are playing on dates where they hire me and I don't open my mouth at all. I love it! I can sit in the back and just play."

He is 100% serious about his guitar-playing. He uses an unorthodox tuning that is unique to him, which gives him more bass range than the standard Spanish guitar–tuning. The tuning Grosz uses, reading the strings from low to high, is: B-flat, F, C,

G, B, D. The lowest string is lower than the standard E on Spanish guitar, and contributes to the satisfyingly solid sound characteristic of Grosz' work. He can play in a trio without a bass player—or even in a duo if need be—without the music's sounding as thin as one might expect.

Grosz *never* uses an amplifier. "I'm about the only guitarist left that does it acoustically," he notes. He believes an acoustic rhythm guitar can generate a propulsive sense of swing that no electric guitar can duplicate. The physical resistance of the heavy strings, set high off the fingerboard, contributes to the generation of a swinging beat. "A lot of my friends have electric guitars where the strings are lying down on top of the fingerboard. And you have no resistance; I mean, you touch the strings and they play. But when you have the strings high off the fingerboard, and they're heavy-gauge strings, you've got to push more with the left hand, which is tough; that's not so much fun. But you don't get the swing—you don't get the drive—unless you've got to force this a little bit. It's got to be a little hard. If playing is too easy [and now his voice lapses into an I-couldn't-care-less type of mode], then it's just going to sound like this. Well, the same thing has happened with the basses. The old basses, with the strings high off the fingerboard, had a lot of resistance. But now the bass player has got the amp jacked up, you know, and he's sitting back on the stool, with the solo strings on his bass. [Grosz scats a light run.] It all sounds a little bit like slack spaghetti. Slack. Dripping. It doesn't have that old [he scats, articulating each sound forcefully: pa-tong, tong, tong, ta-ta-tongtong].

"That sort of change has happened all through jazz. The way a guy like Cootie Williams or Louis Armstrong played the trumpet, there was a lot of resistance. It was painful, but it's what gives it that impact—even on a slow tune [he scats to demonstrate, forcing out each individual sound]. It's like if you sing open throat or closed throat; there's a resistance if you sing closed throat. [He sings an example, constricting his throat to roughen the sound.] That's the way Cootie Williams, you know, *pushed*. And you could see the rings on the lips. Guys don't play that way anymore. Guys play with the horn right on the mike, you know. And they all play [scats a real effortless line] sort of laid back, cool. Over the years, it seems like everything in jazz has gotten lighter—faster and lighter and cooler. You know, the tenor saxophone players in the early '30s got a very big, fat sound, compared to players today—they sounded almost like a baritone. I like the fatter sounds better."

From his vintage guitar, Grosz gets a beauty of tone that to my ears no electric guitar can surpass. He generates infectious rhythmic patterns that conjure up bygone times. He's good at what he does. And knows he's just about the last one left doing it. He says with a sigh: "I would have been *dynamite* in 1933." No doubt. But catch him, the next time he's at a jazz festival in your vicinity, or pick up one of his recordings. I think you'll agree, he's not doing too badly in the 1990s, either.

1992

"Pops was the fountainhead . . ."

"Even if I dropped dead tomorrow, I played with Louis Armstrong. That means so much to me." Joe Muranyi stands as he talks, occasionally pacing in his Manhattan apartment. Shelves filled with classic jazz records—78s and LPs—cover one wall. A framed color photo of Armstrong hangs on the wall at one end of the room. A statuette of Armstrong stands in front of the opposite wall. On a small table is a portable manual typewriter. Muranyi, who was a member of Louis Armstrong's All-Stars for about five years preceding Armstrong's death in 1971, has been spending time each day of late, typing out his recollections of Armstrong for a proposed book.

"He was wonderful—absolutely," Muranyi says. "He was just quite something. A wonderful player. Defined a style. Set down a musical idiom. . . . He was the fountainhead.

"When he died, I was very distressed. I was really in tears, the first time in my life, I mean really. I remember my wife at the time said, 'I understand you loved him and he was a great guy and all that—but *really*.' I said, 'Well, you want to hear how great he is?' I put on the dumb FM radio. I said, *'Wait!'* I swear to God it was like 10 seconds, the *Muzak*. I said, 'Hear that lick!' It was a Louis Armstrong phrase in the Muzak. You don't have to look very far for his influence."

Muranyi, 57, has played clarinet and soprano sax with no small number of jazz greats. He is currently one quarter of the Classic Jazz Quartet, along with Dick Sudhalter, Marty Grosz, and Dick Wellstood.[1] He spent most of the 1970s playing nightly alongside Roy Eldridge. And in earlier years he played, at one time or another, with such venerable jazz stars as Bobby Hackett, Red Allen, Danny Barker, George Wettling, Yank Lawson, Bob Haggart, Herman Autrey, Edmond Hall, and Wingy Manone. But he states simply: "Working with Louis Armstrong was the biggest thrill of my life; I was absolutely knocked out by the fact. I kept thinking, 'Here I am, the immigrant's son—my father came from Hungary in the '20s—with Louis Armstrong.'" For one who grew up treasuring the classic Armstrong recordings of the '20s, to be accompanying Armstrong was the ultimate musical reward.

As a student at Brooklyn Tech High School (from which he graduated in 1946), Muranyi recalls, he got "into old records, Hot Fives and Gennetts and Clarence Williams records. I joined a hot jazz club—we met once a week after school. Everybody brought in their records and played the 78s. It was kind of esoteric then; it was really underground.

"We had various factions. There was a crowd that liked the 'Nicksieland' stuff—you know, Nick's and Condon's stuff. I didn't care for that; I liked the black stuff. I liked New Orleans and Clarence Williams records, black blues records and all that kind of thing. I loved Johnny Dodds. Jimmie Noone. You'd go junk shopping. You'd go to Harlem—it was safe to do back then—secondhand shops, and just look through the piles of 78s.

"By then I was playing the clarinet. I got into the high school band and tried to fool around, playing with the old records. By the time I got out of high school in '46, I think the first live session

---

[1]This interview took place prior to the death of Wellstood on July 24, 1987, which resulted in the dissolution of the Classic Jazz Quartet; since then, Muranyi has free-lanced.

I ever played, Dick Wellstood was playing piano. We were teenagers. In Nola Studios in New York, above the original Lindy's."

The 1940s saw the emergence of bebop. But it also saw the emergence of a new interest in early jazz—"the revival," as some termed it. Today, it seems easy enough for many jazz fans to appreciate both bebop and earlier (or "traditional") jazz sounds. But in the mid '40s, it seemed an either-or decision. "There was that 'moldy fig' versus the beboppers kind of thing, which was a clear and pronounced political kind of thing," Muranyi recalls. "Then, people interested in bebop or modern sounds considered Louis Armstrong or anything like that just absolute shit; they would laugh at it. There was no middle ground."

Muranyi was firmly in the revivalist camp. He found a cadre of white musicians of his age who were committed to the earlier forms of jazz. "There were a lot of young guys around. Wellstood was one of them, and I remember meeting Bob Wilber then. Marty Grosz was in that early crowd, too. The same bag, interested in the old music. Johnny Glasel, who's head of the 802 union, was one of those guys. Irving Kratka—played drums—he ended up with Music Minus One, Inner City and all that, that record label. Jerry Blumberg played cornet. Bob Mielke, he's on the West Coast now, and Ephie Resnick, trombone players. And a piano player, Hank Ross, he's a court reporter now. There was a whole scene. We'd play, re-create old records."

For the revivalists, one of the major events in jazz in the '40s was the rediscovery of veteran New Orleans trumpeter Bunk Johnson. Newspapers from coast to coast reported how, outfitted with new false teeth and a new horn, Johnson could still knock 'em dead.

Muranyi recalls: "I was there opening night when Bunk Johnson came to town [1945], and I went every weekend for two years. At the Stuyvesant Casino. That was great. I got to know the whole band. George Lewis and Jim Robinson and Baby Dodds and Slow Drag and Alton Purnell. There was great dissension in that band. Bunk hated that band. And they hated him. He used to call them his wartime emergency band—putting them down.

"Bunk considered himself way above them musically, and he was. With the exception of Baby Dodds. Jim Robinson was very limited harmonically. Had a wonderful kind of thing. But he would play through the changes, ignoring chords. George Lewis also played kind of out of tune and he missed a lot of chords. They were both charming, and I think George was much more of a talent than Jim Robinson, but they had their limitations, whereas Bunk was a very good musician. He was quite accomplished and could read. Alton Purnell didn't really know that much about that style of music. He played like a Swing Era piano. Slow Drag, the bass player, was kind of primitive. And Lawrence Marrero couldn't tune his own banjo.

"Bunk was a very good player, but Bunk was a very frustrating kind of guy. He would get drunk; he wouldn't play. He wanted to play pop tunes. He wanted to play, you know, 'Bell Bottom Trousers' and all kinds of pop songs. He didn't want to play those old numbers. No, it was a very strange band, torn with dissension. And the only one that held up for me was Baby Dodds. He was the most wonderful drummer. He would just play the hell out of it. And get swinging, you know, and he'd do that shimmy beat. He'd be sitting on the stool and he'd get up and do like a bump and like a grind. Get up and shake his ass and do the thing. He was just wonderful. The sounds and stuff. He was a genius, really wonderful.

"And in 1946, I'm like 18 years old. George Lewis said, 'Come in sometime and bring your horn.' So I brought my clarinet, and Bunk said, 'Okay, boy, tune up!' The piano plays a note and I play a note. I'm flat as a pancake. And Bunk Johnson says to me, 'You're sharp! Pull out!' I was so disillusioned. He couldn't tell whether I was sharp or flat. But I was terribly flat, and I didn't enjoy it at all on account of that. We played the two songs, and all my friends thought it was great. Big applause. The kid clarinet player, you know, sitting in with all the old guys from New Orleans.

"From '46 to '49, I was in the Air Force, and in the band. I got stationed in Westover Army Air Force Base in Springfield, Mass., so I could commute back and forth to New York, and maintain my activities. Irv Kratka got a gig, almost the first gig

I ever played, in Trenton, New Jersey. The bass player was Pops Foster.

"Then I went to college, to Manhattan School of Music and to Columbia. I got a bachelor's and a master's in music from Columbia. And I took all kinds of lessons. A guy named Louis Braun, a Hungarian guy. I studied with Simeon Bellison, who was like the first clarinetist with the New York Philharmonic for 35 years. I wanted to become a classical clarinet player. I played jazz, but I wanted to be a classical player; that's why I studied. But somewhere in college I realized there are so few—only two clarinet players in a symphony orchestra—and then about ten of them in the whole world that make a living. So that means I'm looking for one out of 20 jobs in the whole world. And I kept playing jazz all this time. And I got a day job, working for RCA International in record and phonograph sales.

"I started to play with a group called the Red Onions, with Bob Hodes, around New York. We made a 10-inch LP on Riverside in 1953, which was reissued recently. We played at Jimmy Ryan's on 52nd Street on Monday nights for a long time. And that was a great joy because we played opposite the Wilbur De Paris Band, wonderful group, and I got to know Omer Simeon, one of my favorite clarinetists, there.

"Then I went to Bethlehem Records and I used to write a lot of liner notes for all kinds of records: classical, jazz, etc. But I kept my hand in the playing the whole time. Then by the late '50s, I had a band of my own called the Gutbucket Six, and I played around New York. George Wettling played drums. I would hire him, he would hire me. Also I got to know Johnny Windhurst, and between Windhurst and Wettling, I got involved with Eddie Condon and that crowd. And I played some with Yank Lawson, who had a band for a while in which Bob Haggart played the bass (before their 'World's Greatest Jazz Band'). Jimmy McPartland used to hire me. Through George Wettling I got to know Herman Autrey, a wonderful guy who used to play with Fats Waller. We got to be great friends. I was lucky enough to play with guys like Joe Thomas, the trumpet player. I went on the road with Wingy Manone in Toledo, Ohio, for a couple of weeks. I had a gig in Harold's House of Dixieland in

West Orange, New Jersey. I first played there with the Red Onions, and then I had the band there for a while.

"From RCA, I went to Bethlehem Records, then to Atlantic, and then to Esoteric Counterpoint. At Atlantic Records, I was manager of the foreign department. Then I got involved with Danny Barker. We made an album, with Danny Barker on banjo, Wellman Braud, Walter Johnson, and Don Frye. I played clarinet. That was in '57, '58 somewhere. Danny would hire me and vice versa; we'd gig around.

"I paid my dues. I really knocked around New York. I collected all the old-timers. I played a couple of times with Sandy Williams, the alkie trombone player that played with Chick Webb. I played with Higginbotham. I got to be known and I knew them, so that later when I was with Louis, everywhere we went I always knew a lot of the people that came around and said hello.

"I played Central Plaza, played a lot with Red Allen, a wonderful player. Played with Conrad Janis. I played there one night with Wingy Manone and George Brunis. It was like a vaudeville show, two real characters. Brunis would say, 'And now we're gonna play "The Tin Roof Blues."' And Wingy Manone says, 'Ah, you can't kid me, you didn't write that song.' And Brunis says, 'Well, I'm collecting the royalties!' And Wingy would say, 'You guys'—meaning the New Orleans Rhythm Kings that Brunis had been part of—'you guys didn't write that song. I remember that song in New Orleans when it was called, "Don't Get Funky, 'Cause I Got Your Water On."'" Muranyi laughs and starts singing, to the melody of "The Tin Roof Blues": *Don't get funky, 'cause I got your water on.* . . . It fits, you know."

In the '60s, Muranyi gave up his record company day jobs to become a full-time jazz musician. He toured with Bobby Hackett and Vic Dickenson.

"Then I got involved with a group called the Village Stompers, which had that big hit, 'Washington Square.' We toured with that group—'64, '65, '66, something like that. Went to Japan. Marty Grosz was in that band for a while. Al Hirt hired us to play his club in New Orleans. Between shows, I would go to Preservation Hall and hang out—there were a lot more old-timers around then than now. I got to know Willie Humphrey, the clarinetist, Punch Miller, Cié Frazier, Sweet Emma, and others.

"They had just changed the law about equality; you couldn't refuse service to anybody. I liked Willie Humphrey; he had good vibes on him. I said, 'Why don't you come in and hear us at Al Hirt's?' He said, 'Oh no, I can't go in there.' I said, 'Yeah, come on. Fuck it, the law's changed.' He said, 'The law might be changed, but you're going to go back North. I got to live here.' I said, 'Ah, man, come on.'

"So lo and behold, he comes in one night and sits down, and they serve him, and I got on the mike and said: 'Ladies and gentlemen, how about a hand for one of our great New Orleans jazz pioneers, Willie Humphrey.' And he stood up to a round of applause. And he told me later that I was the first guy ever to do that in New Orleans.

"We played New Orleans quite a few times with the Village Stompers. Joe Glaser booked us. He only managed Louis Armstrong, but he was a big booking agent for everybody else. So that's how I met Joe Glaser and, eventually, that's how I got to play with Louis Armstrong.

"I joined Louis Armstrong in '67, replacing Buster Bailey, who had died. I was with him almost five years [with Tyree Glenn, trombone; Danny Barcelona, drums; Buddy Catlett, bass; Marty Napoleon, piano; and Jewel Brown, vocals]. I'd met him before. I thought, I still think, he was one of *the* greatest jazz musicians ever. No question. With all these cats I had played with, it was almost like 99.9% unanimity—especially the old-timers, they spoke of him with such deference and awe. There was no doubt to me, Pops was the fountainhead.

"I remember, he asked me, 'How the fuck do you pronounce your name?' I said '*Ma Rainey*, like the singer—Joe Ma Rainey.' He liked that. He lit up. He liked the fact, you know, that I knew about Ma Rainey. He never had any trouble after that. He'd roll up a storm: 'Joe Ma-*Rainey*.'

"He had been sick when I joined him. He'd been working on his chops. He sounded quite good. I mean, he didn't sound like on a 'Hot Five' record—he was at least 66, 67 years old. Jazz trumpet-playing is like jazz drumming in that it's a young man's game. Really, when you get down to it, you know, it's a physical activity. I think reed players last longer, or piano players," Muranyi reflects. "But he wore well, because his style became in essence simpler and simpler. He pared down."

The number Muranyi most enjoyed playing with Armstrong was "Give Me a Kiss to Build a Dream On." Muranyi recalls: "He liked that very much. He only played that on the nights he felt good. When his chops were in good shape."

By this stage in Armstrong's career, Armstrong was playing pretty much the same material night after night. "There were numbers he would substitute for others. But after being on the road for 10,000 years, it wasn't a jam session. When you get up at dawn and you take a bus to the airport and travel 2,000 miles or wherever you go, and then you get off and get on another bus, and you have a choice of either having a nap or something to eat, and then you've got to go play—you're not going to be making great big changes in your program. You've got to have a set thing that you can do with your eyes closed—whacked out, tired, and with no sleep. And a lot of that stuff was that way. It was an endurance contest.

"We played sometimes one-nighters, sometimes a week or two. And all over the world. I played Africa with him. Tunisia. I think that was the biggest crowd of people I've ever seen in my life. We played a concert the night we arrived. The dressing room was a tent with Arabian rugs. And they gave us all *dashikis*. We get up on the bandstand—outdoor thing, Tunis—and it looked liked miles, the people are like little dots. It was 20,000, 25,000— I don't know the figure but it was enormous. And they went on and on and on. And I wondered, what does this mean to them? They don't go for jazz particularly. I guess that he was just such a personality."

Muranyi recorded with Armstrong, the most memorable album being *What a Wonderful World*. They did numerous TV spots, including two BBC programs, which were frequently re-broadcast in Europe.

"Before Louis died, I started playing at Jimmy Ryan's. I was playing with Pops' band, but we didn't work 52 weeks a year, so I went into the house band at Ryan's, and then when Louis got a gig, I would get somebody to play for me at Ryan's." The band at Ryan's at that time featured trumpeter Max Kaminsky and drummer Zutty Singleton, who had worked with—and been quite close to—Armstrong in the early days. "So I was playing with Zutty and Louis at the same time. And they weren't friends then. They had separated. Their wives didn't get along," Muranyi recalls. "And behind the scenes, in a quiet way, I brought them together again. I talked to Louis about Zutty, and Zutty about Louis. And Zutty would say, 'Say hello to Pops.' Finally, Zutty took sick, Louis called him, and they got together.

"I had dinner with Louis four days before he died. And I took my tape recorder. And I taped the whole afternoon. Telling jokes and laughing. And he says grace at dinner. I've played it for a couple of people. I don't like to play it because it's sad; I cry all the time.

"I think Louis Armstrong's death was very bad news for any kind of trad or middle-of-the-road jazz. Because there was no other major show biz figure that was playing jazz, that kind of jazz," Muranyi reflects. "So that, as part of his personality—he was so cute and nice and had the personality and stuff—he would expose that kind of music to the public. That was one of his big roles. And when he died, there was nobody else to take his place, to expose the music that way. And that was a very, very big loss to traditional jazz. Nobody took his place. You can't."

Muranyi gets pessimistic at times about the future of jazz. "There are people now, grown people, spending money on entertainment, that have never heard a live jazz band," he notes. "It's very rarely exposed. On TV, there's no jazz. Jazz will never die, but I think it's a continually eroding, smaller and smaller base."

After Armstrong's death, Muranyi continued playing at Jimmy Ryan's. Roy Eldridge took over the band, and Muranyi played with Eldridge for more than a decade. He cut an album with Eldridge in this period, as well as an album under his own leadership with some of his colleagues from the band at Ryan's.

"Roy's a genius. He's a wonderful, wonderful player. Playing with him was an education. He sort of dragged me kicking and screaming into—not into the modern world, but I can now play bebop lines," Muranyi says. "Just as the history of jazz supposedly is—Louis is the big early influence, then Roy Eldridge is the middle figure and develops into Dizzy—that was my experience as a musician: playing with Louis Armstrong and getting what I could, and then with Roy. I'm very lucky to have played with them both.

"Roy's rather difficult. Just the opposite of Louis Armstrong in many ways. We fought like cats and dogs, the whole band. Roy and I fought a lot. He used to refer to Louis Armstrong in my presence as 'your man.' But we ended up pretty mellow. I remember this night I played something particularly good, and he turns to me and he says, 'You *have* learned a lot from me.' Well I guess I *have* learned a lot from him.

"But I never read the writings of any one person that picked up at all what was going on at Ryan's. It was a wonderful, unique band. We played all the Dixieland things, swung the shit out of them. Played swing things. We got a little more modern things. It was a totally unique band, stylistically. And everybody wanted to pigeonhole it: 'Roy Eldridge is stuck playing that Dixieland music. . . .' But if he didn't want to play it, he didn't have to— he loved it. We had a nice repertory ensemble there. We played a million songs. All kinds of different bags. And with Roy's leadership, we played the shit out of it. And we had our own harmonic way of doing it, too. There was a whole sound to that band that nobody ever picked up on. It was all head arrangements. Sometimes we'd play a song we had never played before, and play it in perfect three-part harmony. It was that tight a band. We played five, six nights a week. I think the music was very good and very, very, very underrated. We played 'em our own way. Out of the players came the form, not the other way around. Then Roy had a heart attack, and Spanky Davis, who was a real strong, good player from the midwest, took over for two or three years.[2]

"At Ryan's, I met the whole world. I think I started there in 1970; I was there until Ryan's closed in December of '83. At Ryan's, the whole world sat in. From Ella Fitzgerald to Oscar

---

[2]Eldridge died February 26, 1989.

164

Louis Armstrong and Joe Muranyi (photo by Jack Bradley, courtesy of Joe Muranyi).

Roy Eldridge and Joe Muranyi (courtesy of Joe Muranyi).

The Classic Jazz Quartet: Richard Sudhalter, cornet; Dick Wellstood, piano; Joe Muranyi, clarinet and soprano sax; and Marty Grosz, guitar (courtesy of Joe Muranyi).

Joe Muranyi joins Doc Cheatham at Sweet Basil in New York City, June 7, 1992, for a celebration of Cheatham's 87th birthday (photo by Chip Deffaa).

Peterson, all the way down to Sonny Stitt—and Cleanhead Vinson, I remember, had a wonderful drunken night in there, singing the blues. Zoot Sims. Scott Hamilton.

"Then Ryan's closed, and in recent years I've been going to Europe and playing with European musicians. Almost every year I go over, to Germany and Scandinavia mostly. I was to Hungary once, too. This past year, I've been gigging around."

As for the recently formed Classic Jazz Quartet, Muranyi notes, "I'd known Wellstood and Grosz for a long time. Old buddies. Sudhalter's fairly new on the scene. I always felt compatible with him. He subbed at Ryan's a couple of times.

"We played a party up in Westchester for an East German Dixieland Band, just for the fun of it. We had this quartet, and it sounded good. We jokingly said, 'Hey, we ought to do something with this.' And then Dick Sudhalter got a couple of gigs, and the four of us played. We're really peers in a lot of ways. All of us have gone to college and it's not your usual old type of music. Pretty sophisticated bunch. We all have a sense of humor and we're pretty comfortable with each other. So it just sort of snowballed and it looks like a very good thing. It had the feeling of a winner right away.

"I think there's sort of room for a group like this. We're not exactly the elder statesmen, but we're not a kid band; let's put it that way. We're all enthusiastic about it. I think no matter how diminished the base for jazz becomes, if you come in near the top there'll always be some kind of work."

1985

For the Love of Bix

I sometimes wonder whether having multiple talents is a blessing or a curse. Take the case of Richard Sudhalter, who has an assortment of talents that many would envy.

First, he's an excellent jazz critic and historian—erudite, never shy about expressing his opinions (and he writes from a definite point of view, preferring lyrical, understated jazz of pre-bebop traditions), and always a pleasure to read. Indeed, he's one of the few real prose stylists among jazz critics. His liner note writing has earned him a Grammy. The biography of Bix Beiderbecke, which he coauthored with Philip R. Evans, *Bix: Man and Legend*, remains a model for jazz biographies. And he's got several book projects under way or planned, the most significant being a history of white involvement in jazz, which he is writing for Oxford University Press.

Sudhalter is also a dedicated player of the trumpet, cornet, and flugelhorn. He's been a familiar presence on the traditional jazz scene, whether leading lively groups of his own or as a sideman for others. If you've never had the pleasure of hearing Sudhalter play "live," a fair number of recordings of him have been released—the most recent being *Get Out and Get Under the Moon*, with Connie Jones (Stomp Off 1207). Two particular older favorites of mine, that ought to be reissued on compact disc, are

Dick Sudhalter and His Primus Inter Pares Jazz Ensemble (Audiophile AP-159) and *The New Paul Whiteman Orchestra Live in '75, Volume Two* (Monmouth Evergreen, ES-7078). On the first, he leads a septet including Dave Frishberg, Dan Barrett, and Howard Alden on new versions of numbers he's most comfortable with, such as "I'll Be a Friend 'With Pleasure,'" "Blue River," "From Monday On," and "Waiting at the End of the Road." On the latter, he leads a Whiteman re-creation orchestra on such numbers as "Lonely Melody," "Mary," and a never-before-recorded Lenny Hayton arrangement of "Dusky Stevedore"—all of the original arrangements but with brand-new solos. These two albums capture well what Sudhalter likes to do: offer fresh reinterpretations of classic jazz of the 1920s and '30s.

And if that weren't enough, Sudhalter is also an excellent concert producer. He's done some of the best retrospectives I've attended; his star-studded 80th birthday tribute to Hoagy Carmichael at Carnegie Hall is a standout in my memory. The intimate "Vintage Jazz at the Vineyard" concerts he has hosted and produced in New York have been carried on many American public radio stations. And he periodically finds time to lecture at colleges as well.

The downside of trying to go in so many different directions at once is that you're not likely to get as far in any one direction as you might if you were going in only one direction. That is to say, if Sudhalter were only a writer, he'd probably get books finished faster. If he were only a musician, he'd probably record more and come closer to realizing his full potential as an instrumentalist. If he were only a concert producer, he no doubt would have made a bigger name for himself in that field. He likes tackling a lot of different activities simultaneously—even if, as he's aware, a certain amount of frustration inevitably follows. It's not always easy, he'll tell you, being both a writer about jazz and a player of jazz. But now in middle age—Sudhalter was born December 28, 1938—it would probably be too late to change his habits even if he wanted to. And he doesn't want to.

There is one common theme to all of his different projects. Whether he is writing, playing, or producing, he is championing the kind of jazz in which he ardently believes. No, he doesn't hold much hope for its becoming widely popular in this rock era. But he is doing his bit to keep the tradition alive.

On a visit with him one afternoon in New York, he recounted not only how he became involved in the world of traditional jazz but active in so many different areas.

"I was born and brought up in the suburbs of Boston, in a place called Newton. Steve Kuhn lived there for a long time—I knew him when I was growing up. Roger Kellaway and I were in high school and junior high school; I was one class ahead of him. But I've known Roger since I was about three feet high. Both Steve and Roger went on to become major forces in contemporary jazz," Sudhalter notes.

"We were right outside Boston, which in those years was a very thriving jazz town. Musicians were always coming in from New York. There was a lot of local action. We had a couple of bands in high school—a big band and also a small Dixieland combo.

"We would go down on Friday afternoons to Storyville, which was run by George Wein, when he was running the teenage jazz club. And the idea behind that was to bring in ranking jazz artists of all sorts to play at afternoon sessions for the youngsters, the kids who ordinarily couldn't go into clubs because they were under 21. And then let the young musicians bring groups into the sessions as well. So, for example, if there was a big band at Newton High School, say, we went on the same bill as Clifford Brown and Max Roach. Our group would play and they would listen to us and give us encouragement and comments—and in some cases, we might sit in with our idols, too. It was all a very good arrangement. It was like from three to six on a Friday afternoon. This was around 1953, '54, '55, '56."

As a teenager, Sudhalter got to see and sit in with some top jazzmen. "Pee Wee Russell, Vic Dickenson, Bud Freeman, Buck Clayton—those stand out in my mind. And I remember one Friday afternoon that we went in, Max and Clifford and their quintet were there, and Serge Challoff, and Serge played a set with Clifford and that rhythm section . . . and wow—what music that was! I'll never forget that because it was really an electric

172

kind of thing. Even though in those days I was very parochial and very partisan in my tastes, good is good—and you couldn't listen to Clifford Brown without realizing that you were in the presence of a major jazz improviser. Same thing with Serge."

The music Sudhalter responded to most deeply, however, came from an earlier era and tradition.

"I discovered jazz through Bix, through having found a record in my father's cabinet. A Whiteman record, 'San.' And all through my early years, I had my little place, down in the cellar of our house. A phonograph. We had a piano, I practiced down there. And I lived in my own dream world. I played the records, I played along with the records. Before I started playing the horn, I actually built a toy trumpet out of the remnants of a model airplane kit, and I would turn a light, a spotlight on myself, and pose in front of a wall with this horn like that [holding it up to his lips] and think, oh God, you know, and mime along with Bix records and whatever records I had. I was twelve.

"And throughout my junior high school and high school years, all I wanted was to play jazz. I was aware of popular music to the point where people are always surprised, even now, that I know all of the tunes from those years. If somebody comes up and asks for 'How Important Can It Be?' or 'Moments to Remember' or anything, I know those songs because they were in the air, they were around. One of my favorite ballads is still 'You Belong to Me,' that Jo Stafford sang. We knew all those songs. But that wasn't what I listened to. I would be down in my cellar listening to Goldkette and Whiteman and Fletcher Henderson and McKinney's Cotton Pickers. Interestingly enough, I didn't discover Jelly Roll Morton until later, courtesy of Stan McDonald, with whose band I used to play weekends at the University of Massachusetts. I didn't discover Billie Holiday and Lester Young until later. And I didn't even know about Louis Armstrong then. I mean, to me Louis Armstrong was the guy who sang 'Kiss to Build a Dream On' on the radio. I didn't know about the Hot Fives and Hot Sevens and all that stuff; that came later too," he acknowledges.

"My father, Al Sudhalter, was an alto saxophone player and a wonderful one in the Trumbauer idiom. And of course, those were his gods, those white New York hot jazz players. And so I was kind of late in getting started with appreciation of the others. I didn't find out about Benny Carter until years later. My father was a professional—in fact, he was one of the three major young white alto players to come out of Boston in the late '20s— the other two being Toots Mondello and Ben Cantor. And he turned down, for various reasons, a number of major opportunities to do things abroad and in New York and everything, deciding—partially out of family loyalty—to stay around Boston. But he had his own sustaining radio show and I've got transcriptions and stuff of his playing. He was marvelous. I did two LPs with him when I lived in England. I set them up, and they came out as *Sudhalter and Son, Volumes One and Two*."

Because of the old records he discovered in the basement, Sudhalter sought to become a musician. "I remember my father came home from work one day and I said to him: 'What is this?' You know, this Bix record. And he said, 'Well, that's Bix.' 'What is the instrument? Is it a trumpet?' He says, 'No, it's a cornet.' And I said, 'Well, I'd like to play one of those.'

"And by this time, of course, I'd hacked away at the piano for five years, the obligatory middle-class piano lessons for which, by the way, I'm very grateful now. But at that time my parents were both very skeptical. They said: 'Oh God, you haven't made that many inroads with the piano, now you want to try the cornet?'

"I said, 'Well, just give me a chance.' So they rented one from Carl Fisher for three months, at the end of which, if I didn't make any significant progress, the cornet was going to go back and that would be the end of that. And they got me a teacher, a local Boston trumpet player named Harry Fink, who played one of those old Conn peashooter trumpets with a very thin bore and a sort of narrow, nanny-goat tone. And he'd come in and very carefully lay down newspapers on the living room rug and then we'd sit there and I'd play along with him, and he'd go, 'nyaaaa,' and I'd go, 'buhhhh. . . .' It wasn't very inspiring, but it was a beginning.

"I played cornet from the beginning. I was 12, 13. I remember I got the horn and I ran around the corner to a girl in the neighborhood on whom I had a crush and I took it out of the case and I said, 'Look!' And she said [in a flat voice], 'So, what can you do on it?' And I went, 'buhhh,' you know, and said, 'Well, that'll come, but isn't it beautiful?' She said, 'No, not particularly, it's just a piece of metal.' She wasn't very impressed with it.

"I played third cornet in the junior high school band. I still know all the third cornet parts on 'El Capitan' and 'Washington Post' and 'On the Mall' and 'Stars and Stripes Forever,' and all that stuff."

Not only did Sudhalter start playing in a jazz group as soon as he could, but he still has a record he made with some of his friends in high school. He puts it on for me: a driving, Dixieland-type thing, his enthusiastic horn coming through strong.

"We were all high school kids. The pianist is Steve Kuhn. The clarinet player was 13 at the time. This is Kuhn you're hearing now; he was 16, he was older than we were. For kids in their early teens, it's all right. It's a good thing that youth is confident, because it doesn't have much else sometimes.

"And out of that evolved a Dixieland band that was not bad. It became sufficiently popular at Newton High that our popularity rivaled that of the football team. That was kind of funny! We used to play out on the lawn between the buildings during lunch hours and everything, play at special assemblies and music club concerts or something. We had a faculty member, a dance band clarinetist, who helped organize our big band and stayed on a couple of extra years beyond his contract because he just liked having a bunch of kids who were keen—interested in what they were doing."

Sudhalter attended Oberlin College (class of 1960), where he studied English literature and music. After graduation, "I went right to Europe. I lived first in Salzburg, Austria. I taught English in a Berlitz School and played in jazz bands in Munich. I worked at Bavarian State Radio on staff there, playing cornet. I joined UPI in 1964. I was with them until the end of 1972, reporting news from Europe and managing bureaus in different places," he recalls.

In the meantime, Sudhalter also free-lanced articles for *Jazz Journal, Storyville,* and other jazz publications, as well as for

175

general interest publications such as *Punch*, using the pseudonym of "Art Napoleon." "I just thought Napoleon was a great name for a jazz writer . . . Phil Napoleon, Marty Napoleon, Teddy Napoleon, and you know, it just seemed right," he says.

In London in 1968, Sudhalter heard on the radio that Soviet troops were moving to the border of Czechoslovakia. He flew to Germany, drove a rented car to Czechoslovakia, and became the only Western journalist in the country when the Soviets invaded. The exclusive front-page stories he filed over the next few days made him a star at UPI. For a while, he continued covering Eastern Europe for UPI, based in Belgrade, Yugoslavia, then moved back to England.

As time permitted, he played music professionally, working with both British and visiting American musicians. He formed the "New Paul Whiteman Orchestra," using copies of original Whiteman Orchestra arrangements—both the well-known recorded ones and some never-recorded ones he obtained from the Whiteman Archives at Williams College in Massachusetts. The orchestra, which gave concerts, made some records, and broadcast "live" on the BBC, gave him a chance in effect to *be* Bix Beiderbecke, whose solo spots he filled.

In the meantime, Sudhalter had begun his collaboration with Philip R. Evans of Bakersfield, California, on a biography of Beiderbecke. Evans, a die-hard Beiderbecke fan, actually did most of the research for the book. (And his exceptionally thorough research has been relied upon by all—this author included—who have ever written anything about Beiderbecke since then.) Over a span of more than 15 years, Evans had devoted countless hours of his free time to tracking down people who may have known Beiderbecke, however slightly. He managed to interview—either in person, over the phone, or by mail—an incredible total of 684 people concerning Beiderbecke. He compiled a diary, unprecedented in jazz research, that accounted for Beiderbecke's whereabouts practically day by day throughout his career. Using this material, Evans wrote a first draft of the Beiderbecke biography before connecting with Sudhalter. But Evans was not a professional writer—he worked for the government—nor a musician. Because Sudhalter was both—as well as, of course, a fellow Beiderbecke enthusiast (he had begun researching Beiderbecke himself while in college)—he seemed an ideal partner for Evans. Sudhalter quit his job at UPI so that he could concentrate on the Beiderbecke book. The collaborators communicated mostly by mail, meeting in person only briefly when Sudhalter paid a visit to Evans' home. Evans mailed pages to Sudhalter; Sudhalter put them into polished form, adding whatever he could on the basis of his own research and knowledge as a musician, and (after getting Evans' approval on them) passed them on to the publisher. In addition, William Dean-Myatt of Walsall, England, contributed discographical research for the book. The agreement Evans, Sudhalter, and Dean-Myatt ultimately reached was that although Dean-Myatt would receive third billing as a collaborator on the book, he would not share in the royalties; Evans would get a somewhat larger share of the royalties than Sudhalter, and a small percentage of the royalties would also go to the Beiderbecke family.

While it is impossible for an outsider to determine exactly how much of the credit for the book's success should be given to Sudhalter and how much to Evans, it seems safe to say the following. *Bix: Man and Legend* is about as well researched as any jazz biography that has yet appeared; that would not have been the case without the contributions of Evans. It is also about as readable as any jazz biography that has yet appeared; *that* would not have been the case without the contributions of Sudhalter. Both Evans and Sudhalter, then, made crucial contributions. The book received deservedly high praise from reviewers. (It is one of my own two favorite jazz biographies, the other being *Benny Carter,* by Morroe Berger, Edward Berger, and James Patrick.)

Why then, one might ask, is this major jazz book unavailable today?

Although publishers have expressed interest in bringing the book back into print, Evans (who shares ownership of the copyright with Sudhalter) says he would consent only if he were given top billing, which he expected to receive when he and Sudhalter originally agreed to collaborate but did not receive when the book was published by Arlington House in 1974. In the years since then, Evans has gone on to other writing projects, including collaborating with Larry Kiner on *Al Jolson: A Bio-Discography* (Scarecrow Press) and writing a soon-to-be-published biography of Beiderbecke's frequent musical partner Frank Trumbauer. Both Evans and Sudhalter would like to do a revised edition of their Beiderbecke biography someday, correcting errors in the original one—but neither is willing to accept second billing and the project remains deadlocked.

The publication of *Bix: Man and Legend*, combined with Sudhalter's tributes to Beiderbecke in concerts and on records, put Sudhalter on the map as a Beiderbecke authority. And Sudhalter felt particularly flattered when trombonist Bill Rank, who had played with Beiderbecke in the '20s, generously compared Sudhalter's playing favorably with Beiderbecke's. Though Sudhalter continued dividing his time between playing jazz and writing about it, he gradually began focusing more of his energies on playing.

I wondered if Sudhalter's goal had ever been to become strictly a professional musician. Did he really feel content maintaining music as a kind of adjunct to a writing career?

"When I was growing up, I was getting a twin set of signals from my father," Sudhalter recalls. "One of them said, 'Don't go into the music business; it's lousy, it's a cutthroat business, it's ultimately frustrating, it will strip you of your idealism and all that, and leave you with nothing'—and of course he was right. But on the other hand, there was this rather more subliminal set of signals that said, 'There is no greater endeavor in all the world than making music.' And of course he still played until his last days. He was an extraordinary saxophone player. In fact, we used to have jam sessions in the cellar. He would wait until the opportune moment, you know, and then he'd come down and say, 'Would you fellows mind if I'd sit in for a number?' And he'd just cut everybody up. I mean, he was just wonderful. Played with a real sort of full, creamy sound, and a beautiful, lyrical style, and all of that. He had been a fiddle player first and that was the approach he used on the saxophone too.

"My problem was only that I never really thought that I would ever equal my father as a musician. And indeed, when it came to recording together, I think—without purposely setting out to do it—I played under my best. Because it's a kind of unwritten law of parent-child relations that one does not meet one's father on the field of gladiatorial combat and vanquish him. You just don't do it.

"It's interesting to note that the ground behind us is littered with the corpses of sons who tried to make it in the same business as their fathers, and either did themselves in or took left turns or whatever. Somehow, there's something in the dynamic between a son and his father. If I were to be coming up as a jazz musician, playing the same music as my father, indeed in the same stylistic incarnation as his idol—you know, he was a Bix fanatic—sooner or later it would have to have come to a contest. A contest for prestige, a contest for stature. And one doesn't do that," Sudhalter insists. And that reluctance to compete with his father on his father's own turf, he feels, kept him from devoting himself more deeply to music.

"What happened was kind of haunting in a way. While I was living in England, I did two records with my father. Then in 1974 I organized the Whiteman orchestra and my parents were supposed to be at the concert; they were supposed to come over to see me play. And at the last minute, I got cold feet and asked them not to be there. Bobby Hackett was there but they weren't. And I always regretted that. My father was very guarded about the praise that he had to give for the record that the orchestra made as a result of that concert.

"Then the following spring I got a call from Bob Wilber, asking would I be interested in coming to New York and participating in a New York Jazz Repertory Company concert honoring Bix Beiderbecke. I would devise the shape, write the script, narrate it, and play some cornet. Sure! You know, Carnegie Hall. So I came on a Friday and talked to my father; he said he and my mother would be there at the concert—which was to be the following Thursday—and then the next day, on Saturday, I went to an all-day rehearsal. I got back to the apartment I was staying in, along about seven o'clock or so; I walked in and the phone was ringing. I picked it up and it was my mother. I said, 'Hi, how're things?' And she said, without much preamble: 'I'm sorry to have to tell you, your father died an hour

179

ago.' He had a heart attack, he just fell over and died, the Saturday before the concert, the day after I came into town. I had to go up to Boston and bury him, and then come back and do the concert.

"If you think of it—Carnegie Hall, me as Bix, you know, this whole thing which meant so much to him, and it was funny because when the concert came—of course it was a very highly emotionally charged thing for me. I can't even to this day think about it without kind of choking up—I got through the first half of the concert and I was standing in the wings, just looking out at the audience, feeling about as bad as I've ever felt—desolate. And just at the moment when it was worst, I felt a big sort of arm around my shoulder, and a big hand, and it was Jimmy McPartland, who was on the bill as well. And I didn't know Jimmy very well at that point, but I talked to him—he knew the circumstances—and all he said was, 'Don't worry, kid, he's out there and he's proud of you.' And McPartland made a friend for life out of that.

"I went out in the second half of the concert and played the solo on 'Clementine,' you know, the Goldkette re-creation arrangement. They had a band with [Goldkette alumni] Joe Venuti and Chauncey Morehouse and Spiegle Willcox and Bill Rank and all those guys, who were still alive at that time. I played, I guess, like a man possessed, because people are still talking about that solo. And to me that was sort of, I suppose, a requiem."

Richard Sudhalter made quite a splash in the mid '70s. His American debut as professional musician, performing in the Beiderbecke concert, was at no less than Carnegie Hall. The book he and Evans coauthored, *Bix: Man and Legend*, was nominated in 1975 for a National Book Award—the first jazz book ever so nominated. By the end of 1975, Sudhalter had moved back to the U.S. for good, after living in Europe for 15 years. He was soon busy writing, playing (everything from club dates to radio and TV commercials to Dixieland small groups to big bands), and producing concerts. By 1978, he was the jazz critic for *The New*

York Post—and still performing, whenever opportunities arose, on cornet and trumpet.

To the outside observer, it appeared as if Sudhalter had made a name for himself very quickly. From his perspective, however, it felt as if things were proceeding much more slowly than hoped for. After all, in England he had led a "New Paul Whiteman Orchestra" that made records, broadcast frequently on the BBC radio, and even made a 90-minute BBC-TV special. Sudhalter did a couple of Whiteman concerts in the U.S. shortly after moving back here—and won some new respect for Whiteman's music in the process—but he found the U.S. costs were so much higher that he could not keep an orchestra going financially as he had in England. He could do a concert once in a great while, but that was all. The scales of payment for musicians were higher in New York than in London, and U.S. radio and TV stations weren't interested in Whiteman's music.

And if he had imagined he would take the New York musical establishment by storm, he was soon disillusioned. Yes, he had done a splendid job at the Beiderbecke concert; yes, he had gotten some quite favorable critical attention—Whitney Balliett of *The New Yorker* suggested Sudhalter was the best lyrical cornet-ist to emerge since Ruby Braff. But no, that did not mean he'd be able to pack jazz clubs or concert halls as a bandleader.

"It took a couple of years to kind of catch hold," he says. "It's taken me a long time to establish my identity here, for a number of reasons: first, because I think I probably got off on very much a wrong foot by coming on too strong, assuming that a lot of what I'd achieved in England and Germany and other places would precede me, which it hadn't, and also because I had a lot to learn. I had not been in the music business full-time before that. I had worked as a news correspondent for UPI, and all that stuff. And I had to pay my dues. It's taken a long time, also, to get a real focus on the horn and what I want to do with it. I've been through a lot of ups and downs," he notes.

For a while Sudhalter led a band billed as the New California Ramblers.

"That was something that happened for a minute, after I got

back. I had started going to rehearsals of Vince Giordano's band and we became friends. He didn't really seem to be going much of anywhere and was on the verge of abandoning it, and I took it over for a while and said, 'Well, I'll try it.' I added a lot more jazz people and changed its bias from really a dance band to a hot repertory ensemble. We worked, did some things at clubs around town and odds and ends, but again, the economy was against it. And after a while, I had other fish to fry and other things I had to do. And I couldn't afford the luxury of trying to keep a 10-piece band afloat.

"The *Post* thing came along in 1978. Bob Kimball [a music critic for *The Post*], whom I'd known through Max Morath and Sam Parkins before that, called me one day and asked me if I felt like doing any reviewing. And I said, 'Sure'—I needed the money and I wasn't doing that much at the time. They liked me, so I stayed on. I did it for five years. And found that it almost wrecked my career as a player—whatever career that is.

"And it didn't really help to focus my ideas about what I wanted to do with the rest of my life. Because I never aspired to be a jazz critic. My God, no! The last thing in the world! I had always shared the jazz musician's instinctive contempt for critics and commentators and reviewers—and all of a sudden I found myself doing just that. And trying to justify being two people at once—being in the middle and at the same time being out there on the firing line as a player.

"And it was, I think, an ultimately untenable situation, and sooner or later this collision course I'd set with myself was bound to result in the necessity of making a decision. And of course, sooner or later it did. At the end of the Kool Festival, in the summer of '83, I went away for the summer again, to play in Rhode Island with Daryl [Sherman], and really did some hard thinking and finally told *The Post*, 'That's it, I don't want to do it anymore.' I had to systematically cut all my ties with the persona of the reviewer. Just not be seen in the places, not be identified, just kind of turn aside—even for a while, turn aside requests from other clients to write things that would be critical pieces, and everything—like magazine reviews, even in some respects record sleeve notes and everything. I do them now. But there

Richard Sudhalter, alone and with Bobby Hackett (courtesy of Richard Sudhalter).

The top photo (courtesy of Richard Sudhalter) depicts a 1956 gig by Sudhalter's group: Fred Giordano, piano; Roger Kellaway, bass; Sudhalter, cornet; Harvey Simons, drums; and Frank Nizzari, clarinet. The bottom photo (by Chip Deffaa) shows Sudhalter in 1984 with two of his frequent musical collaborators: Joe Muranyi, clarinet, and Marty Grosz, guitar.

The top photo, taken in England, shows Laurie Wright, Henry Thins Francis, Sudhalter, Bill Rank (alumnus of the Jean Goldkette Band of the '20s), John R. T. Davies, and Neville Scrimshire; the bottom photo, taken in New York, shows Sudhalter with Hoagy Carmichael (for whom Sudhalter had organized an 80th birthday salute) and an assistant to Mayor Edward Koch (courtesy of Richard Sudhalter).

Richard Sudhalter leads a group with drummer Ronnie Bedford, bassist Jay Leonhart, and pianist/vocalist Daryl Sherman in the top photo (courtesy of Richard Sudhalter) and with tenor saxist Al Klink, guitarist Marty Grosz, and clarinetist Joe Muranyi in the bottom photo (by Chip Deffaa).

was a time when I really backed off from it altogether. I still am loath to do any reviewing, as such. Because I just don't feel that that's where I belong. And as long as people are at all ambiguous about where I stand and how to deal with me, I can't afford the luxury—even though it's cut out a good, I suppose, $20,000 a year from my income."

Sudhalter realized it was hard for people to take him seriously as a musician. He was generally perceived as a jazz writer who moonlighted as a musician.

"And it happened again and again, where my name simply would not be included among prominent horn players in my field—and I knew, because people really didn't consider me anything but a writer who played sometimes, and played OK, but wasn't a full-time professional. And argue as I might against that, those were the facts," he says. The reality was also that, as one who divided his time between playing and writing, he was not likely to achieve the same level of technical mastery of his instrument as someone who devoted himself exclusively to playing could.

Sudhalter's playing was controlled, thoughtful. It could be quite tender and moving. There is—not surprisingly, in view of both his fondness for Beiderbecke and his overall attitude towards the world—a bittersweet quality to the best of his work. He seemed most comfortable playing music from the era of Beiderbecke and young Louis Armstrong (and later originals by such fellow traditionalists as Dick Wellstood and Marty Grosz that sounded as if they could have come out of that era; think of the recordings of the Classic Jazz Quartet). The truth was, though, no matter how well he played in that idiom, no matter how well constructed or heartfelt his phrases were, he was not likely to attract a mass audience or a major record deal. The times simply weren't right for his kind of music.

Indeed, in talking with Sudhalter, I sometimes get the feeling he might have been happier had he been born in an earlier era. Ask him, for example, why he periodically revives the music of Paul Whiteman, and he responds with considerable intensity: "I believe in Paul Whiteman. I believe in the elegance of that music. What was it that Twyla Tharp said of the late '20s: 'It was a time when style mattered, almost sometimes at the expense of content.' And I'm a believer in style. I believe that the world in which we live now has lost a sense of style. You know, you get to a point where you can say 'anything goes' just often enough and then people start believing it and forgetting detail.

"I did an interview with Benny Goodman for *American Heritage* magazine and he made a wonderful statement in there, where he said that the loss of detail is an imperceptible thing. You don't notice when people stop holding doors for people or saying thank you or knowing which fork to eat a dish with or dressing so that their clothes are an ensemble, or any number of things like that. And you look at them as individual points and you think, 'Oh, that's not important,' but one day you simply wake up and realize that all those details have amounted to an aggregate body of what constitutes style, of what constitutes elegance, of what constitutes class—and we've lost it. So we're in the middle, instead, of a tyranny of the least common denominator. And you know, maybe we get what we deserve and maybe we don't. I don't believe that that's the best of all possible worlds."

Style is important to Sudhalter, as is striving to play purely, melodically, economically. But he fears he is in an ever-diminishing minority. "Because the voices of the Michael Jacksons and all of that are far more deafening." In the building where Sudhalter long had an office, he saw Tin Pan Alley oldsters move out and be replaced by writers and record producers of the rock world: "—these ragamuffins who have become rich just catering to the least common denominator and not caring a jot, not caring a fig, about taste and dignity and integrity and all those things that are now impossibly old-fashioned types of values." No, he's not impressed by current American popular culture.

I ask Sudhalter what it is he most wants to do with his life.

"They talk about mid-life crises and I suppose I'm having mine, because I know more specifically what I don't want to do than what I do. And what I don't want to do is be a jazz critic. Or a critic of any sort. I enjoy writing. I want to write fiction at some point or other—I suppose everybody does, sooner or later. I've been approached with a couple of book ideas. I want to continue to play but I don't want to have to depend on playing to meet my monumental overhead. . . . And I still write for major clients, such as Reader's Digest Records and Time-Life, Book of the Month Club, and all that, doing essentially anonymous but decently paying jobs. Writing notes for those great boxed sets, those large eight-volume collections of Kate Smith records and such things." Sudhalter's expertise on older jazz and pop music, as well as his notable grace as a writer, comes through clearly in all of his liner notes.

He also observes: "The entrepreneurial thing is not without promise: the organization of concerts—producing, especially as regards establishing a beachhead for traditional jazz in as many places as possible. I do have some unique capacities, I mean, to play and also to talk and to convince people. And all of that must add up to something. I'm also interested in the world of academe, which has already begun to beckon in some respects. Maybe it'll all come together.

"It's all a very disparate picture. You know, I sometimes envy those people who can do one thing, and have done it so well that they've become the world's greatest authority in something that's immediately salable to a grateful public. Christ, I mean, the guy who devised Tofu-ti—it was just an idea: take tofu and make some kind of flavored Popsicles out of it. And yet he found his market and he's selling it, and he's gotten rich off of it."

Sudhalter is justifiably proud of the concerts he has produced at the intimate Vineyard Theater, edited versions of many of which have been broadcast on American Public Radio. Each concert features just a handful of musicians. Everyone gets ample solo space. And a highlight comes when Sudhalter chats with the leaders. The combination of music and reminiscences makes for unique programs. Listeners hear distinguished veterans make music and talk about their careers. He hopes to continue the concerts and broadcasts indefinitely, provided sufficient financial support can be found.[1]

Sudhalter says of his concerts: "I'd like to touch everything

---

[1] The series has come to an end since this profile was written.

which can be defined as traditional jazz. It is not a very narrow definition, a sort of small-band Dixieland type of thing. That's included in it, but traditional jazz is a much wider, much broader category than that. It can be Cootie Williams and his Rug Cutters, it can be Frankie Newton's Uptown Serenaders, Stuff Smith's Onyx Club Orchestra, and on the other hand it can be the California Ramblers and the Charleston Chasers, and all the rest of it." He's tried to cover as many bases as possible, often presenting older players such as Eddie Barefield, Doc Cheatham, Jimmy McPartland, and Spiegle Willcox, sometimes presenting younger revivalists. Among the older players, some are black, some are white. The young revivalists tend, almost without exception, to be white.

Sudhalter comments: "The matter of black artists is worth discussing a little bit. From what I can gather, when they cast *Ain't Misbehavin'* on Broadway, they wanted a young black stride piano player to be sitting on stage with the Fats Waller hat on, playing 'Alligator Crawl' or whatever it was he was playing, and, look as they might, they couldn't find one. And I, in all my travels, have very seldom come across—I mean, talk about competent or incompetent—just come across traditional jazz players under the age of 50 who are black. All the players seem to be white, middle-class musicians. Why is that? Well, the answer delves deep into the nature of black and white sociology, the fact that black culture, because of the way it's lived and because of its particular history in this country and in, you know, white-dominated society, has no conservationist tradition. When was the last time you met a black record collector?

"Somehow, black culture seems to depend upon acknowledgment and cultivation of today, and couldn't care two hoots, with exceptions here and there, about yesterday. Somehow yesterday is a retreat into the shadows. I think it's very significant, for example, that some years ago, when Jane Goldberg first started talking about a tap dance renaissance, she approached some of the older black tap dancers to help her and was almost universally turned down. They said, 'Oh, who wants that old stuff, it's dead, let it go. Nobody cares about that anymore.' She went ahead and started putting on little shows, and interest was generated to the point where she began to be able to convince some of the older dancers to join her. Cookie Cook, Honi Coles, Bubba Gaines, Buster Brown, a lot of those guys who were still around and really able to cut it, and lo and behold, people started coming and there was a real rebirth of interest, to the point where Honi became a star all over again on Broadway and all sorts of things have happened. But it wouldn't have happened had it not been for this white, middle-class girl who had no sociological associations with the music or the form but for the fact that she could dance and she loved it and it spoke to her.

"And I think that's very significant because in a sense she was coming to it from outside. She hadn't lived through all the attendant sociology, and all the discouragement, and all the heartbreak, and all the rest that being a black in show business has always carried with it. And I sort of think that you find your answer to the questions I asked somewhere in there. You're not going to find a young black coming along and sounding like Coleman Hawkins did in 1929. Or playing like Rex Stewart did in his Ellington days. Because somehow it doesn't square with the sociology of black American culture. I think that's a pity because they're missing out on a very important key to their own legacy, but that seems to be the way it's worked out.[2]

"Anyway, this is all by way of explaining the preponderance of white musicians in these traditional jazz concerts and in this kind of programming. Believe me, if tomorrow a young black guy came along—or even better, a young black woman came along—playing piano in the style of James P. Johnson and Fats and the Lion and everybody, and really playing it well, she could clean up and I would think it would be wonderful. Because we're all waiting for that. We're sort of waiting for black culture to grab its own music in a real sense by the shoulders and shake it, and say, 'Look, we can do this, we've done this,' because, quite

---

[2]Since this interview took place, one major black revivalist has emerged, clarinet-ist Michael White of New Orleans, who has organized concerts celebrating the music of King Oliver, Johnny Dodds, Jelly Roll Morton, and others. In addition, pianist Marcus Roberts, while not a revivalist, has recently begun performing and recording works by James P. Johnson and other early greats, besides his modern originals.

clearly, most of the really great innovators in the past were black players. There was no white trumpet player to approach an Armstrong. What Beiderbecke had was individual and beautiful and influential—and certainly shaped my life—but he's not to be compared in any kind of apocalyptic importance to an Armstrong. And I'll be the first person to acknowledge that. Bechet, Dodds, Morton, Ellington, Henderson—name them—Don Redman, Benny Carter, Lester Young—you know the litany as well as I do. . . ."

What sort of music does Sudhalter enjoy going out to listen to?

"I don't much enjoy listening to jazz, I'll say that," he acknowledges. "Because really when I go hear some music, I want to emerge with a catch in my throat, or with my heart thumping a little more strongly, or feeling that—in some way that maybe I can't even define or describe—I'll never again be the same. I don't particularly want to just sit there and listen to a bunch of people indulging in musical onanism at the expense of the public. I don't need that. I had a lot of that when I was writing, and I had to sit in the front row with my note pad and listen to a whole bunch of people who had no story to tell and who were jiving the audience. And I don't want to ever have to do that again. As a result, I will sooner go to a performance by the New York Saxophone Quartet, for example, whom I know to be artists of surpassing brilliance, and who always leave me breathless, because they're wonderful musicians. Or go see a performance of the Brahms Requiem, which has always been a work that moved me greatly. . . . Or just sit at home and listen to things like those Grieg string pieces. I love the impressionists. Above all, I love Brahms.

"I have records of old saxophone solos by Rudy Wiedoft, which I adore because that's a very pure way of playing. It comes directly out of the whole French method of approaching a saxophone. I like Rumanian and Hungarian music featuring the taragota, a wooden soprano saxophone which comes apart in joints like a clarinet and is fingered more or less like an Albert system clarinet. It has a great musical tradition which in some particulars parallels the development of the soprano saxophone in jazz. I got very interested in that music in the years that I was living out there. And so forth and so on it goes. I mean, I don't draw lines. Good is good. And it doesn't have to conform to any musical profile. But also, bad is bad. And I don't have any great interest in going to hear some tired Dixieland band flogging the life out of 'That's A Plenty' yet again. Because there's no point to that.

"The idea to all music is honesty. Honesty and integrity and dignity. And an awareness of the fact that we are all striving for excellence and all striving to create beauty. You can define beauty in lots of different terms, but let's not fool ourselves. The people who say, 'To hell with beauty—beauty's not important. We don't have to be beautiful, we have to represent life as it is.' I don't believe that. And I never will. Because if I believed that, if I believed that the sounds of traffic on the street or the sounds of people screaming at each other and arguing at each other, and the sounds of steam shovels digging up New York City had the same value in my ken as let's say the Second Movement of Brahms' Fourth, that beautiful string theme—I think I'd jump out of a window."

1984

DAN · BARRETT

Hot Jazz and
Smooth Swing

"I call myself a *musician*. Somebody else can put the category on me," declares Dan Barrett when asked if he considers himself more of a "traditional" or more of a "mainstream" jazz trombonist. We're sitting in his Roselle Park, New Jersey, apartment. "What's funny is that whenever I go back to California, I'm confronted by people who remember me playing in traditional bands out there and they'll say—and I love this line: 'Oh, Dan, you've gone *modern* on us.' But that's not the case at all. If I get called to play with Scott Hamilton or Dave McKenna or something, I'll say, 'Great! Sure, I'll take it.' And I'll do my best to fit in with that environment. But recently at Michael's Pub, you know, Terry Waldo did a show re-creating Jelly Roll Morton, and that's been some of my favorite music since I first started listening to jazz, so I enjoyed the opportunity to play in that kind of a vein." Barrett also frequently plays Chicago-style jazz, whether in concerts organized by Dick Hyman at New York's 92nd Street Y or on recordings with saxist Rick Fay and others for the Arbors label (for which Barrett currently serves as musical director). And he seems at least as "at home" playing that kind of boistrous hot jazz as playing smooth, polished small-group swing with the well-known Alden-Barrett Quintet, which he co-leads with his close friend and longtime collaborator, guitarist Howard Alden. "I just try and adapt myself to whatever's going on," Barrett says.

He certainly succeeds. In the fields of traditional and mainstream jazz, Barrett, born December 14, 1955, in Pasadena, California, is clearly one of the best all-around trombonists of his generation.

So how did he choose to become a trombonist?

"I didn't," Barrett admits. "When I was in fifth grade, Mr. Kenneth Owen, who gave music lessons and directed the junior high band, asked our class if we'd ever given any thought to playing a musical instrument. I told him my first choice was to play trumpet. He asked why. I said, 'Because they always get to play the melody in school bands.' He looked me over and said, 'Well, you *could* probably play the trumpet—but I think you'd be a lot better trombonist, given your embouchure.' So I started taking trombone lessons each week with Mr. Owen. It was only when I got into junior high school and was in Mr. Owen's band program on trombone that it occurred to me why he actually wanted me to play trombone—because he already had about 20 trumpet players and only three or four trombone players. I realized that a trick had been played on me—that I could very well have played trumpet but he really needed trombone players—but I don't blame him at all, now." And besides, Barrett *does* play a little trumpet on the side these days.

Barrett's interest in music, if not trombone, predated Mr. Owen's invitation to take lessons. "I grew up in Costa Mesa, California, during the southern California Surf Rock craze, when Dick Dale and the Del-Tones, the Beach Boys, and various other groups were playing in and about Malibu. Around 1960, '61, my brother Mark, who's around 10 years older than I am, was leading a Surf Rock group called the Tridents that worked professionally around Newport Beach. I was the band mascot, which I think they wanted like a hole in the head. You can imagine these 17-year-old guys with this 6- or 7-year-old kid tagging around. But they were all nice about it. Surf Rock was sort of based on the blues. And it was my brother Mark who taught me what a blues progression was. He played enough piano so he could do that, although he played guitar in the band."

When did Barrett become aware of, and interested in, jazz?

"In the summer after eighth grade, a piano player named Doug Bradford, who was one of Mr. Owen's former students— Doug's younger sisters went to school with me—said he was going to hear a jazz band one night. I said, 'What's a jazz band?' He said that there was this South Frisco Jazz Band, playing Friday and Saturday nights at a place called the Pizza Palace in Huntington Beach, California. He said they played music by Jelly Roll Morton and King Oliver and Lu Watters and Turk Murphy— names that were all completely foreign to me. We got permission from my parents to go; Doug would have me home at a certain hour. And he drove me over. I remember opening the door to the Pizza Palace and—well, the band played very loudly. I mean, you could even hear them out in the parking lot. And when you opened this wooden door, it was like *blissfully* loud! Exciting. It just sounded great. That was the first live jazz band I had heard, and I soon knew that that was the kind of music I wanted to hear. I wound up spending every Friday and Saturday night I could listening to the South Frisco Band. That band, by the way, is still playing, although the lineup has changed. But that was my first exposure to the music of Jelly Roll Morton and the San Francisco revival. And through being there night after night, I learned their arrangements and the tunes and everything. And the Pizza Parlor was a fun place. On the breaks, they used to show Laurel and Hardy movies and stuff like that. The adults could have a pitcher of beer and the kids could have Coca-Cola and eat a pizza.

"Frank Demond, who's currently playing with one of the Preservation Hall Jazz Bands in New Orleans, was the South Frisco Band's trombone player at the time. And Frank was a big first influence on me, both as a person and as a musician. Then one time Frank had to go to New Orleans to sub for Big Jim Robinson, and I wound up subbing for Frank in the South Frisco Band. I was 15 and that was one of my first professional experiences. It was pretty exciting. I had to borrow my Dad's necktie and all that stuff.

"Around the same time, my folks and I found out that there were various jazz societies all over southern California, where people could get together and enjoy each other socially but also listen to jazz. And the thing that made them exciting out there was that at almost every one, you could see—and if you were a musician, you'd get an opportunity to play with—some of the second-generation New Orleans jazz musicians who had moved from New Orleans to the southern California area. My theory is that when King Oliver's Band went out to California in 1921, they probably returned to New Orleans raving about the climate, and then, one by one, musicians started moving out there.

"The jazz societies in southern California all met on Sundays. You could actually go every Sunday to a different jazz society meeting and play. You'd enter the club, sign on a clipboard under the instrument that you played, and then a musical director would assign you to certain sets. And it was there that I met—oh gosh, Barney Bigard [noted clarinetist who had played with Duke Ellington and Louis Armstrong] would show up at several of these societies; he'd be just one of the guys, playing with both professionals and amateurs. And clarinetist Joe Darensbourg was out there. There was a trumpet player who had played with Piron's Orchestra in New Orleans, Mike DeLay. And Alton Purnell, the piano player from George Lewis' New Orleans band, was a frequent guest. Drummer Alton Redd from Kid Ory's band. Montudi Garland was out there on bass. Sylvester Rice, who was a drummer. At these societies, they'd play just for fun—no money. Each set would be a different style. If all of the old-time New Orleans players got on a set, of course that's the type of music they'd play. And then the next set might be more of a mainstream bag, and some moldy figs would stomp out in disgust because it was too modern for them! It was all kind of fun.

"When I was between 15 and 16, a trombonist named Gordon Mitchell got me working with these musicians on the outside. Gordon led a group called the Crown City Jazz Band, which had a double front line and one rhythm section, and we worked a dozen or more jobs around L.A. The front line generally included Joe Darensbourg and Barney Bigard on clarinets. The trumpet players were George Orendorff—he had played behind Louis Armstrong on some of the famous Les Hite records and later was in Louis' big band—and Andy Blakeney, who had been a member of Ory's band in the '40s and was a very strong, powerful New Orleans–style player. And then Gordon and I played trombone. How exciting it was to play with some of these New Orleans veterans! And, you know, I grew up in an all-white neighborhood. So at an early age, I was getting an exposure to different cultures. And I have to credit my parents with raising me to believe that people are people and shouldn't be judged on their color or religion or anything."

Initially, Barrett's tastes fell exclusively into the "moldy fig" category. He liked hot, old-time jazz, as played either by New Orleans veterans or by younger West Coast revivalists who had adapted the traditional New Orleans style. Gradually, however, he also became interested in the somewhat smoother and more modern sounds of swing music. "Here's how I got interested in swing, briefly. One night at the Pizza Palace, Mike Baird, who's one of my favorite clarinetists, couldn't make it. So a fellow named John Smith, who played soprano saxophone, came in as a substitute, and when he played—well, I didn't understand what he was doing except it just made me stomp my foot and made my heart beat faster. But I found out later that he was playing in more of a swing style. I got to know John, and found he had an enormous record collection and knew about the whole history of jazz. So John would make me cassettes, and that was like the first that I'd heard of, oh, Billie Holiday and those small-group sides with Teddy Wilson and Lester Young and stuff.

"And in this period, I happened to hear the guy who I still think is probably my favorite living trombonist. His name is Al Jenkins. About the only recordings you'll find of Al were made in the late '40s with Doc Evans' band in Minneapolis. I heard Al in southern California and it really turned me around. Because at that time—I was still in high school—I hung around with some college guys who had convinced me that the only way to play trombone was sort of like Kid Ory or Turk Murphy or Big Jim Robinson. And, incidentally, I still love those players. However, one night I heard Al Jenkins with a local Dixieland band, and he wasn't playing anything like that, and yet it was just so terrific. His playing was more out of Jack Teagarden and Lou McGarity and Miff Mole—although Al puts it together his own unique way so it sounds like Al Jenkins. But I mean, he approaches the horn more like those trombonists than the traditional players I had been admiring. And so he made a real significant impact on me."

Barrett bought more records, gradually amassing a magnificent collection, teaching himself the history of jazz—particularly early jazz. He loved the playing of Jack Teagarden. (In this period he also became good friends with a banjo player named Bill Campbell, who had worked with Teagarden.) He dug the famed Ellington trombonists Lawrence Brown, Juan Tizol, and Tricky Sam Nanton. The expressive Vic Dickenson impressed him greatly, and he added some of Dickenson's effects to his repertoire. He enjoyed the playing, too, of such departed greats as Dickie Wells, Miff Mole, and J. C. Higginbotham. He admired such lyrical players as Tommy Dorsey and Jack Jenney. Among more modern stylists, one he found particularly enjoyable was Bill Harris. Even Frank Rosolino's unique modern approach held some intrigue for him. But invariably, he found himself drawn more to stylists of an earlier era: Lou McGarity, Cutty Cutshall, and many others. "I call it the golden era of trombonists, like in the '30s and '40s," he says.

"I've seen it written so many times that when bop came along, the trombone was liberated. And certainly J. J. Johnson accomplished a lot; he brought his own technical ability to the instrument. But as far as the bop movement goes, I'm not sure that it was liberating the instrument as much as confining it. Because prior to the advent of bebop, the trombone was doing all kinds of things. You know, you hear Dickie Wells and Vic Dickenson, and even the tailgaters with the smears and the slides. And among all of that, in the trombonists' bag of devices to use, was the ability to play strings of eighth notes, in a bop way. But then it seems like by the mid or late 1940s, when bebop got established, all of the other things that the trombone could do were set aside just for this virtuoso technical approach—to make the trombone sound like Charlie Parker. Well, that's a noble endeavor. But for one reason or another, I sort of gravitate toward what the guys were doing before then, in the '30s and '40s. It just hits me more." He could listen to some bebop and enjoy it—he says there are some mornings when he'll wake up and feel like listening to a Charlie Parker record, others when he'd rather hear early Fletcher Henderson—but his preference was basically for the sounds of earlier eras. Even today, he notes, "Louis Armstrong is my favorite musician."

In addition to playing, Barrett began arranging music while still in high school. He was essentially self-taught. "My high school band director, Richard England, called me into his office one day and said, 'Hey Barrett, when's the next time the pep band is going to play?' I said, 'Two weeks from now.' He said, 'Well look, I'm getting tired of hearing "On Wisconsin" and "Navy Blue and Gold" and these various marches we've been playing that pep bands have been playing since the 1920s. I know you're interested in swing. The pep band has three saxophones and a couple of trumpets and you on trombone. Why don't you write some arrangements like that for the pep band?' I said, 'What are you talking about? I don't know how to do that.' He told me to ask for help from a kid in the band who had been studying orchestrations: 'He'll tell you the books to buy. You've got two weeks. I want you to have three arrangements ready.' And I said, 'But, but, but—' He said, 'Nah, get out of here. I'm busy.' And he knew what he was doing. He was a military-type disciplinarian. I stayed up all night trying to figure out how to transpose an alto part, you know, reading a book and so on. 'Oh my God, this is the hardest thing I've ever done.' I sort of transcribed the Luis Russell record of 'St. Louis Blues.' And then did charts for 'Shine' and 'It Don't Mean a Thing (If It Ain't Got That Swing).' So our pep band is up there in the Newport Harbor High School bleachers during a basketball game and we started playing 'St. Louis Blues.' And after we finished, there were a couple of seconds of silence and then the gymnasium burst out into applause. That was the first time that anybody actually clapped for the pep band—usually we'd have apple cores thrown at us—so we were all pretty proud."

The musical association for which Barrett is best known—and certainly the most lasting of his career—is with guitarist/ banjoist Howard Alden. Alden's pure tone, rather measured musical statements, and overall good taste make him a considerable asset in any group, whether he is adding just a few choice notes to embellish someone else's solo or carrying an entire number alone—as may be heard on any of his many recordings. (Public recognition came when *JazzTimes* magazine instituted its annual Critics' Poll in 1990; Alden promptly won in the category of best emerging guitarist.) There is a remarkable "rightness" about the best of Alden's improvised work, a sense that each note is falling into place with an indisputable logic.

Barrett recalls, "I met Howard when I was about 18 and he was 14. Actually, even before then we may have both been at the Pizza Palace watching the South Frisco Band on some nights—for he knew about that band—but we didn't know each other back then. The first time Howard and I met was when he subbed for an older banjo player on a strolling job we had taken at a Costa Mesa shopping center. And here's this young fellow taking the banjo out of the case. And the rest us in the band were sort of snobbish because we could play things like 'Mabel's Dream'— old jazz tunes nobody else knew. There's a self-righteousness to being a staunch moldy fig! And yet it turned out that Howard knew 'Mabel's Dream' and he knew 'Papa Dip,' and he knew all of the other old numbers. And then on the breaks, I'd *also* hear him practicing these more modern Charlie Christian guitar solos on the banjo! Of course I didn't know what I was hearing then— but that's what it was. For the first couple of sets, he just played rhythm for us. And then finally the leader turned so Howard could have a solo. And at 14, Howard was playing essentially similar to what he's doing today. I mean, that marvelous technique on whatever he plays, banjo or guitar. He's just 14—and here's all this talent coming around! During the next break, I went over to one of the fellows leading the band and I said, 'Who *is* this guy?' He answered in this matter-of-fact voice, 'Oh, that's Howard Alden.' I said, 'Yeah? Where'd he come from? *Mars?*'

"And again, he says to me in that flat tone, 'Oh—what, you like him?' I said, 'What!? I've never heard anything like it. Have you?' And he says, 'Well, he plays sort of *modern.*' And I wanted to say, 'Well, modern schmodern—jeez, just listen!' So, Howard was only hired because he knew the tunes, you know what I mean? And they sort of disparaged his approach to the banjo. Someone in the group said, 'Well, he doesn't really play it like a banjo.' I said, 'Well, jeez, come on, guys—listen, open your ears!' But anyway, then Howard and I started talking and we found out we had similar views on music and the jazz scene and everything. He'd recommend me for jobs and I'd recommend him for jobs.

"And let me say this about Howard—and I don't say this lightly. If you play with a musician for a long time—and certainly for as long as I've known Howard and played with him—you tend to know what they're going to do. Some musicians are more predictable than others, but generally you get a feeling for how a guy is going to approach a solo or how he is going to approach a tune. And all I can say is that Howard still continues to surprise me. And I still find myself listening to everything he has to offer because there is still so much to learn there." He also credits Alden with helping him eventually become a full-time musician.

"After high school, I went to Orange Coast College, a two-year college, and then on to Long Beach State, where I majored in music teaching. I thought I'd become a high school band teacher. I mean, I liked music, but the thought of playing professionally—well, that just wasn't working for me then and I couldn't see a way to change the situation. But I met a banjoist, Lueder Ohlwein, who was putting together a band to go to the annual Breda, Holland, Jazz Festival. He asked, would I like to go to Holland in May? And there was going to be a tour of Germany after the Breda Festival. So we'd be gone a month, which would necessitate my taking off a semester at college. And I wasn't having a good time at all in college! I convinced my folks, 'Look, I'll just take a semester off and go over. This may be

my only opportunity to see Europe.' Europe was like a fantasy—
someplace you only see on TV. So I told Long Beach State that
I wouldn't be coming back that semester. I was never more
relieved to leave a place in all my life! And it was during that
trip, in Holland in 1977, that I decided to try to be a professional
musician. I never went back to Long Beach State. But it wasn't
until 1983, when I moved to New York, that I actually started
making a living, fully supporting myself, in music." In the meantime, Barrett and Alden worked together as much they could.
They even got to record together occasionally as sidemen for
Dick Sudhalter (on his 1981 Audiophile album, *Friends with Pleasure*) and Doc Cheatham (on a 1982 New York Jazz album, produced and conducted by Eddy Davis, *Adolphus Anthony "Doc"
Cheatham: Too Marvelous for Words*).

"Meanwhile, Howard got called to play with Red Norvo's
Trio in Atlantic City. And on their day off, Howard would take
the train from Atlantic City up to New York and he took a liking
to New York City and decided that he'd move. In fact, he came
back to California and said, 'This is it. I'm moving to New York.
It's the only place to be if you want to play.' And we all kind of
said, 'Yeah, sure, Howard, OK, fine.' And I don't think it was
three weeks later that I got this phone call and Howard says,
'Well, I'm here in New York. I'm all settled in in my new apartment.' I said, 'What?! What are you talking about, New York?'
He said, 'Well, I told you I was moving to New York.' I said,
'Yeah, but man, that was less than a month ago.' He said, 'Well,
here I am.'" Alden moved to New York in January of 1983 and
kept urging Barrett to join him. "He said if I wanted to make a
living playing music of any kind, but especially jazz, I'd better
come out to New York. But see, I was still living with my parents
and I couldn't make enough money to move out and be on my
own. I was playing with some very good bands, but they were
all avocational bands; the fellows would get together once or
twice a week for fun. I was making $40 each Sunday afternoon,
playing at the San Juan Capistrano Depot with Dick Shooshan's
Golden Eagle Jazz Band. Incidentally, that's one of the very
best—along with the South Frisco Jazz Band—traditional bands
on the circuit. And then I'd go up the coast and play a couple of

nights a week at the Hotel Laguna with a guitarist/singer named Tony Romano. Between those gigs and the occasional outside jobs I'd pick up, I wasn't making a whole lot of money.

"But Howard finally convinced me to move to New York. I saved what little money I had and bought a one-way airplane ticket to New York City, and packed up one box with my 'desert island' records and just a few clothes. Howard said that I could stay with him until I found a place of my own; we'd split the rent. I was all set to go. And my folks wrote me off as certifiably insane! They did everything they could to talk me out of it. But finally I convinced them that they couldn't tell me what New York was going to be like, any more than I could tell them what it would be like. And we all agreed that I was spinning my wheels in southern California. Howard had moved to New York and was doing OK. My parents and I all respected Howard's judgment—so if Howard thought I might be able to make it, why not give it a shot?

"Then, a few weeks before the date of my plane ticket, David Lillie called me and said that he was affiliated with the Widespread Depression Orchestra—I'd known them from some records—that their trombonist was leaving, and David had heard from Howard and a couple of my other friends in the New York area that I might be interested in the trombone chair. And I said yes and sent an audition tape. And he called back and said the guys all liked the tape and you can have the job. And the band was on a salary at that time—which was almost unheard-of, except for maybe the Basie Band or something. Well, he asked me how soon I could get my affairs in order to come to New York to play with the band. I said, 'Well, how does three weeks sound?' I started working with the band as soon as I moved to New York [in February of 1983]. And that made quite a big difference. Because we all know stories of otherwise good musicians' coming to New York and not being able to make it, just due to circumstances; it's like the roll of the dice. But here I had this ready-made job waiting for me. And that enabled me to have the dough to hang out at Eddie Condon's Club. And there I met Ed Polcer, who got me working at Eddie Condon's—subbing for Tom Artin—only two weeks after I got to town. So that was real nice. In Los Angeles, I'd met all sorts of guys who took my number but I never heard from them again. But I sat in one night at Condon's and Ed said, 'Give me your number and if Tom Artin ever has to take a break, I'll call you for a sub.' I thought, 'I'll give him my number and I'll never hear from him again.' But sure enough, two weeks later Ed called and asked me to play at Condon's.

"I played at the closing night at Eddie Condon's, July 31st, 1985, in Ed Polcer's band. Boy, that was a wild night! And I didn't know it but I wound up sort of auditioning for Benny Goodman that night, too. I remember, I was standing out on the sidewalk for a bit because it was so hot inside. Of course it was jam-packed—the club's final night. And this Checker cab rolled up and like the biggest guy I'd ever seen got out of the back seat: Benny Goodman. And I say 'big' because he seemed larger than life. He stopped all conversation. There were about 20 of us out on the sidewalk, trying to cool off. And I mean, here Benny Goodman gets out of a cab and there's this silence. And he nodded to everybody and sort of smiled. I think he enjoyed being the center of attention as he walked in the place. And he got a seat right in front of the band. And shortly after that, I started working with Goodman's last big band."

A number of former Goodman sidemen have described Goodman as rude, self-centered, cheap, and mean. But Barrett will not join the Goodman-bashers. He says simply, "I was taught to judge—and I have always judged—people by the way they treat me. Sure, I'd heard all the stories about Benny and I was certainly intimidated by playing for him. He's an icon. But all I can say is that he treated me fairly and featured me quite a bit and was always real pleasant to me. He knew that I was fond of Jack Teagarden and he'd talk about some of the old records that he was on with Teagarden. And he took the time to share a couple of anecdotes with me. Here's one story he told me, from when he was in the Ben Pollack Band in the 1920s. Of course the saxes were in front and the brass section sat behind the saxes. Well, Jack Teagarden had just joined the band, and he was really on that night. (I mean, was he ever not on? You know, I haven't heard those records; he always sounds great.) But on that night

Jack stood up to play, and Benny said he just started playing some stuff that—well, Benny had never heard anything like it come out of a trombone before. And Benny told me he turned around in his chair and was just sort of staring at Jack. And then Teagarden stopped playing and sat down, and Benny just kept staring at him—trying to figure out what made him tick and how does a guy play like that. And finally, Teagarden got a little upset and said in that Texas voice of his, 'What you looking at?' And Goodman said, 'Well, I'm sorry—you know, I just—man, I think you just play great.' And Teagarden told him, 'Yeah, well, just turn around. You're making me nervous.'

"Benny was always a pretty eccentric guy. And I do think that some of the things he did that people attribute to malice, maybe I would attribute to an absent-mindedness or perhaps an insensitivity. I don't know if there was an evil streak. A lot of people will say there was. But I really think that he just had his mind on music and he was sort of an eccentric individual.

"I like to think he liked me. And musically, for a man that age—he lived to be 77—to inspire the band the way he did . . . I mean, there wasn't a moment where he didn't give it his all. And all he was thinking about was the future; he was talking about a trip to Japan and Australia. He seemed happy with the band." The Goodman Band made carefully selected concert appearances, often several weeks apart; members were free to take other gigs between concerts. Among the major Goodman Band concerts in which Barrett participated were ones at Yale University, December 8, 1985; the Kennedy Center, February 15, 1986; Radio City Music Hall (with Frank Sinatra), March 16, 1986; the University of Michigan, March 22, 1986; and Wolf Trap, in Vienna, Virginia, June 7, 1986.

At most of these concerts, singer Carrie Smith, backed informally by a handful of members of the band (allowing Goodman to take a bit of a breather), was featured on several numbers, such as "Gimme a Pigfoot," "Ja-Da," and "You've Changed." Barrett says of Smith, "She's marvelous. She can sort of turn on a crowd. A big, powerful voice." Barrett wrote a big band arrangement of "You've Changed" for Smith, and Goodman okayed its use. "I was very pleased that Benny let us play my arrangement because there were other instances where guys would bring in charts they had written and he didn't seem interested. You know, the band already had so many great old arrangements by Fletcher Henderson and others to play. But at least he let us perform that one I had written. I had dreams of starting to arrange for the band! Well, we played my arrangement of 'You've Changed' for the first time at Wolf Trap on June 7th. But that turned out to be our very last concert, because Benny died the following week, on Friday, June 13th, 1986. We had no idea, in his last performances, that he was so near death." Goodman left explicit instructions that the band should not continue to perform after his death; he did not believe in "ghost bands" that exploited the memories of departed leaders. The members of Benny Goodman's final orchestra went their separate ways.

After the passing of Goodman, Barrett focused his attention increasingly on the Alden-Barrett Quintet—known to fans as the ABQ—which by then had already been in existence for a couple of years. (They had flipped a coin to decide whether the name would be the Alden-Barrett Quintet or the Barrett-Alden Quintet.)

"We organized the quintet in New York in 1984. Actually, Howard and I had put together a prototype of it back in California," Barrett points out. "That was just born of the fact that there was really nowhere where we could hear that kind of band. We figured if we couldn't go out and hear a band like that, we might as well put one together ourselves. Because Howard was playing with more quote-unquote modern groups than I was; I'll say 'post-bop.' And I'd been playing with avocational jazz bands and Dixieland bands. There just didn't seem to be anyplace in the L.A. area where you could go hear a group playing like swinging arrangements or in more of a swing style, and that was where Howard and I sort of came together musically; I mean, that was our common ground. Because Howard knew more about post-bop music than I did. And maybe I had the edge on him, as far as very early jazz. And so we sort of met in the middle there. We both had a healthy respect for, oh, the John Kirby Sextet and the Goodman small groups, and of course the Red Norvo groups, through Howard's experience with Red. And we kept thinking, 'Gee, wouldn't it be great if we could have a band that plays stuff like that—like have little things worked out so it sounded like a band, and yet have enough room for improvisation to let things happen.' So, our group had a couple of rehearsals in California, but we never worked a job with it out there. However, shortly after I got to New York, we set about putting together a group like that with New York musicians.

"The unusual instrumentation—trombone, guitar, alto sax, bass, and drums—was Howard's idea. I have to give him credit for that. And I tried to talk him out of it because I was more traditionally oriented and I guess I had Count Basie's four-piece rhythm section in mind. But Howard thought that he had a little more freedom without a piano. And he thought that an alto sax, being a lighter instrument than a tenor, would be more of a contrast to the trombone. And Howard sort of had that sound in his mind and finally he convinced me to try it and I said, 'Yeah, sure; OK, that'll be fine.' In New York, Howard and I talked about which musicians we wanted. We decided upon Jackie Williams on drums and Frank Tate on bass. I couldn't come up with a reed player, and Howard said, 'There's only one guy to get and that's Chuck Wilson.' And at that time, I really hadn't heard that much of Chuck. I had subbed in Vince Giordano's band—that's always fun; I like playing with that band—and Chuck was playing lead alto there. This was back before Chuck and I became members of Benny Goodman's band. So I really didn't know Chuck except from having heard him in Vince's band. I knew he played the instrument very well and was a very good lead player, but I had no idea that he was also an improviser. And Howard sort of chuckled—I can hear him chuckling now—and said, 'You just wait. You just wait until the rehearsal.' I said, 'OK, Howard, if you like him, I guess we'll give him a try.' The first thing we played was a blues in B-flat or something. Howard took a couple of choruses, I took a couple, and Howard pointed to Chuck to play—and of course it was marvelous. And I realized Alden was right once again, that Chuck was probably the only guy for the band. The quintet first appeared at Condon's as a group, and we played a few festivals. After we appeared at the Conneaut Lake Festival, producer Joe Boughton booked us for a regional tour. And we began working from time to time at the club J's; I'm glad to give them a plug because owner Judy Barnett has always been very supportive about giving us dates."

The popularity of the quintet led to Barrett's being asked to do recording sessions. "The late record producer Harry Lim was quite fond of the quintet; he saw us back when we were at Condon's. So Harry recorded me a couple of times for his label, Famous Door Records—not as a leader but as a sideman on Butch Miles' dates. Then the first recording I did for Concord was on Warren Vaché's album *Easy Going* in 1986. That was when I met Carl Jefferson, the president of Concord Records, and got connected with the company. Gus Statiras actually produced the first Alden-Barrett Quintet record, *Swing Street*, but it wound up coming out on the Concord label, rather than on Gus' label; Carl bought the rights to the recording from Gus and put it out," Barrett recalls. The Alden-Barrett Quintet's first album included numbers that had originally been recorded by John Kirby, Benny Goodman, Duke Ellington, and Thelonious Monk, as well as a few new numbers in a classic swing vein composed by Buck Clayton. The distinctive originals by Clayton, one of the elder statesmen of the jazz world, helped draw attention to the group. Clayton, who had first risen to stardom in the 1930s as featured trumpeter with the Count Basie Band, had been in retirement in recent years. Writing for Alden and Barrett provided his reentry onto the current jazz scene.

The quintet's next Concord album, *The ABQ Salutes Buck Clayton*, was devoted entirely to music associated with Clayton: mostly new material that he had composed and arranged expressly for the quintet, plus some numbers he had recorded many years before, which Alden and Barrett arranged. Alden and Barrett were showcased beautifully playing Clayton's music; their association with Clayton proved beneficial to both them and him. Listen to how effectively Barrett states the melody, getting a rich, dark wine tone, on the haunting "Winter Light." Savor his bluesy trombone work on "Claytonia." And for an elegant example of Alden's sensitive work, listen to "A Beautiful Yesteryear." Barrett comments, "Buck Clayton was legendary. It was Howard who actually met Buck first, when Howard was working with pianist Joe Bushkin at the St. Regis Hotel [in early 1983]. Later on I got to work with Joe at the same place. Buck and Joe were old friends, going back to their days at the Embers in the '50s, and when Buck came in one night to hear Joe, someone introduced Howard to Buck. Howard got to talking about the quintet and asked if Buck could write some arrangements for the group. Buck said that when he had time, he would. When Howard told me this, we both figured, well, Buck says 'when he has time'—this could take years, if ever. About two weeks later, Buck called Howard and said, 'I've got a couple of charts for your group.' And he kept writing more arrangements for us, contributing 20 or 25 originals in all. Buck was there the first night that we played at Condon's, and we played his arrangements. And we were sort of flattered that when he subsequently started writing arrangements for his big band, many of the things that he arranged for that band were things that he had written initially for our quintet. He liked the sound with the quintet, and then he went on to expand the numbers for the big band. 'In a Parisian Mood,' 'Pretty Peepers,' and 'Winter Light,' for example, were all tunes that he wrote initially for our quintet, then later for his big band."

Clayton told me a few years ago: "Howard and Dan were the real reason that I got back into having a band of my own because Howard was the first one to approach me to make some charts for his band—which I think is the best little band since John Kirby's. I wrote some things for them, and then the word got around." Clayton wound up composing and arranging for various other bands. "And after that, I decided I might as well do it for myself." Barrett and Alden both became charter members of the Buck Clayton Swing Band, which won high praise internationally in the few years that it existed prior to Clayton's death in 1991. Barrett may be heard on the band's Stash album *A Swingin' Dream* (Alden was unavailable on the date that "live" album was recorded).

Other noteworthy albums on which Barrett has played in

Dan Barrett (courtesy of Judy Jack).

Dan Barrett leads a band at the 1986 Conneaut Lake Jazz Festival including guitarist Howard Alden, bassist Phil Flanigan, tenor saxist Eddie Miller, and trumpeter Billy Butterfield (photos by Chip Deffaa).

The top photo (courtesy of Judy Jack) shows the Alden-Barrett Quintet: Jackie Williams, drums; Frank Tate, bass; Howard Alden, guitar/coleader; Barrett, trombone/coleader; and Chuck Wilson, alto sax. The bottom photo (by Chip Deffaa) shows Barrett playing on one of Richard Sudhalter's gigs, with Joe Muranyi, soprano sax; Marty Grosz, guitar; Ronnie Bedford, drums; Sudhalter, trumpet; Barrett, trombone; and Betty Comora, washboard/vocals.

Dan Barrett with his son, Andy (photo by Chip Deffaa).

recent years include *Strictly Instrumental*, an octet session under his leadership, which he made for Concord, and *Jubilesta*, his first album as a soloist backed simply by a rhythm section, which he made for Arbors, the label with which he is currently affiliated. Arbors President Mat Domber uses Barrett as musical director, soliciting his advice regarding musicians to record. For Arbors, Barrett has been featured on various Chicago-jazz recordings with reedman Rick Fay, with whom he had first played in southern California as a teenager. The sessions have been spirited, with pleasingly full-sounding ensembles (using as many as nine musicians), although not all of the other musicians have always been up to Barrett's level. One could also question the need for still another casually jammed version of some of the more familiar tunes; aficionados of this type of music are likely to already own superior older recorded versions. In this regard, Barrett's craftsmanship as an arranger has proved an asset to the label—an asset one hopes the label will more fully exploit in the future. The few sides that he has arranged have been more focused and more interesting than the loose, jam-session-type sides. Listen to Barrett's arrangement of "Roll On, Mississippi, Roll On," on the Arbors CD *Rick Fay and Friends: Rolling On*. The performance is a kick from start to finish; it has both vitality and a sense of forward movement—no wasted motions. Or check out Barrett's refreshing original, "Possum Jump," which sounds a bit more modern than most other numbers on the CD, and shows he's listened to his share of jump blues and boogie-woogie over the years. (Barrett's arrangements, by the way, are available for purchase from Arbors Records.) I'd like to see CDs devoted solely to music arranged and/or composed by Barrett.

Besides the records he has made, Barrett has occasionally been heard on the soundtracks of TV commercials (for the likes of American Express and Wendy's) and motion pictures (such as *The Cotton Club* and *Brighton Beach Memoirs*). He is gradually acquiring more and more of an international reputation as a jazz musician. This has taken some time to build, since the labels for which he has recorded have not had nearly the distribution of a major label like, say, Sony. But if you're good, the news eventually spreads. I learned of the Alden-Barrett Quintet's success at the Edinburgh Jazz Festival a few years ago via a transatlantic phone call from Clarrie Henley, a jazz correspondent for England's *Daily Telegraph*; he had been so taken by their music that in one week he had gone back to hear them seven times. And as Barrett notes, the news is creating demand. "I just got back from working in England and now I'm getting ready for a tour of Germany with a 14-piece band, for which I'm writing some charts, that will include Howard Alden, Chuck Wilson, Randy Sandke, Harry Allen, and Jon-Erik Kellso." And in the past 10 years, Barrett has become a highly sought-after trombonist at traditional jazz parties. He's keeping busy. To the casual observer, his career would seem to be evolving quite nicely indeed. But Barrett sees cause for concern.

"The jazz parties are not going to be around a whole lot longer," he believes. "I'm very thankful that the ones that are still here *are* here. I remember a conversation that took place among Ken Peplowski and Howard Alden and myself four years ago; we didn't give the jazz parties more than five to ten years. And since then, several of them have gone. The Minneapolis Jazz Party is defunct, because Scotch 3M withdrew its sponsorship. And the Triangle Jazz Party, for which I was the musical director, in Raleigh, North Carolina, is now defunct; we're hoping maybe next year we can revive it, whether it's in Raleigh or not. I just got a letter from Bev Muchnik of the San Diego Jazz Party; she had to cancel that one for next February, for personal reasons. And the Midland Jazz Classic in Texas had to let one year fall by the wayside. So it doesn't really bode well for the jazz parties. But even if all of those parties were healthy and strong, the median age of the audience is about 65 or so.

"And unfortunately, I don't see any avenues for kids' getting exposed to traditional jazz today. Like for instance, in Manhattan, when Eddie Condon's Club went—that was like the last real bastion of traditional jazz. There are still a couple of places in town where you can hear traditional music, but perhaps played by more avocational bands. Back when Ed Polcer was running Condon's, I proposed that he have at least one night be sort of a family night, where you get the house band to play several hours earlier—maybe start at six o'clock—and offer a kids' menu.

Just have an evening where minors could go hear jazz. I was lucky to have a place like the Pizza Palace where I could discover this music when I was growing up. And there were other places in southern California where minors could go and hear music. In New York, I really don't know of any places playing live music that welcome minors. And you certainly need places where young people can be exposed to *this* music—or how else are you going to develop new audiences?"

1992

Cornetist and Club Owner

"It's America's greatest art form; our greatest contribution to the arts in general is this thing called jazz. It's all over the world now. You go to Japan and you're treated like a king, whereas here in our own country you're sort of a second-class citizen," Ed Polcer, jazz cornetist, bandleader, and club owner, is telling me.

We're sitting on the veranda of a turn-of-the-century hotel in Conneaut Lake, Pennsylvania, midway between New York and Chicago. I've flown here to cover the 1986 Conneaut Lake Jazz Festival; Polcer has come to make music. He's a good man to have at these festivals. He plays a driving cornet with a direct, simple attack, and he never seems to tire. That final point is important. He's been playing until two in the morning the last two nights, and he was up early this morning to lead an informal session at brunch. As a leader, Polcer works hard to make the whole band sound good, not just to get his own solos heard. He's a solid ensemble player, who helps provide the framework so that other soloists are heard to their best advantage. He knows all the tunes. And there are times this weekend when he's the glue holding things together. Producer Joe Boughton has assembled a marvelous collection of musicians, including Bud Freeman, Billy Butterfield, Eddie Miller, Ray McKinley, and more, but some of these great veterans simply no longer have the stamina to play all-out throughout a three-day bash. With his strong and consistent playing, Polcer covers for some of the older jazzmen whose energies have flagged a bit by the final day of the festival.

You may spot Polcer at jazz parties or festivals in Odessa, Texas, and Wilmington, North Carolina, and Decatur, Illinois. He also likes to take a band to England every year, if he can. But most of the time, Polcer stays in New York, where he has been the co-owner of one of the best-known jazz clubs in the world: Eddie Condon's.

"People will pay thousands of dollars to charity for the local opera," Polcer is saying now. "And it's prestigious for Joe Doakes, businessman, to have his company donate $10,000 to the Toledo Symphony. But God forbid they should donate $2,000 to the Toledo Hot Jazz Society for programs. Because jazz is a kind of music that people have fun with. And it can't be quite taken seriously. . . ."

Polcer has been an outspoken advocate of jazz for a decade. He's a trustee, for example, of the International Art of Jazz, Inc., which puts jazz programs into public schools and public parks. His concern over our culture's lack of appreciation for jazz, over the future of jazz and the precarious economics of it, is hardly new. But these days, there's something more specific fueling Polcer's anxiety over the future of jazz in America—and more specifically, of traditional jazz. In July of 1985, Polcer's club, Eddie Condon's, was forced to close. Its lease ran out and an office building is now going up in its place. And Polcer has had a devil of a time trying to find an affordable Manhattan site so that the club can reopen. As we talk, Polcer is expressing confidence in reopening Eddie Condon's sometime in 1986, but admits he has still not yet found a viable location. And as he gives me a background briefing on the situation—he'd seemingly rather talk about the jazz club scene than himself—there is little reason for optimism.

A New York without Eddie Condon's? To many fans of traditional jazz, Polcer realizes, the idea may seem almost unthinkable. There always was a fraternal spirit in Condon's. And

219

there's never been a cover charge. You'd walk in. You'd listen to the five or six musicians on the bandstand; a house band played on most nights but the specific personnel shifted from night to night. If you liked what you heard, you stayed. If not, you moved on without having spent a nice sum just to get in the door—as is the case at most jazz clubs these days. Polcer notes that the city's other major traditional jazz club, Jimmy Ryan's, which had a history nearly as proud as Condon's, lost its lease shortly before Condon's did and found reopening elsewhere economically impossible. Property values have been rising so much in midtown Manhattan that it is becoming increasingly difficult to maintain jazz clubs, particularly clubs like these two in which patrons could drop in to hear music without a cover charge or minimum. And Condon's and Ryan's always had *bands*, not like the less-expensive but comparatively anemic duos and trios you find in many of the city's jazz rooms. Musicians, club owners, and knowing fans get justifiably apprehensive when they see towering office buildings and luxury apartments replacing the smaller, older buildings that once housed jazz clubs like Eddie Condon's. Lovers of jazz feel a real loss that not even one room in New York devotes itself on an exclusive basis to high-quality traditional (or "classic") jazz.[1]

Many businesses now being squeezed out of Manhattan by the rising land values and other economic factors can easily relocate out of state. But you could not so easily disperse Manhattan's 40 or so jazz clubs and the extraordinary concentration of musicians who live in Manhattan—not without affecting the liveliness of jazz in general. And it's not just jazz club owners and musicians in New York who are voicing concern these days; you'll hear similar fears expressed by people involved in off-Broadway theater, and dance, and art of various kinds. Office buildings, condos, and hotels are putting a squeeze on theater

---

[1]Since this profile was written, another club named Condon's, but having no connection to the clubs that were run by Eddie Condon and Ed Polcer, has opened in New York. Featuring modern jazz, it is co-owned by a man—no relation to Eddie Condon—who happens to be named John Condon. Friends of Eddie Condon unsuccessfully appealed to John Condon to call his club something else to avoid confusion.

and dance companies and related businesses such as costume and scenery makers. Rehearsal halls and art galleries find it increasingly hard to pay commercial rents. Manhattan may simply be getting too expensive for some of the often-only-marginally-profitable facilities for the arts that help make it our nation's cultural center. Those in theater and dance have done a better job of bringing their concerns to the attention of New York politicians, who generally seem more aware of the importance of keeping theater and dance healthy in the city rather than jazz.

Polcer comments: "It's wonderful to have great hotels in New York and new office buildings and stuff to accommodate people who are coming to New York—but somewhere along the way, if New York loses some of its vitality, the people will have no reason to come. The soul of New York is nightlife—theater and cabaret and night clubs and entertainment. Real estate prices are so astronomical in midtown now—we were quoted at a thousand dollars a day rent, you know, for a place about twice the size of what the old Eddie Condon's was. I mean, if you want good ground-floor space in midtown Manhattan. The problem that jazz clubs have is that you have to generate an awful lot of people coming in there to even pay the rent. You can do it by sticking stiff cover charges, but then that defeats the purpose. If a person wants to feel free to come into a jazz club, they don't want to get stiffed with a $10 or $20 cover charge. And most of the places in New York now have these cover charges. We tried to keep it at Condon's so people could say after the theater, 'Let's go have a drink at Condon's.' They'd come in and have two or three drinks and we'd end up doing about as well as if we'd had a cover charge—because they liked what they heard." Polcer sees irony, too, in the fact that the Hilton Hotel Corporation, together with the Prudential Insurance Company, is putting up the office building where Condon's once stood. There were ten hotels within three blocks of Condon's and its former neighbor on West 54th Street, Jimmy Ryan's. New York's midtown jazz clubs drew many patrons from the nearby hotels. And the midtown hotels have traditionally been attractive to many people because of their proximity to nightlife. That a major hotel firm like Hilton's should be a party to the driving of nightlife out of midtown Manhattan strikes Polcer as madness.

For fans of the music one heard at Jimmy Ryan's and Eddie Condon's, New York has been diminished since their closings. For decades, fans had taken it for granted that they could find those older jazz sounds every night of the week in the "Big Apple." When Condon's closed, July 31st, 1985, reporters noted that countless jazz greats had played at some point in Condon's. Some, remembering the heyday of nearby 52nd Street—"Swing Street"—recalled how many vibrant jazz clubs had once enlivened the area but that skyscrapers had replaced them; Condon's was the last big-name jazz joint in midtown. Reporters mentioned, too, celebrities who had been known to drop in to catch the music at Condon's, figures like Johnny Carson, Walter Cronkite, Frank Sinatra, Dinah Shore, Jackie Gleason, and Liza Minnelli. Polcer, though, stresses now he'd been particularly proud that the club had long been a *musicians'* hangout. When the Basie Band had a gig in the area, Polcer reminds me, half the band might drop into the club after they were done working for the night. Joe Williams would frequently come into the club to sing— for free—after finishing his paid jobs in the area. On one evening at Condon's earlier in the year (a party honoring jazz writer George T. Simon's 50th year in the business), Benny Goodman, Sammy Kaye, Gerry Mulligan, Les Paul, Marian McPartland, Cab Calloway, and Tony Bennett had been present. And rising younger artists who are expanding upon older jazz styles, such as Scott Hamilton and Howard Alden, found Condon's a congenial place in which to build a following. Condon's, in its various incarnations at various locations in Manhattan over the past four decades, had been a gathering place for musicians and fans, young and old, with an interest in traditional jazz.

No area south of 96th Street in Manhattan is cheap anymore, but some areas are less expensive than others. Why not, you may ask, simply relocate a midtown jazz club like Condon's to a relatively less expensive, if somewhat out-of-the-way, spot? Well, for starters, Polcer says, you'd lose the after-the-theater crowd. He also believes you'd lose many of the tourists who play such an important role in sustaining New York's nightlife. Some nights you could go into Condon's and find a quarter of the patrons were tourists from Japan, where American jazz is well appreciated. If jazz clubs are located too far from midtown hotels, Polcer believes, some tourists simply won't get to them (although it should be noted that a significant number of patrons at the Greenwich Village jazz clubs are always tourists, some from abroad).

Well then, why not join the trend and simply tack on healthy cover charges, the way so many clubs now do? The problem, according to Polcer, is twofold. If jazz clubs charge steep cover charges, they wind up catering primarily to the well-to-do and favoring mostly established artists. Condon's drew some young jazz buffs and young musicians in the audience precisely because it didn't have a cover charge, and it needed them if the music it offered were to survive. A club with a cover charge does *not* become a gathering place for musicians, especially younger ones, who may be barely getting by economically. Condon's could present a band led by an "unknown" but promising younger musician on a Sunday night and still be sure of drawing a crowd. The musicians' friends, club regulars, and a certain number of tourists would drop by, safe in the knowledge that if they didn't like what they heard they wouldn't be out any money. But if patrons have to pay $10-$20 just to get in a club's door, they'll usually want to be sure they'll like the music. Condon's has helped provide needed exposure for younger musicians. Talented, but not yet famous, younger mainstream players such as Howard Alden, Chris Flory, and Loren Schoenberg could lead groups at Condon's and build a following.

Polcer remarks, "I'm dedicated to this kind of music—classic jazz and swing—and I feel that there are plenty of people out there who want to hear it." In the long run, Polcer believes, "the music is going to survive, regardless of ebbs and flows in popularity. I believe that good music will survive, whether it's good rock or good bebop or good traditional jazz or whatever."

But in the short run, he seems a bit worried. It's not enough to have talented musicians and people who enjoy their music. In the real world, you have to have clubs to showcase the musicians. And the clubs have to be able to at least break even. Jazz clubs have never been gold mines, but dedicated owners could at least make a go of them. Now the economics are more precarious, he says. The rents are getting so high that the future for establishments like Condon's is questionable. And although audiences turned out nightly to hear the Condon's Gang at Eddie Condon's Club, they haven't followed the same musicians to their occasional bookings at other locations since the club's closing. Polcer and I are relaxing this afternoon, conversing at a star-studded jazz festival fully 500 miles from New York City. But Polcer's thoughts, now, are very clearly back in New York. He hopes maybe a hotel will provide the space he needs at an affordable price. He feels he's got to get that club reopened.

When Polcer says clubs like Condon's have helped pass along a musical legacy to new fans and new musicians, he's not just speculating; he's drawing upon personal experience. Polcer recalls that he first started going to Condon's—drinking underage, he admits—while a teenager growing up in northern New Jersey in the early '50s. Polcer was born in 1937 in Paterson, but soon moved to nearby Prospect Park. Nights spent in Condon's and in Jimmy Ryan's—where the intermission pianist, Don Frye, sometimes would let him sit in on cornet—were invaluable to his development as a musician, he says. He learned classic jazz from the veterans.

Polcer's favorite cornetist back then was Wild Bill Davison, long a mainstay of the late Eddie Condon's renowned house band. Polcer says that in his youth he deliberately modeled his playing on Davison's, although Polcer's playing has evolved so that today a listener would no longer think of him as a Davison follower. Polcer has absorbed influences of Louis Armstrong, Bobby Hackett, and others in developing his approach to the horn.

Traditional jazz enjoyed a certain revival of popularity in the 1940s and early '50s. As a teen in the early 1950s, Polcer played cornet locally with one Walt Lawrence and his Knights of Dixieland. They provided music for dances not just at Polcer's own Hawthorne, New Jersey, High School but also at high schools in nearby towns such as Fair Lawn and Ridgewood.

Polcer went to Princeton University on a scholarship because, while he was still in high school, he had learned about jazz at Princeton and the phenomenal commercial success of Stan Rubin (class of 1955) and his Tigertown Five. That undergraduate band was in demand at colleges all up and down the East Coast, and had taken a summer cruise to Europe, providing entertainment for passengers on a Holland-America Lines ship. No campus jazz band anywhere had stirred up so much interest since the Jazz Age, when polished bands such as the Yale Collegians and the Princeton Triangle Jazz Band cut records and drew fans beyond their own campuses. On the Saturday morning radio show that Polcer listened to as a high school senior, disc jockey Ted Husing played recordings by Rubin's Tigertown Five.

Polcer was eager to make his mark at Princeton when he arrived on campus in the fall of '54. "I think the first week of class, I opened up my window and started playing along with jazz records, thinking that maybe somebody would hear me and discover me," he recalls. "I'm in the middle of a chorus and a guy, Dennis Brady, comes knocking on my door, saying, 'Holy crow! What's going on here?' He hired me to work in his band." Before the year was over, Polcer says, Brady had flunked out and Polcer had taken over the band, which he continued to lead through the remainder of his four years at Princeton.

Polcer also worked often with Stan Rubin. "Stan's was the most famous and popular of all the Ivy League jazz bands, and he commanded the highest price. He was a good promoter. Either through prep school or through the summer camp he had gone to, he had friends in all the Ivy League schools. He'd write letters to them: 'Hey, get our band to play for Dartmouth's Winter Carnival,' 'Get our band to play for Yale.' And Stan promoted our band, the Nassau Jazz Band, too. In 1955 or '56, Stan booked the Nassau Jazz Band to play Carnegie Hall, in a program with his Tigertown Five and a couple of other bands. That was a big thrill, the first time playing Carnegie Hall. Then I played a couple times with Stan's band at Carnegie Hall."

While attending Princeton, Polcer made about $2,000 yearly as a musician, playing 30 weekends a year for four years. He went to Europe with the Nassau Jazz Band in the summer of '55, playing aboard a Holland-America Lines ship, a gig arranged by Rubin. "Then in April of 1956, Stan got booked to play at Grace Kelly's wedding—we were the only American band there— which was the highlight of my early life," Polcer recalls. "It was really an incredible affair. Up until this recent wedding of Lady Di, it was really the wedding of the century. We played on Onassis' yacht, too, over there," Polcer recalls. The trip was a heady experience for Polcer—although he very nearly flunked out of Princeton because of all the classes he missed.

Polcer and his campus musician friends headed into New York as often as they could. Their favorite hangouts were Eddie Condon's and Jimmy Ryan's. Ryan's was preferred because every Monday night—the traditional musicians' night off—it would hire college jazz bands, such as Eli's Chosen Six from Yale, or the Spring Street Stompers from Williams, or Polcer's Nassau Jazz Band, or Rubin's Tigertown Five. (Today, incidentally, Rubin still occasionally hires Polcer and another Princeton musician from that period, trombonist Tom Artin, to work with him.)

Polcer had arrived at Princeton in 1954, just before rock 'n' roll did. In his four years there, he saw rock 'n' roll hit and grow in popularity until it overwhelmed everything else. Prerock pop music was largely swamped in rock 'n' roll's wake. And the traditional jazz that Polcer liked was all but obliterated. Polcer particularly remembers the "Rock Around the Clock Riot," which occurred in his junior year. As Polcer recalls it, somebody organized it so that 30 hi-fi sets all around the campus were turned on at midnight, all playing "Rock Around the Clock" at full blast. No place on campus was out of range of that loud new anthem of American youth. Students poured out of the dorms to release their pent-up energies. Spring riots were not all that unusual at Princeton in those years, spurred on, some said, by the high academic pressure and the absence of females on campus. But this particular night stands out so vividly in Polcer's memory because it seemed to symbolize how completely rock 'n' roll was taking over. The music was inescapable. A generation had claimed it as its own.

Princeton social life revolved around the Prospect Street eating clubs. Fewer of the clubs were hiring jazz bands for parties

*Ed Polcer, cornet, and Bob Haggart, bass, at the 1985 Odessa, Texas, Jazz Party
(courtesy of Ed Polcer).*

Ed Polcer at the 1986 Conneaut Lake Jazz Festival, with tenor saxist Bud Freeman, bassist Phil Flanigan, clarinetist Bob Reitmeier, and guitarist Howard Alden (photos by Chip Deffaa).

now. When Polcer had started at Princeton, it was not unusual to find a half dozen clubs hiring jazz bands, whether student bands like the Tigertown Five and the Nassau Jazz Band or professional groups from New York. Princeton's proximity to New York and the fact that the students had money meant that top players such as Buck Clayton and Bobby Hackett could be hired to lead groups. Jazz and fall football-weekend parties had seemed to go together naturally. But by Polcer's graduation in 1958, rock 'n' roll was omnipresent. Polcer came back to Princeton two years after he graduated and found that not one club was still hiring jazz bands. By 1960, the music of bands like the Tigertown Five or the Nassau Jazz Band, so popular just a few years before, had become archaic in the minds of the students.

Polcer, meanwhile, had opted for the route his parents and Princeton thesis adviser had thought best: he had put jazz on the back burner, to pursue a "respectable" career. He took jazz gigs on weekends, but tried to convince himself his future was in business. "For 10 years, more or less, I was a purchasing agent for different companies," he recalls. "I became purchasing manager for a paper bag manufacturing company." It was not a rewarding period for him. "And then when I guess I was about 34, 35, I went through my mid-life crisis. You know, if the company was dyeing paper bags green that day, the river looked green. If I was going through life once, I decided, I didn't want to chalk it up pouring dyes into a river."

Polcer quit the paper bag manufacturing company, and increasingly focused on working as a jazz musician. He took temporary day jobs as needed, to just scrape by financially. For a while, he did telephone soliciting for a firm that waterproofed basements. Eventually, enough music gigs came in for him to wean himself from the day jobs. When, on the recommendation of Bobby Hackett, Benny Goodman hired Polcer for a series of concerts, Polcer decided he would try to make it strictly in jazz. "My opening concert with Benny was before 18,000 people, up in Cape Cod," he recalls. And when you're playing for 18,000 people—and with Benny Goodman, no less—you know you've got to be able to cut it."

But jazz gigs still came in sporadically. Polcer sacrificed a great deal financially to try to stay with the music. "Working as a musician created a big economic trauma. That, probably more than anything, brought an end to my first marriage," he says. And for musicians who worry about the popularity of jazz today, he recalls that things were far worse in the late '60s and early '70s. "Rock had done its number on jazz. In fact, jazz in New York was almost nonexistent then." At the nadir, he says, there were perhaps 15 clubs offering jazz in New York.

Polcer worked frequently with guitarist Red Balaban, in a band which they called Balaban and Cats. Meanwhile, in 1973, veteran jazz guitarist/club owner Eddie Condon died. Condon had closed his club a few years before his death. Balaban and Polcer had both known Condon, and both played in the vigorous older style he had favored. They got the consent of Condon's widow to carry on the Condon name. They reestablished Eddie Condon's Club in 1975. The timing was good. Jazz was beginning to rebound in New York.

Balaban owned the club. Polcer initially confined his activities to playing cornet in their house band. But within two years he was managing the club, and by 1979 he had become co-owner. He and Balaban alternated as resident band leaders, with Sundays given over to guest bands. Master trombonist Vic Dickenson made the club his home and was a favorite of audiences until his death in 1984. Dickenson's alternate was Tom Artin (Princeton class of 1960), who had played with Polcer as an undergraduate. Like Polcer, Artin had tried to find satisfaction after Princeton in a "legitimate" career—in his case as a college professor—before finally concluding that jazz was what he wanted to do most.

Most of the time, the music in the club was in the traditional vein that the late Eddie Condon himself had favored. The house bands would play such Jazz Age classics as "Wolverine Blues" and "Sugar," not all that differently from the way Condon's own bands might have tackled them over the years—there'd be an ensemble opening and closing, and in between, successive solos by the members of the band—and they'd also play ballads and swing things of somewhat more modern 1930s and '40s vintage.

Polcer offered a driving hot lead cornet, with a lip trill he had borrowed from Louis Armstrong. On a number like "Sweet Sue," he could particularly make you think of Armstrong. House musicians were always free to take off, as opportunities arose. On any given night, there might be one or more alternate players in the band, which helped freshen the music. If Polcer was sometimes outshone by soloists, such as the ever-expressive and inventive trombonist Vic Dickenson, he didn't seem to mind. He was working steady now, in a solid band.

Polcer's own playing has evolved over time, becoming slightly more modernized. Polcer began breaking out of the traditional mold a bit on Monday nights, a night he used to experiment. At Condon's on a Monday, Polcer might trade phrases with a guest mainstream soloist such as saxist Kenny Hing of the Basie Band. The music probably would have sounded unacceptably modern to the late Eddie Condon, but it seemed to go down just fine with listeners in the club. Sunday bookings showed great variety. Polcer would occasionally even hire beboppers. On a given Sunday, you might see Milt Hinton and Jane Jarvis coleading a band, with Warren Vaché on trumpet. Or Norris Turney or Harold Ashby offering Ellingtonia. Or a new group created by up-and-coming players such as saxist Loren Schoenberg or trombonist Dan Barrett. The names of the musicians who had played at Condon's over the years were placed up on the walls near the entrance; it was an awesome list.

Polcer has made occasional recordings with the likes of Red Balaban and the late trombonist Big Chief Russell Moore. He's also backed singer Leon Redbone. And he has the makings of a new album in the can now, he says, with a band including Kenny Hing and trombonist George Masso. But he hasn't recorded much; he's concentrated on playing nightly and on helping to keep the club alive. He adds, "I'm not just dedicated to preserving a lot of the older musicians. I'm very serious about encouraging younger musicians. I mean, if you don't have younger players, you won't have jazz. You can have all the fans in the world, but if you don't have the guys playing it, forget it." When Polcer's Condon Gang band gets a gig someplace these days, it usually includes a mix of seasoned players, such as perhaps pianist Red

231

Richards and drummer Oliver Jackson, and rising younger ones, such as Ken Peplowski and Dan Barrett. Polcer says: "If Condon's reopens, I do believe that the young, up-and-coming players deserve the exposure. That's always been an important part of my philosophy."

If Condon's reopens. Note that moment of doubt on Polcer's part. The economic situation in New York, particularly in midtown, is not encouraging for jazz club operators these days. And the older music Polcer favors appeals mostly to older listeners— a shrinking audience, and one increasingly less inclined to spend late nights in jazz clubs. But enough of such reflection. Polcer has got to get ready to play now. He can't be brooding over the fate of his jazz club back in Manhattan—not this afternoon, with fans who've traveled hundreds of miles to Conneaut Lake, Pennsylvania, waiting to be entertained.

You catch Polcer a bit later, leading 20 by-now-rather-weary-looking musicians in the final set. There's a lot of jazz history up there in the front of the room, from pioneers like legendary saxophonist Bud Freeman, 80, to rising stars like guitarist Howard Alden, 26. Polcer's holding the somewhat ragged ensemble together with his forthright lead. The music, you suppose, is taking his mind off the fate of Eddie Condon's Club.

But maybe not. Polcer calls out what will be the very final number of this jazz festival. It's "September in the Rain." That was the very first number, he mentions by way of introduction, that was played when the original Eddie Condon's Club first opened in the 1940s, and the very last number played when Condon's closed—for what we have since accepted was for good—in July of 1985.

1986

Undecided

"My father always said to me, 'You can do it all, Stan.' When I was trying to figure out if I should become a musician or a lawyer, he'd say, 'You can do both, Stan; you can do it.' I don't know whether that was good advice because I spread myself thin—psychically, emotionally, physically. I was exhausted all the time," clarinetist/bandleader Stan Rubin recalls. "I think if that had been my son, I would have said, 'You've got to make a choice.'"

For as long as possible, Rubin put off making a choice between a career in music, which was always a great source of pleasure for him, and a more conventional career in law or business, which he sensed his family expected him to pursue. And yet, despite his less than wholehearted commitment to music, he reaped tremendous commercial success in the field, first with the Tigertown Five Dixieland jazz combo he formed before he was even out of his teens, and then with the big swing band that he still leads today. By the time he finally committed himself exclusively to music, however, it was later in the game than he had realized. A brain tumor robbed him of—among other things—his ability to play the clarinet.

He has continued fronting his big band nonetheless, and working to expand his library of note-for-note Swing Era re-creations. "Vince Giordano stands for the 1920s, and I stand for the '30s and '40s," Rubin maintains. And if he never quite hit the heights he might like to have hit as a clarinetist, he can take satisfaction in the long list of other musicians whose careers he has helped nurture through the years, ranging from Tommy Newsom and Ed Polcer to Randy Sandke and Spanky Davis.

"My father was a frustrated bandleader—a cute stride piano player who became a lawyer. He worked his way through law school with a band back in the 1920s: Irving Rubin and his Moonlight Syncopaters," Stan Rubin recalls one afternoon at his comfortable Larchmont, New York, home. His father and uncle went on to head a successful law firm: Rubin and Rubin. As a youth, Stan was given to understand that someday there would be a place in the firm for him. Of course, if he preferred going into medicine or business instead of law, that would be all right, too. The essential thing was that he become a success; that was the message he always got.

His father also expressed satisfaction in young Stan's prowess on clarinet. Born July 14, 1933, in New Rochelle, New York, Stan grew to greatly admire Benny Goodman. He still proudly shows a picture taken of himself with Goodman when he was just a boy. By sixth grade, he was already playing simplified versions of hit big band swing arrangements by the likes of Goodman, Glenn Miller, the Dorseys and so on, in a grade school band.

At Blair Academy, a prep school in Blair, New Jersey, Rubin not only played in a big swing band but also became cocaptain of the basketball team, captain of the golf team, and valedictorian. His father said he could do whatever he put his mind to, and it seemed to be true. "I was a very highly motivated, driven kid. You almost had to be, if you wanted to get into Princeton," he says.

At Princeton, which Rubin entered in the fall of 1951, he decided to focus his energies on music—particularly after being told he was not really good enough at basketball for the Princeton team. Rubin comments, "If I had been a basketball star, I wouldn't have had to be a musician. Because sports guys got the girls. Dig it? I think that may be underneath everything." Academically, he was doing well; in his first term, he was in the top 8% of his class, and he told his family he planned to eventually become a doctor or a psychiatrist. But he was skinny, suffering from unusually severe acne, and his self-confidence was shaky; his hope was that if he could make a big name for himself on campus as a musician, he would be able to impress girls.

When he joined the school's marching band, which performed in halftime shows at football games, he felt he was in the spotlight. Princeton had never before had as successful a football year as 1951. The Princeton team was ranked third in the country—an astonishing achievement for an Ivy League college team—and consequently a lot of media attention was focused on Princeton. Princeton's football star, Dick Kazmaier, even made the cover of *Time* magazine.

When Rubin formed a Dixieland quintet, the Tigertown Five, he discovered to his surprise that newsmen were willing to give him publicity; it was almost as if, in the current climate, anything connected with Princeton was newsworthy—including young Princeton students who were supposed masters of hot, old-time jazz. The ironic thing was that Rubin actually knew little about the music beyond the fact that Dixieland was enjoying a vogue on many college campuses, Princeton included; over the last couple of years, trumpeter Johnny Dengler's Intensely Vigorous Jazzband had established a healthy following at Princeton. (Eventually, Rubin would hire Dengler to play in his own band.) Rubin, whose own personal preference was more for swing music—to this day, his all-time favorite jazz group is the Benny Goodman Sextet—didn't know the Dixieland repertoire, but he diligently went about learning tunes from a book he bought and from records his drummer owned. He acknowledges frankly, "I knew nothing about the history of jazz. Everybody assumed I knew. But I never even heard of Bix Beiderbecke until I was at college. I was not a student of American jazz. I was just a kid who was precocious on an instrument, who was lucky enough to see Benny Goodman, you know." But he set a goal for himself;

he would make his quintet the best-known college jazz band in the country.

By soliciting friends at other colleges whom he had known from prep school or summer camp, Rubin was able to secure gigs for the Tigertown Five at Dartmouth, Cornell, Penn, and other prominent colleges. He also got the band a live radio show of its own on the Princeton University station, which helped it to develop a growing campus following.

With borrowed funds, Rubin put out the Tigertown Five's first 10-inch LP; the band's trombonist, Bill Spilka, designed the cover. By Rubin's own admission, his band was not great, but the album, featuring the most familiar of Dixieland numbers like "When the Saints Go Marching In," "Royal Garden Blues," "Panama," and "Tiger Rag," sold unexpectedly well on many campuses. Rubin notes, "I wasn't looking to making money from the record. I used it as a business card, giving copies away to get work. I thought of it as a self-liquidating promotion; in other words, you're using it to promote yourself, but you might also be able to sell some copies, recovering your costs. I just figured, having an album gave the band credibility." But popular New York disc jockey Ted Husing gave the album a lot of play. The Tigertown Five made prize-winning appearances on bandleader Paul Whiteman's radio and TV shows. Rubin recorded two more self-produced albums, including numbers like "San," "Margie," "St. James Infirmary," "Basin Street Blues," and "Blues My Naughty Sweetie Gives to Me," which his musicians had simply copied off old records. A record company, Jubilee, bought the rights to Rubin's three 10-inch LPs and repackaged them into two professionally designed 12-inch LPs, which sold surprisingly well throughout the East.

When, during Rubin's sophomore year, the Tigertown Five was invited to play one Monday night at Jimmy Ryan's popular jazz club on 52nd Street in New York, some 400 enthusiastic Princeton students turned out, forming a line along 52nd Street, which wrapped around onto Sixth Avenue. The New York World Telegram took photos and gave the band full-page coverage. Rubin knew his band was hardly the match of professional jazz bands playing the same sort of music in New York, but his seemed to be doing better business, at least partly because young people would support someone of their own generation. On a trip to Europe that summer, Rubin's Tigertown Five played at Maxim's on the French Riviera and at private parties that socialite Elsa Maxwell gave for King Farouk of Egypt and Jack Warner of Warner Brothers. Then, under Maxwell's wing, they played all over the Riviera, chauffeured from gig to gig in a Rolls-Royce and performing for celebrities including Hedy Lamarr, Claudette Colbert, Lady Ashley, and Prince Bernadotte of Sweden. At one point, Rubin even got to appear with Edith Piaf. When he returned to college in the fall, he wrote about his summer adventures—he couldn't imagine anything surpassing them—for the Princeton *Tiger* magazine.

Rubin told his family he had decided to become a lawyer like his father and uncle, which he figured would please them. He didn't imagine they had spent all that money to send him to Blair Academy and to Princeton just so he could become a musician. But the popularity of his band kept snowballing. When he joined Louis Armstrong onstage during an Armstrong concert appearance at Princeton, he proved such a hit with the crowd that Armstrong got him signed to a high-powered booking agency. Rubin wound up working so many different college dates as a bandleader in his junior year, he barely had time to study. One February weekend his band played Hamilton College on Friday, Lehigh University on Saturday, and Vassar College on Sunday; his Monday morning classes at Princeton became almost an afterthought.

That summer, his band was invited to play in Europe once again, but he opted to stay home and accept bookings in the New York area. In his stead he sent to Europe a second Princeton band, the Nassau Jazz Band with cornetist Ed Polcer and trombonist Tom Artin (both of whom were to be associated with him professionally in years to come).

In the fall of his senior year, Rubin's Tigertown Five and new Swing Sextette gave a concert at Carnegie Hall, sharing the bill with the Spring Street Stompers from Williams College. "I never was a Dixieland purist," Rubin says, in explaining his decision to also play some swing music. The concert, the first of its kind in Carnegie Hall, sold out in 11 days, and booking agents took notice. "It was the beginning of the whole youth thing. The rock 'n' roll era had hardly begun. My success at Carnegie Hall opened up people's thinking towards the youth market per se. We got coverage in *Life, Look,* and *Time,*" Rubin recalls. The press liked the idea that a Princetonian set on a career in law could be so involved with hot jazz. Gilbert Millstein wrote in *The New York Times*: "Mr. Rubin was sufficiently good that he may be forced to give up Blackstone for Condon" (referring to noted jazz band leader Eddie Condon). Rubin's father assured Stan that, once he became a successful lawyer, he would have no trouble playing music for pleasure on the side.

RCA Victor Records soon signed the 21-year-old Rubin; a "live" album of his Carnegie Hall debut was his first release for the label. Demand for his band was so strong, he was off campus playing somewhere almost every weekend of his senior year. His grades were plummeting, though. While trying to study for exams, Rubin got a call from someone at RCA Victor saying that Mannie Sacks wanted him to play at a party the next day. He declined, saying he didn't know any Mannie Sacks and he had an exam to worry about. He was informed that Sacks was the president of RCA Victor, and one did not say "no" to him. The next night, Rubin's band was playing for Sacks' party at the Cherry Hill Inn, in southern New Jersey. When Rubin saw that Sacks' date for the evening was Grace Kelly, he dropped his lobster Newburg into his lap. Rubin's Princeton class had voted Kelly, who had recently won an Academy Award for *The Country Girl,* as its favorite actress. To Rubin, she was a goddess. When he cut in on Sacks and danced with Kelly, his highly impressed trombone player snapped photos. "And Grace became a fan of the band," Rubin recalls. "We corresponded for a year."

Graduating from Princeton in the bottom fourth of his class, Rubin was accepted into Fordham Law School. The dean cautioned him that if he wanted to succeed at Fordham, he would have to commit himself to his studies more than he had at Princeton. Rubin gave assurances that law was really much more important to him than music; in fact, he was pretty sure he wanted to give up music—although not quite yet. In the summer of 1955, Rubin's Tigertown Five played at the second annual Newport Jazz Festival, along with the bands of such jazz immortals as Louis Armstrong, Coleman Hawkins, Roy Eldridge, and Count Basie. Rubin appeared on Stan Kenton's CBS-TV special, *Music '55*, sitting around the piano as an ostensible peer with Kenton's other guests, Hoagy Carmichael and Ella Fitzgerald. Rubin had no doubt been included in the program as a come-on for young viewers and for Dixieland enthusiasts who might not be much interested in Kenton's progressive jazz, which Rubin admits sometimes got too far-out for his own tastes.

When Rubin started at law school in the fall, he continued gigging with his band on weekends, despite the predictable effect it had on his grades. And in his second concert appearance at Carnegie Hall, he introduced, in addition to his Tigertown Five, his 17-piece big band. He had bought the big band library of Bob Friedlander, an arranger who had written for Harry James and others, and who had tried to run a big band of his own. (His association with Friedlander has continued to this day.)

"Then Grace Kelly got engaged to Prince Rainier of Monaco, and she called me to play at her wedding," Rubin recalls. He took a leave of absence from Fordham Law School so he could accept her invitation; he vowed to start again as a freshman the following fall. He still maintained that he was not planning on a career in music—but an opportunity to play at this royal wedding, which was drawing worldwide attention, simply could not be turned down. He and his musicians would give Grace Kelly—who was giving up her acting career to become Her Serene Highness, Princess Grace of Monaco—a jazzy American send-off.

Although only one member of the band that Rubin took to Monaco in April of 1956—Ed Polcer—was actually then a student at Princeton, Rubin still called his band the Tigertown Five, and its members still wore the Princeton colors: orange blazers and black slacks. Rubin recalls, "The Grace Kelly wedding was such a big event of our century, I was in the front pages of every newspaper practically for three weeks. They all wrote, 'Grace brings young boys from Princeton.' Even though I wasn't at Princeton anymore, you know, they milked that Princeton angle.

Playing that was the high point of my career with the band—and 'high point' is an understatement. It changed my life.

"But that experience was so stressful—it was too much pressure—that actually it was not enjoyable for me. For starters, on the way over, our plane lost engines and we almost had to ditch. It was very scary. We were flying over the ocean at about 200 feet. And I was thinking: how could the greatest event of your life lead to your demise? We had to land in Ireland, and we lost a day, but we couldn't sleep. So we arrived in Monaco for the wedding having had no sleep in 26 hours.

"Meanwhile, 1,800 correspondents had shown up to cover the wedding and they were not being allowed into any of the private affairs. Well, I get off the plane and it's like they're all coming to me. Earl Wilson, the famous columnist, is shouting, 'Stan! Stan!' I'm going, 'Stan? Stan? I don't know you.' He says, 'Stan, you're the biggest story up here! Tell us about this party you're playing tonight.' I tell him, 'We're not playing tonight. We're not due to play until. . . .' And I find out—this was the hardest part—that somehow we've been scheduled to do 12 more things than we had been contracted for. And we *did* have a big party we had to play, just three hours after we arrived. I not only did private parties, I did concerts for the people, and radio shows. We were the hottest thing over there.

"For me, the greatest part of that whole experience was meeting Aristotle Onassis, since I already knew Grace. It was a thrill playing for Onassis day after day on his yacht, for lunch. And one time my piano player got drunk, and my father, who had come over with us, had to sub for him in our band," Rubin recalls.

The Prince's mother, Charlotte, presented the Tigertown Five at one gala party for Grace Kelly's American wedding guests—a little touch of home for the Americans. As Rubin's straw-hatted musicians brashly ripped into repeated choruses of "Tiger Rag," they elicited especially boisterous cheers from Princetonians in attendance—the tiger being a symbol of Princeton—and Kelly had a lot of Princeton friends. "Things got a little out of hand," Rubin acknowledges, although he remembers the Prince as smiling throughout, nonetheless. The next day, however, Jinx Falkenburg of *The Today Show* called Rubin, saying she had heard he'd been kicked out of Monaco in tears after playing too loudly, despite requests from the Prince's mother to tone things down. Rubin was aghast at the untrue account; rumors were obviously ballooning because no reporters were being allowed into the parties. He feared his career might be ruined, but his agent had a hunch that the publicity would work to his advantage; every debutante in America would soon be clamoring for the hot young jazz band that had played Princess Grace's wedding. Which of course is exactly what happened. The play that Rubin got for three weeks on the wire services, in major magazines, and on the NBC, ABC, and CBS networks, established his band as a "name attraction." Elsa Maxwell, whose good taste was unquestioned, assured readers of *The New York Journal American* that Rubin's men had provided "as perfect a bit of Americana as you could ever get in France." Rubin's participation in the "wedding of the century" greatly increased his market value. Even society bandleader Lester Lanin asked if Rubin would like to work for his organization. But Rubin had more tempting offers to consider.

"After the wedding, George Hamid, who ran the famed Steel Pier in Atlantic City, asked me to play at the Steel Pier. That was my first real popular gig. And I decided to go in there with a big band. We could still feature the Tigertown Five as a band within the band—sort of like the way Benny Goodman had had his sextet and Tommy Dorsey had had his Clambake Seven. But I had a decision to make as to what musical format I wanted for my big band. Should I strive for a new sound? I wasn't a modernist. Guys like Maynard Ferguson and Woody Herman were modernists. I mean, they were the greatest musicians in the world— but they weren't *my* kind of musicians. I was still a Dixieland/ swing musician. Bebop was good, you know, but to me it was too individualistic.

"So at that point in time, I decided to preserve and re-create—with a mission—the sounds of the Swing Era. I remember saying to my arranger, Bob Friedlander, 'You don't change Bach, Beethoven, and Brahms. Let's look at the Swing Era as something. To me, the arrangers of the Swing Era were the Bachs, Beethovens, and Brahmses. The songwriters gave the melodies, but the arrangers took it over and created the identities of the different bands—you know, a Glenn Miller sound and so on.' So I made a decision, instead of seeking a new sound, to begin having Bob transcribe the classic arrangements. He has this great ear. I mean, it's difficult to hear all of the lines when you've got 13 to 15 parts. But Bob could do it. We tried a few and I loved them. My first arrangement was 'Begin the Beguine.' 'Big John Special' was the second. Then 'Moonlight Serenade.' I wanted to do the ones that were instrumentally sound—not necessarily the most popular; I didn't get 'In the Mood' for years—and also ones that featured the clarinet. So gradually I built this library of arrangements. It was expensive. I played the Steel Pier in August of '56, using about 30 Swing Era re-creations of uptempo things and fox-trots, plus Bob's original arrangements of ballads; Bob's got a great style of his own, you know.

"My agent got me a booking to play the Sahara Hotel in Las Vegas—I was to open there on September 8th, '56. The agency could get me a lot of work for the next year if I were willing to work full-time. They wanted me to go to Hollywood after the Sahara. But September 8th was also the opening day of Fordham Law School. So I had to choose. I elected to return to law school instead of pursuing a real show biz career. That was a very significant decision.

"When I went back to law school, I still kept getting calls to play and I gigged every weekend. I didn't think of the music as a business. I was just enjoying doing it while I was preparing for my life—presumably to be a lawyer. Frankly, I didn't know what I wanted to do. And the Tigertown Five gave me options," Rubin says. Meanwhile, his agent kept working on building up his name as a musician.

On December 1st, 1956, Rubin headlined a concert, "Dixieland at Carnegie," in which five bands participated. He was billed above jazzmen far more experienced than he was, including Henry "Red" Allen, Cozy Cole, Max Kaminsky, Jacques Butler, Tony Parenti, Joe Venuti, and Willie the Lion Smith. At a subsequent Carnegie Hall concert, he was given billing above such masterly jazz improvisers as Buck Clayton and Bud Freeman. Appearing on Art Ford's TV show, he was given billing above the gifted singer Maxine Sullivan. On strictly musical grounds, Rubin certainly did not merit being billed above such talented and dedicated artists, but he was, at least for the time being, a highly marketable commodity. His youth and his association with Grace Kelly worked in his favor. Rubin and his Tigertown Five made guest appearances on leading network TV shows, including Ed Sullivan's, Jackie Gleason's, Perry Como's, Ernie Kovacs', and Steve Allen's. In all, Rubin made some 50 television appearances before the hype died down.

Although he continued to use the "Tigertown Five" and "Tigertown Orchestra" billings throughout the '50s, Rubin employed the best available musicians for his dates, not the college kids he had started out with. Among the many highly respected players (most of whom were alumni of "name" big bands) who either recorded with or played in Rubin's bands at one time or another were trombonist Lou McGarity; trumpeters Billy Butterfield, Bobby Hackett, and John Frosk; reedmen Eddie Barefield, Boomie Richman, Hank D'Amico, Tommy Newsom, and Bob Wilber; and pianists Hank Jones, Derek Smith, and Marty Napoleon. Although Bob Friedlander was Rubin's primary arranger, Rubin also bought arrangements from Wilber, Newsom, Dick Cary, Matty Matlock, and others. On Rubin's Coral album *Dixieland Goes Broadway*, for example, the billing was Stan Rubin and his Tigertown Orchestra, but the 14-piece studio orchestra he led through hits from shows like *My Fair Lady*, *Li'l Abner*, and *Bells Are Ringing* was arranged by Deane Kincaide (who had arranged for such top bands as Benny Goodman's, Bob Crosby's, and Tommy Dorsey's) and included such seasoned pros as Bud Freeman on tenor sax, Cutty Cutshall on trombone, Mel Davis on trumpet, Bunny Shawker on drums, George Barnes on guitar, and Milt Hinton on bass. As a 24-year-old law student, Rubin felt honored to be in such company.

"Meanwhile, because of the Grace Kelly wedding, I was also getting a lot of calls to provide dance music for debutante parties," Rubin recalls. "So, while staying in law school—I really postponed decision making—I began moving into the quote unquote society dance field. Playing society dance music, which is basically up-tempo fox-trots, laid perfectly into the Dixieland concept. With the Tigertown Five as the band within my big band, I'd add some Dixieland jazz to the expected Cole Porter, Gershwin, and Kern standards. Society music in those days was medleys, and we'd end up the medleys with Dixieland. We might play, say, 'Cheek to Cheek,' 'From This Moment On,' and 'The Lady Is a Tramp,' and then—staying in the same tempo but ending the medley with a lot of pizzazz and excitement—we'd go into 'Dixieland One-Step.'

"I worked at building my big band library of re-creations, and also building a society band library—not re-creations but new arrangements of standards. We weren't simply faking numbers, which is the way most society bands work. The society band business is built around putting together large numbers of musicians and then just faking the music. Of course you can't do that and get it to be very musical. If you put Lester Lanin, Meyer Davis, Peter Duchin, and most of them back-to-back, you would pretty much say they were the same. I have respect for their business acumen, but I never aspired to do what they were doing. I wasn't interested in taking 'Cheek to Cheek' and trying to play it [he snaps his fingers in a mechanical, unhip way] in its lowest common denominator rhythmically. So Bob and I began writing a society library. So I was building all this up, and business was getting bigger.

"I kept working with my band throughout law school— every weekend. I don't know how I got through. But my Dad would say, 'You can do it all, Stan.' In retrospect, I think my going to law school probably was the wrong thing to do. Why did I do it? I think there was a fear involved, of making the commitment to being something. To me, music was a kick. It was fun to tell your friends you had played at Grace Kelly's wedding or whatever. The Princeton people got off on it. Everybody had a ball. I did. But to say, 'I am going to be a bandleader. I am going to work full-time in night clubs'? I mean, in those days, it usually meant working from like nine at night to three or four in the morning. That didn't seem appealing. When I decided to go back to law school, theoretically that was going to

Stan Rubin enjoys a 1977 reunion with Princess Grace of Monaco. When she selected his band to play at her wedding in 1956, which was the focus of worldwide attention, she gave his career an enormous boost (courtesy of Stan Rubin).

The top photo shows Atlantic City's famed Steel Pier, during one of Stan Rubin's engagements there. The bottom photo shows Julie Andrews, borrowing bandleader Rubin's clarinet, at a 1956 Christmas party for the cast of the Broadway hit My Fair Lady *(courtesy of Stan Rubin).*

Stan Rubin and his Tigertown Five play for President Lyndon Johnson at Madison Square Garden in the top photo and for comedienne Phyllis Diller on her ABC-TV show in the bottom photo (courtesy of Stan Rubin).

Albums Stan Rubin has recorded for RCA Victor, Coral, and other labels (courtesy of Stan Rubin).

give me greater options," Rubin explains, adding after a moment, "although, as it turned out, I didn't pass the bar exam."

That was one outcome he had not foreseen. Trying to keep options open in the fields of both law and music, he wound up with less options than he had expected. As the '50s wore to a close, he realized that he would never be joining his father's law practice. Well, he could live with that. But he also realized, with some regret, that he had not established himself as deeply in the music business as he might have, had he committed himself fully to music. And the great interest bookers had shown in him right after the Grace Kelly wedding had cooled off. The wedding was now yesterday's news. The offers to play Las Vegas, which he had turned down in 1956, were no longer coming in 1960.

Rubin started the 1960s more uncertain about the future than he had ever been. "It was clear to me that the music scene was changing. Rock 'n' roll was coming in everywhere. And the debutante thing was beginning to fade. With colleges, I still was getting some work. I would call up some of the schools that had had me the year before and say, 'Do you want us back?' You see, up to that point, I had never even had to make a phone call; the phones rang for nine years. But now I would call up, say, Washington and Lee, and maybe they would say, 'We love you Stan but we're going to have something a little different this year,' you know. And then I heard that from enough people. So I'd say to them, 'Well, what do you want? And how are you getting it?'

"In 1960, I realized—with pain—that except in isolated instances I was no longer a college commodity. I mean, I was still getting college concerts and I was still doing a fair amount of dances with the big band, but it certainly was not a growing business. I had to make a living. I didn't have a law degree. I was married and had a kid. And I sensed this need of colleges to have somebody buy talent for them. So I started a college entertainment company. I would purchase talent for the colleges. I knew all the agents and managers from my own career. I knew a lot about how the business operated. Within four years, I had about 20 accounts, including Notre Dame, Syracuse, Lehigh,

Colgate, and Cornell, and the business was growing. I'd get them contemporary acts. And very often I would open for those acts. I became the prime booker of Motown. Groups like the 'Four Tops' and 'Temptations' traveled with just four rhythm musicians. But they liked to also use horns and saxes, if they could. So—survival—I kept my band alive, backing up other groups. And we'd play on our own when we could. I always would say, 'Hey, let me open the show with my big band.' And the acts would always be late so I was there to save the day. For instance, I opened up at Penn State for the Four Tops and played 'One o'Clock Jump,' 'Sing Sing Sing,' and Count Basie's version of 'I Can't Stop Loving You.' I'll never forget the ovation we got. And the audience didn't know this type of music. Whom had they come to hear? The Four Tops, of course. And Woody Allen was the comic. I was also the director of the Forest Hills Music Festival. I booked the shows—and I also opened the shows. So I'd put the different hats on—producer, contractor, booker. And I'd fit my musicians and my own musical statement into whatever we were doing. And still, every chance I could, I would add more music to my band's library. In my heart was, 'I'm not giving up, yet. I'll wait this out.' In those days, we didn't know if rock 'n' roll was going to last.

"I never got entirely out of being a bandleader, but there were about 10 years when I was out of really trying to *make it* as a bandleader. From 1960 to 1970, I concentrated on my firm, College Entertainment Associates. I worked with my own band when opportunities came up. Like when the Riverboat, a brand-new room, came along in New York City—I opened the Riverboat in 1964 and I kept it seemingly forever. I always had a good name in New York. But College Entertainment kept growing," Rubin recalls. The money was pouring in. By most people's standards, he was living quite well.

Rubin's business success, however, brought him surprisingly little gratification. "Eventually I had 110 accounts, 11 people working for me—and headaches I couldn't deal with. I couldn't deal with the pressure of big business; the artist in me was coming out," he says.

"Then suddenly my dad died, I got a divorce, and College Entertainment Associates just seemed a very big headache. It was knocking the hell out of me. So I sold it to one of my employees. I got married again—to Judy [Rubin's present wife]. And with the money that I got from selling College Entertainment, I bought two years to unwind. For those two years, I knew my rent and other expenses were going to be paid. I wanted to smell the proverbial roses. I think my dad's sudden death showed me how quickly it can all go. So I was creating new values. And I enjoyed those two years." They were the first pressure-free years he had felt, he says, since he was a student at Blair Academy, some 20 years before.

Rubin felt he wanted to try something new with his life, but he wasn't sure what. In the next couple of years he made abortive moves in several directions. He got an insurance license, toying with the idea of selling insurance. He spent part of a year at Columbia in pursuit of a teaching certificate, thinking of becoming a teacher but unwilling to commit himself fully. "Then, in the midst of studying for exams at Columbia, a friend of mine, a Princetonian named Lon Harriman, who had become a super-agent—for James Taylor and others—called me and asked how I was doing. I said, 'Lon, I'm not happy. I don't know what I want to do.' He says, 'Why don't you come work for me?'" So Rubin tried that for a year. Then he thought he would try becoming a personal manager for performers on his own and went through $30,000 of his money before abandoning the notion. He considered going back to law school. But one day, on the street in New York, he chanced to run into Aristotle Onassis, who reminisced with him about Monaco and expressed regret that Rubin had given up music. Onassis added that if there was one thing the world did not need it was another lawyer. For Rubin, that line had a curious resonance.

"Meanwhile, I was going through money; I needed money," Rubin recalls. "Then in 1973, I got a call from Ernie Morris, president of the Saratoga Race Track, to do a big private party for him. I had done parties for him years before, and he didn't realize that I had left the band business. At that point, I hadn't done a big band job in about two years—I didn't think I wanted to be in the spotlight anymore—and my library of arrangements was in storage, in suitcases in the cellar of my best buddy, in Tenafly, New Jersey. But I accepted the job offer and hired musicians. The day before the job, I went to get the music—and found it was sitting in three inches of water in that cellar! If I hadn't gone to get it then, it would have all been ruined. I still have the music—you can see that 'Moonlight Serenade' and all of these old charts have this three-inch waterline. I put the music over a heater to get it dry for the job the next day.

"And then when I went in there with the big band, I had a calling which said to me simply, 'This is what you love doing. This is what you can do.' And I had a big talk with my wife. I started telling her, 'I don't know what I want to do.' I had different options. I had an insurance license. I was supposed to study for the bar exam again. And God bless my wife, we both made the commitment that I was going to become a bandleader. Finally. In 1973, I made my first real commitment to becoming a bandleader in my life."

Once he began concentrating on getting work as a bandleader, Rubin found there was more work to be had than he had anticipated—although not always for great money. "I called the Riverboat, having left them for seven years; they accepted me with welcoming arms, to alternate with another band. I called Roseland, which I'd never played before; they were thrilled. Then a place opened up in New Canaan, Connecticut, called Fat Tuesday—no relation to the New York City jazz club Fat Tuesday's—and they wanted me. So between the Riverboat, Fat Tuesday, and Roseland, I was in business within a year," he recalls.

"What was my goal? To re-create the Swing Era, to preserve its music. To use all of these places to let me do—at least occasionally—my big band thing. The Riverboat wanted only a six-piece band. I agreed to put a six-piece band in there five days a week—but only if they'd let me do a big band once a week. Roseland wanted only a 10-piece band. I said, 'But you've got to let me do once a week with the 15-piece band.' Fat Tuesday wanted just my Tigertown Five Dixieland band. I said, 'You can get it, but you must do my big band once a week.' At Roseland, it was Friday that I appeared with the big band; at the Riverboat, it was Monday; at Fat Tuesday, it was Thursday. See, that was my purpose, in 1973–74, creating a demand for the big band." But he was swimming against a strong current, trying to maintain a swing band in a world dominated by rock. When Fat Tuesday suspended operations, Roseland cut back, and the Riverboat switched to a rock music policy, Rubin put his big band dreams on the back burner again, and took a day job for a year as an A&R man at Audio Fidelity Records.

"Then in 1976 we come to the shot heard round the world for me. The Glen Island Casino in New Rochelle, New York— the most important place in my career—decided to celebrate the nation's bicentennial with a big dinner-dance affair. Although the Glen Island Casino had been the home of the Glenn Miller Band and other top bands in the Swing Era, it hadn't had big bands in years. I was hired. This bicentennial event, July 6th, 1976, was a natural sellout. But the success was so great—my band was doing these numbers that people were thirsting for, numbers they hadn't heard in that setting for 20 or 30 years— that I was invited to do a big band dance there once a month. I played the casino monthly for the next six years—selling out every time—until it closed for renovations. And that's what put me on the map."

Rubin had a knack for creating job opportunities in places that had not considered hiring bands, and in many cases could not have afforded bands had they paid union scale. He was particularly gratified to get some exposure in the borough of Princeton, New Jersey, since his career had had its start at Princeton University. This exposure led to his being hired to provide music for many University-related affairs as well. "I put live music in Princeton's Nassau Inn from 1979 through 1986. They didn't have a lot of money to spend. I said, 'I have an idea, and I will make the price right.' This is how I created work. I told them, 'I will get the best jazzmen in New York to go to your inn on weekends, subject to cancellation if they get better jobs. Give them room and board, along with some money." Musicians would be accepting less cash than would be standard for a gig in New York, but would be getting attractive accommodations for a weekend out of town—accommodations the Inn could make available at relatively little cost to itself. "I agreed to provide a small group every week, so long as I could appear with my big band once a month. See, that was the main reason I wanted to do it, to have another outlet for the big band. And I didn't care if it cost me money to have the big band there.

"Working in Princeton was really great for me. Imagine going back to the 'scene of the crime' some 30 years later. I loved it! I led the big band in person; I didn't have to be there with the small groups. I got lots of jazz musicians down there as guest stars. You name them, I had them down there: Doc Cheatham, Benny Waters, Don Kelso, Warren Vaché. But the union got on my case about that Princeton inn deal. And the Department of Labor—years later they're trying to get my ass, too. I didn't go through the union on that deal because the union would not have let me do it. But I was creating work for musicians, which I wish the union could understand; the union has never been much of a help for the cause of jazz, or swing music. The musicians I used at the inn all made a living wage. And if one of them got offered a $150 job or something, naturally I would let him go and take that instead. But the union tried to hit me for money, like for the pension fund. And pension-schmension! I told the musicians, 'Guys, do you want unemployment insurance or do you want a job? I've got to make a dollar.' If I had the money to lobby, I could show how we could put live music into a lot of places that don't have it now, and everybody would win. I'd be the Lee Iacocca of the goddamn music industry," Rubin declares, becoming impassioned. He has had many run-ins with the union. Then his voice drops very low, as if his energy is fading, and he adds, "If I can survive . . ." Since the operation for the brain tumor, it has been a fight for him just to keep functioning. He does not like having to fight the musicians' union, too.

"I want to go to hotels and to the musicians' union and try to get music back into hotels. But the union would have to be flexible in order for it to make sense economically. I've come up with a formula that would work. You'd have to make the per-

week scale [of how much musicians would be paid] as low as the
room could initially handle. And then if the room succeeds—
if it does good business—you would increase that low scale,
according to justification. If this plan were to work, you'd also
have to allow the musicians to take off for 'club dates,' as musicians call single engagements. I mean, if they get offered higher-
paid gigs on some nights, let them take off; put substitutes who
can sight-read the music into the band. With this simple formula,
we could get bands back into hotels. But if the union's attitude
is that the hotels are part of multinational corporations that can
afford to pay the current scale, it's never going to happen. The
union has to be flexible. I'd like to see bands back in the major
movie theaters again, too. Remember when theaters like the
Paramount presented big bands? There are plenty of musicians
who would welcome the work.

"I have a pretty stable personnel—musicians who want to
play for me. I'm dealing with young people now—the old guys
are too tired—and over the years I've given a lot of green musicians valuable training. You know, the union has activists who
don't see the humanist in me. They want everything to go strictly
by the book, which isn't always feasible. I work really hard to
keep this big band thing alive, and to create jobs for musicians.
I want to be appreciated. I've lost a lot of time and energy trying
to promote the cause." It rankles him that some union people
apparently believe he has sought to exploit musicians. For him,
business has been decidedly up-and-down over the last 20 years.
And he works with a limited budget. Anyone who imagines he
has grown rich doesn't understand the economics of the big band
business today, or even the frequency with which venues that
might book a big band tend to open and close.

The only club that has provided really steady employment
for Rubin's band—and even this club had to take a hiatus of
several years—has been the Red Blazer Too, where Rubin's band
appears every Thursday night. Indeed Rubin's band has been,
along with Vince Giordano's, one of the two bands most closely
associated with the club. Disc jockey Danny Stiles was responsible for getting the club's owner, Denis Carey, to book the band,

and indeed to adopt a big band and Dixieland music policy generally.

"Danny Stiles, who was emceeing for us, brought Denis up to hear my band at the Glen Island Casino in 1979. Denis flipped out, saying he'd never heard anything that great. And with some reluctance—I was worried the union was going to bust my hump—I went into the Red Blazer. I fell in love with the place. I said 'This is my home.' I started in 1979 at the Blazer's old location, up on 88th Street; now, of course, they're on 46th Street." Having a weekly Manhattan outlet brought the band greater media coverage than it had enjoyed before. They made the local TV news; that a club in the disco era would be filled week after week with a crowd digging sounds of the long-gone Swing Era *was* newsworthy.

"My goal was to re-create the Swing Era, market the music from a 20-year period in every which way. We went into the recording studio, did a series of albums called 'Hall of Fame Hits of the Swing Era.' I had no record company behind me, so I marketed the albums myself. For two years I had a commercial on TV, which I filmed at the Blazer. I took out ads for the albums in *The Princeton Alumni Weekly*. And there were good musicians on my albums. Players like Spanky Davis, Randy Sandke—I helped put them on the map. And Chuck Wilson, Joe Mosello, and Bob Kindred. I helped keep these guys alive with my craziness through all these years.

"Jim Lowe of WNEW radio called me 'the Keeper of the Flame' because there was nobody in this business more enamored of that music. I put my money where my soul was. I had a goal. I mean, my arranger, Bob Friedlander, and I—we *have* a goal. Nobody would do what I'm doing, unless they had a love affair with this music. If I had the money that I've put into this over the last 32 years . . . If I'd just used stock charts, like so many other bands have done, I'd have saved a fortune. But I wouldn't do it. We use no stock arrangements.

"I have maybe 400 to 600 Swing Era re-creations, all transcribed from records. Most solos are written out, from the records, too. We play the music I really care about: re-creating music of all the major big bands. My favorite bands were Goodman and Shaw, and Miller, the Dorseys, Krupa, Harry James, Barnet, Woody Herman—I mean, we've got them all. It's the genius of my arranger, Bob Friedlander, that enables me to proselytize for the music that I love.

"I now have maybe 2,000 arrangements in my library in total, including many great songs by Jerome Kern, Cole Porter and the like that were not made famous by any band in particular. But it's the Swing Era re-creations for which the band is best known. We do some numbers that no one else plays anymore. For example, we do the Glenn Miller arrangement of 'Under a Blanket of Blue.' Do you think the official Glenn Miller Band today plays that arrangement? Shit, no. Good luck, official. I know who plays in that band, and I know what they play. You're lucky if they get past 'American Patrol'! If I mention 'Stardust' to you, you think of Artie Shaw's version first, right? But I also play Glenn Miller's lesser-known version of 'Stardust.' And I have three different versions of 'All or Nothing at All': the one Frank Sinatra originally did with Harry James, the more modern Nelson Riddle arrangement Sinatra later used, and also the arrangement Jimmy Dorsey and Bob Eberly recorded. We've got Jimmy Dorsey's 'John Silver' and 'Parade of the Milk Bottle Caps,' too. That's how deep my library is. And I'm still ordering arrangements. You know what I just put in the book? 'Jubilee'— the old Louis Armstrong number—which trumpeter Johnny Letman, who's been associated with me for 26 years, is going to do for the first time when I play the Taj Mahal in Atlantic City for New Year's."

For commercial reasons, Rubin has found it advantageous to stress his band's flexibility to prospective bookers. The brochure for the Stan Rubin Orchestra proclaims it is "America's Most Versatile Musical Organization," and he aims to give listeners whatever they want—including rock, if requested. But he is happy that the demand for his band is primarily due to its reputation as a swing band.

"We have become one of the hottest society and wedding bands in the country. We can play anything. We can go from Swing Era to society style. We will do rock somewhat; you have to give people what they request. Although I will say—good news!—we're getting to a point now where many, many people in their 20s who are having weddings don't want *any* rock. They're saying when they hire us: 'It's my wedding and I want to hear everything that Cole Porter wrote . . . and I love your swing.' So there's real hope. This isn't just hype," Rubin says. He notes that younger audiences are continuing to discover the older styles of music he prefers.

"You know, I'm happy that the Glenn Miller Orchestra's CD *In the Digital Mood* has just gone 'gold.' It proves that Glenn Miller's music has kept. I still get chills when I play 'Moonlight Serenade.' I love Glenn Miller's arrangements. My musicians don't like them; they don't want to play them. But screw them! If you just play music to please musicians, you'll be out of business in a week.

"I'm also happy that Harry Connick is alive. 'The Messiah' I call him because he is helping bring this type of music back. You turn on the radio and hear him singing 'It Had to Be You.' Now young people are saying to me, 'We want Harry Connick music.' That may mean they want a song written many years ago by a Jerome Kern or an Isham Jones, a song someone like Artie Shaw used to do. But now that Harry Connick is singing the song, it's Harry Connick music I'm playing—which is all right with me. By the way, did you see his show on PBS? Was it beautiful?

"My long-range goal is to bring this band to the Rainbow Room. If they hired me, we would be a general dance band. But each week I would feature a special tribute to a different artist; I could do a show, playing things that would be exciting, like 'Well Git It' if you're saluting Tommy Dorsey, or 'Let Me off Uptown' if you're doing Gene Krupa. I'm hoping that someday, someone is going to have the foresight to say, 'Let's open a Rainbow Room where the music is more important than the Hollandaise sauce.'"

Rubin is confident that, properly promoted, well-played big band music can appeal to contemporary audiences. All that's really needed is the proper exposure at an "in" place. He knows what that feels like. "The best job I've ever had in my life was playing at the Red Parrot," Rubin recalls, naming a midtown New York discotheque that enjoyed great popularity for several years in the 1980s. "This beautiful guy, Jim Merry, who just died of AIDS—he was gay—opened the Red Parrot, a gorgeous place with a huge dance floor. The format was disco—a DJ and state-of-the-art equipment—but Jim loved swing and so he was also budgeting for a 15-piece big swing band. He gave my band a try-out for one night—the 'Night of the Gypsy,' a night honoring Broadway dancers—and that night made me. The ovation. My library. Afterwards, Jim came to me and said 'You mean you have Charlie Barnet's "Skyliner"? You mean you have . . .' and he couldn't believe it. He said, 'You're my man.' I said, 'Yes, I am.' I became *the* band there. The sound was state-of-the-art. We had one microphone on every chair, and a mixing board, like in a recording studio. The lighting was state-of-the-art. The audience was ready to dance and have a good time. I was alternating with disco. In the disco sets, I'd put the earplugs in and go upstairs; I couldn't handle all that boom-boom-boom. But then soon it would be showtime again: 'Ladies and gentlemen, Stan Rubin and his Swing Era Band.' And I built up fans of young people who had never heard the music. Eventually, they were asking for every tune—not just 'In the Mood'—because they'd gotten to know my library. People came in, saw the band, the magic; sometimes they hired us for private parties, weddings, and so on.

"I started at the Red Parrot in February of '83. My musicians were getting paid decently. Very often we were working there four nights a week. We were swinging. I had finally *made* it. I mean, in 1983 I had the biggest year of my life financially, and I had hope that things would just keep getting better. And then, unfortunately, in January of the next year—the brain tumor," Rubin recalls. He is speaking with some difficulty now.

"The diagnosis was made by CAT scan in January of '84: acoustic neuroma, the same type of tumor of the hearing nerve that George Gershwin had died from. I had actually had the first symptom way back in July of 1975, but a doctor had not done a good job of diagnosing the problem then. Acoustic neuroma is a very slow-growing, benign tumor. It probably began its growth in 1970 and got into the auditory canal about four years later. The operation for the tumor finally took place on April 16, 1984.

"Jim was good enough to keep my band at the Red Parrot without me. That really helped me to survive, because I was suffering. As I was recovering, I used the club as a place for me to get my bearings again. My band was at the Red Parrot for four years, from 1983 through 1986. I miss that place."

Rubin mentions that some acquaintances didn't seem to want to see him after his tumor was removed. Perhaps they weren't sure how he would change after brain surgery. But, he notes, "I've gotten a lot of support from Princeton people. My 30th Princeton reunion was the year following the operation. I didn't look too great, and I was pretty nervous about it. One classmate I'd never known before, Jim Petrucci, was particularly supportive of me; he's become a big fan, a good friend. And I've played at many Princeton-related events. You know, I've just agreed to play this year's senior prom—the 14th time I've done that. And in 1986, I played a big dance for Princeton alumni and I met Bill Bradley; I almost fainted because I'm a basketball freak and I had worshiped him from afar, back when he played basketball. And then Bill Bradley asked me if I would play for *his* fundraiser. Later I got a letter from him, saying how great the band was, and he added in his handwriting, 'I really was honored to meet you.' Can you imagine that?"

And now Rubin must take a break for a bit. We have been talking for a couple of hours and he appears wiped out. He raises his hand to his head. "My head is a little . . . It's starting to . . . I have a physiological problem," he says, struggling to explain. "You see, my tongue nerve is now hooked up to my extracranial facial nerve. They did that in the second operation. So now everything from here to here moves involuntarily every time my tongue moves. And eventually I spasm; the muscles are overworked. So talking can get to be a strain. I'm on a sixth gear right now, but I'm not going to let you go. Till the pain comes."

He summons his wife. "Where is that book? I want to show Chip the underlining, honey. Would you get it, honey?"

His wife brings me Rubin's copy of my book *Voices of the Jazz*

Age. I'm stunned to see that, like a Princeton senior preparing for final exams, he has made extensive underlinings throughout the text, and repeatedly written comments, questions, and reactions in the margins. I'm impressed by the intensity of the man. Seeing those copious markings, I get a picture of someone who applies himself *hard* to whatever task is at hand.

I tell him, "When I wrote that book, I never imagined anybody would read it this carefully."

"You were telling me things in it that I didn't know," he remarks.

A phone call interrupts us. It is a woman interested in hiring his band for her upcoming wedding; she wants him to send her a tape of his band. He will do that, if she wishes, but he suggests the best thing would be for her to drop by the Red Blazer Too any Thursday night and hear his band in person. He comments to me, after hanging up, "I have recorded 23 albums, which I could send to prospective clients, but how would they know they'd be hearing the band they'd actually be getting? So I invite people to the Blazer. Tapes don't prove anything. I mean, 99% of the bandleaders who compete with me for these weddings and private parties actually have nothing, but they'll go into a studio and make a good tape, which they'll say is their band. Then when they get a job, they put men together and fake tunes. Some of the bandleaders have little interest in music. Their interest is in doing business. In volume. How many jobs can they line up for a given night? I can't get my heart and soul into trying to line up 10 jobs for a Saturday night, and hiring musicians to cover them. I'm concerned with just one entity—well, two, actually: my big band and the small band, the Tigertown Five concept. For that I use guys like Randy Reinhart, Tom Artin, Mark Lopeman. Sometimes I use guys who play regularly in Vince Giordano's Nighthawks. Vinnie and I help each other out," he says. He respects Giordano's commitment to the music Giordano loves. And he is grateful to Denis Carey for providing a regular outlet for his band, and for Giordano's.

"I'm glad there is a place like the Red Blazer Too. Without the Blazer, I'd have nothing. And I have told the musicians in my band, we must thank our lucky stars that Denis Carey can

261

keep his doors open. Because the minute he closes the Red Blazer Too—which he had to do for three years—you're going to miss it so bad your head is going to spin. You're going to be in your apartment thinking you have nothing, your life means zero. Because the life of a jazz musician today, except for the few who are up on top—you're going to have to get day jobs. Which I also tell them to do anyhow."

The Red Blazer Too has managed to survive, despite a lingering recession that has hit New York's clubs very hard. It cannot afford to pay bands what the musicians' union feels would be appropriate. (Rubin cannot generally get musicians as good as those in the best bands of the Swing Era.) Rubin comments, "I have helped Denis by lobbying with the union for years. They were going to move in on the Red Blazer years ago. I begged them not to. Because I knew that if they did, Denis would simply say, 'Good-bye. I can't do it.'" And Rubin knows it would serve the interests of no one if the Blazer were to stop booking big bands. Rubin feels particularly dependent upon the Blazer's survival for the survival of his own band; although his band works many outside engagements, he fears many of those engagements would not be offered to him except for the regular exposure the band gets from playing at the Blazer.

"Of course I don't always appear with my band anymore. Sometimes Tom Artin will front it for me in my absence. It's a contractual thing. If buyers require my presence, they pay extra. But I like to appear with the band when I have the energy. I don't go to the Blazer every week. That's the sad part. I do not have the energy. It takes a lot of energy to fight the physical problems. Before the operation, I never missed going to the Blazer. I'm not contractually required to appear with my band there. I only decide at six p.m. if I'm going to be there on a given night. I go when I can," he says, with some wistfulness.

"You see, it was a very big tumor that I had. It was over the size of a golf ball, in the cranial nerve area," he says. Fatigued as he obviously is, he is determined to make clear the impact the tumor has had on him. "What's the biggest change in my life caused by the tumor? What can I not do anymore? Play the clarinet. Not only was I pretty damned good at the instrument, but I was a performer. I was more of a performer than a great musician, actually. I was potentially great. Never studied, never practiced. Just natural. And yet I had a great sound. And when that clarinet wailed above that big band, and the way I used to hold the clarinet . . . Eventually, I hope I can play piano with my band. I'm trying to get good enough. I played a little, as a boy. But not playing the clarinet is hard for me. I've lost the artistic expression in my soul. Yeah, that's the biggest thing.

"Plus about a hundred other things that I lost. I can't project sound much anymore, so I can't shout over the musicians. And most bandleading is discipline. The musicians are children. They pay no attention. They don't get back on the bandstand on time. And my musicians like me! I'd hate to see what they do to the bandleaders they don't like.

"I also have balance problems, because the tumor was impinging upon the brain stem. After the operation, I was in the hospital for five weeks. I was left with 14 deficits. I had to learn to walk. I was falling all over the place. See, they took all of the hearing mechanism out, so I lost the inner ear. Plus the brain stem is your balance and your computer. I had double vision. And I can't blink my eye.

"I also have to crank my mouth open fives times a day because I have something like lockjaw. Originally I couldn't get it open more than here. And I've been trying. I think we Tigers are fighters, my friend.

"Not smiling is probably the toughest. You know how you feel when you leave the dentist's office after getting novocaine? This is what it feels like, on half of my face. I can't smile. Do you know what that is to a performer? People look at you. . . . And my child doesn't always know what I mean. I can't temper words with nuances, facial expressions—how often a smile tempers scolding.

"On the right side of my body, I have what's called hemisensory deficiency, which means I have no ability to evaluate heat or cold. I could scald myself and not know it. And that won't go away.

"I have a lot of energy problems. It feels like my feet are magnetized to the earth. So every time I walk, it is calculated,

choreographed. It is not a reflex. I don't just walk. I have to—
somewhere my brain is saying, 'Take a step.'

"I live with frustration. And that was never my strong suit.
Being an artist, being a perfectionist, being a highly motivated
achiever, I didn't have too much patience for imperfection in
myself. You went to Princeton, Chip. You had to be *numero uno*,
didn't you? At least that's the message I always got. So I've
made—I'm still making—daily psychological, physical adjustments. I think I will get an A in that."

1990

CARRIE · SMITH

Singing the Blues on Broadway

"Most people would give their right arm and their right leg to be where I am now. Even the biggest star in the world wants to be on Broadway somewhere. Why? Maybe you can tell me. This is my first Broadway show. And it's quite different from what I thought it would be. It's a different animal, I'll tell you that— Broadway." So says traditional jazz/blues singer Carrie Smith, whose ripe, full voice has enhanced numerous jazz parties, festivals, and concerts—often retrospectives saluting the music of some bygone great, because her sound and style evoke memories of classic blues singers. For the past year and a half, Smith has been one of the stars of Broadway's *Black and Blue,* a lavish, hit musical celebration of vintage black jazz and blues. But as we chat this afternoon at her East Orange, New Jersey, apartment, she makes it clear she is less than wholly thrilled about being a "Broadway star."

"Sometimes, I'd rather be doing what I was doing when you first met me," Smith says, referring to the days when she'd play little clubs, backed by four or five pieces and singing into the early morning whatever songs she felt like singing—numbers like "Nobody Knows You When You're Down and Out," "June Night," or "St. Louis Blues." "I was not making as much money—but money ain't everything either." Now, instead of singing to a small audience in a jazz club, or perhaps to several hundred at a jazz party, she is singing the same handful of songs nightly to an audience of nearly 2,000 people in Broadway's Minskoff Theater. She has three featured numbers of her own—"I Want a Big Butter and Egg Man," "I Gotta Right to Sing the Blues," and "Am I Blue"—and sings two more numbers along with costars Ruth Brown and Linda Hopkins: "I'm a Woman" and "Black and Blue."

Although *Black and Blue*'s cast of 43 singers, dancers, and musicians might appear, to the audience, to resemble one big, happy family, Smith has seen plenty of bickering backstage as performers' egos have clashed. At times, in fact, Linda Hopkins and Ruth Brown were barely speaking to each other offstage; each seemed resentful of the attention the other was garnering and there were accusations of "upstaging" and "unprofessionalism." Smith sometimes got caught in the middle of their conflicts. She had never known such hassles when singing on her own in little jazz clubs. "Including the stagehands and all that, there must be 60-some people in *Black and Blue*. I've never worked around all these people before. And to deal with the different personalities . . ." she says, shaking her head in dismay.

A number of cast members, she also comments wearily, have tried to push their religious beliefs upon her. With characteristic frankness, she comments: "All of them are very religious—so they say. Everybody says their little prayer, bla-bla-bla, and then they're trying to give it to you. And I tell them, 'You don't have to pray for me. I can pray for myself. And don't try to shove your religion down my throat because I've been a religious person all my life. My father's a minister. So you just keep your little books and whatever you want to yourself!' So a lot of the kids are a little peeved with me because I'm very outspoken. But if you're going to quote to me what the Bible says, then you do that; you don't do the opposite. You mean to tell me you're going to walk by your brother and your sister and you can't speak to them and say, 'Good morning'? The Bible don't tell you to do that—if you believe that. So, some of them are a little peeved with me, which I don't care."

Smith stresses, though, that despite whatever gripes she

may have about performing on Broadway, she is basically quite proud of this show. She likes its lavishness and dignity, and likes the way it reminds people of the Bessie Smiths and Josephine Bakers who were black stars some 60 years ago. "The producers captured all of the elegance of what the folk were about in the '20s and '30s," Smith notes. Maintaining a sense of dignity and class—even if interpreting risqué songs, as she sometimes does in her work (although not in *Black and Blue*)—has always been important for her. "It's amazing to see the kids in sneakers come into the theater. And when they leave, they leave happy; they have enjoyed something they saw, that some of them didn't even know existed."

Among other pluses connected with appearing on Broadway, Smith mentions, "I have one of the best dressing rooms I've ever had. You know, in those little clubs we work in, they do the best they can but they could do better. I'll never forget working down at Carlos I [in Greenwich Village]. And I used to say, 'My God, clean up the place!' It's funky in that bathroom: You're going to invite somebody to come see you at a club, and they go to the ladies' room or the men's room and then they come back and say, 'My God, what happened?' Anytime you see me, I'm always trying to be elegant like those women were in those days [the 1920s and '30]."

Smith wonders, though, if most members of *Black and Blue*'s audience actually know who she is. When she walks out the stage door, where fans gather after the show to get autographs, she insists she's more apt to hear comments like, "Oh, look, there's the lady who was on the swing" or "the lady who was in that gown with the long train" than, "Oh look, there's Carrie Smith." Here she brings up an interesting point. For the show *is* so spectacular visually, the audience's attention is at times diverted from the singing itself. It's actually easier to fully appreciate Carrie Smith's interpretation of "Am I Blue," for example, if you buy the DRG cast album of *Black and Blue*, than if you see her do the number in the show. Why? Onstage, she sings the song seated on a swing high above the stage, in a gorgeous, heavily beaded white gown with about as long a train as can be imagined. When the audience first sees this elaborate scene, some will invariably gasp in awe. Others may find it camp and chuckle a bit. But in either case, it is the striking scenic display, rather than the singing, that at first commands attention.

"When I'm singing 'Am I Blue' up on that swing, I think of all the old movies that I've seen with Ethel Waters and Josephine Baker—I've never seen Ethel up in a swing, but the song relates to her. I'm showing off the costume there. I really don't think my talent is what it's all about in this show. I really don't. You know, I was chosen to sing these songs. Hector Orezzoli [who, along with Claudio Segovia, conceived the show and designed the highly praised costumes and lighting] saw me four or five or six times in France when I was working on my own. He would just come and sit and watch me. And I think he wanted to add to the show that sort of elegance that Josephine Baker had. This is what he was looking for. Just to show off his costumes, that's what I think. I could be wrong, Chip," she says, but she sometimes feels like she is being used largely as a model for their spectacular, heavily beaded costumes. "And I think I'm about more than that, you know?"

In *Black and Blue*, Smith sings "I Gotta Right to Sing the Blues" while attached to a large disc that moves her across the stage and then slowly tilts back. I must admit that when I first saw this effect, I was wondering how far the disc would tilt back and whether Smith was uncomfortable being attached to it; I wasn't focusing fully on the song. I've now gone back to see the show four times, and have noted with pleasure that Smith varies her renditions of her songs—sometimes doing them more dramatically (or even melodramatically), sometimes with more of a heartfelt simplicity. (The hoofers in the show also vary their performances considerably from night to night—giving *Black and Blue* a bit of an improvisatory quality that is rare on Broadway.) Smith comments, "Because this is a revue, not a book show, you can take a couple of liberties with the lyrics. Or sort of project a different feeling of how you feel about the song. Now when I sing 'I've got a right to sing the blues down around the river,' I might sort of lean forward like I'm going to jump in. And then I'll sort of—you know, it's acting. Acting's important for a singer.

That's what makes Ruth Brown so great, singing 'St. Louis Blues,' because she's acting that song; every word means something, you know."

Smith notes that one song was placed in *Black and Blue* specifically because Orezzoli and Segovia had admired the way she sang it. "I had recorded 'I Want a Big Butter and Egg Man' for Parkwood Records with [trumpeter] Doc Cheatham and [pianist] Art Hodes; we did it with just the two instruments. Well, Hector and Claudio heard this song on the radio and they thought it was so authentic, with just the two pieces—and that is why we do it that same way in the show now, with just a piano [Sir Roland Hanna] and a trumpet [Emery Thompson] accompanying me. I had to work on that number to really make it work onstage because I have three dancers dancing in front of my face. At first I used to step aside and let them do whatever they're going to do, and then I thought, 'Well, this is my song,' so now I sort of move about with them."

That particular song, she notes, she first knew from performances of it by Louis Armstrong and Velma Middleton. Over the years, she has acquired a good-sized record collection, with plenty of rare sides by old-time jazz and blues performers. "I do a lot of studying, listening. Like every day I might play somebody." She hands me a record she's been listening to lately: Sister Rosetta Tharpe, whose swinging, gospel-based singing was popular some 50 years ago. And here's a recording of Eva Taylor, all but forgotten today; once billed as the "Queen of the Moaners," Taylor recorded prolifically with Clarence Williams' Blue Five, back in the '20s. And Smith has recordings of others, still more obscure, I note, like Blind Joe Taggart and the Delta Boys. Framed and hanging on the wall across from where I'm sitting, I note, is an original 1920s 78 r.p.m. record by Bessie Smith, the "Empress of the Blues," a gift from a European fan. Carrie Smith not only has a voice that just naturally happens to be reminiscent of Bessie Smith's, but she also looks a little like Bessie Smith (she beams when I mention that). Bessie is a particular favorite of Carrie's, but in a broad sense Carrie Smith is trying to maintain the legacy of many pioneering jazz and blues singers.

"I'm trying to hold up the banner, because the music is dying—you know that. And I'm one of the few women out here that's trying to keep it going. And doing pretty well with it," she says. I'm pleased, I tell her, that she's so deep into the music. "I've been around this kind of music all my life," she notes. "It's not new to me."

How did she first get into it? She'll be glad to talk about her roots—so long, she adds with a smile, as I don't ask her exactly how old she is. It's a deal.

"I was born in Georgia but my family moved to Newark, New Jersey, when I was about seven. And that means that I was a Newark-ite. I was raised and schooled there. Sarah [Vaughan] lived like two blocks down from me. We used to live on Bergen Street and she lived on Avon Avenue. I went to school in Newark. I've been living in East Orange for about eight years.

"From my childhood, I was brought up in the church. My mother could sing—not professionally, she didn't, but she could sing. In fact, my whole family—they're all good singers. And my father, he's excellent. He was a Baptist minister and he's now in his 80s."

Bessie Smith was always a great favorite of Carrie Smith. "Oh, I knew about her because I had an aunt who used to have all of Bessie's records; they were on 78s. And she would play these songs, you know. And I used to say, 'Boy, I wish I could sing like that one day.' And my aunt, who would play these songs, was like a black sheep in the family. Everybody would look at her sort of cross-eyed because she was *for real*. And she loved music; she loved to dance. She was my favorite aunt, she really was. And she'd play these records and I could see her doing the shimmy, you know. All of this is not new to me—I've seen it. And she used to do the black bottom, and she used to do something like this [dancing in place a bit]—I forget what she called that. But all those dances, she knew them; she could do them all. And she used to tell me how she saw Bessie Smith onstage and what she'd have on, you know, and all these pretty clothes and everything. So I would play the records and I learned

270

Carrie Smith (courtesy of Carrie Smith).

Carrie Smith sings "I Gotta Right to Sing the Blues" (top photo) and "I Want a Big Butter and Egg Man" (bottom photo) in the Broadway musical revue Black and Blue *(photos by Martha Swope, courtesy of Marilyn LeVine).*

how to sing 'Good Old Wagon' from listening to those records. Then I really got into Bessie because I loved her voice and I just wish I could have seen her at least once on stage. I never saw Billie Holiday on stage. I never saw Ethel Waters. I never saw any of these great people.

"My aunt lived in Newark. She was born in Georgia but she moved here when she was very small. She was a barrelhouse mama. Yes, she loved barrelhouse music. . . . My uncle, who was her brother, played piano like [blues pianist Little Brother] Montgomery. He was tall, handsome, and all he did was play for house-rent parties. He was a ladies' man. He'd play for the parties and he'd have the little kitty sitting up on the piano, you know. And he went to Philadelphia and he stayed down there a long time, playing piano. And then I had another uncle who played guitar. And he played like Leadbelly; he played blues and stuff like that. I never heard anything he did on record because I don't think that he was hip to that—but he could have been right there with those guys. He died at the age of 80-something. But my family—boy, they were all musically inclined. My aunt used to have house-rent parties. And she had a piano. And where I was born—a little old house way in the backwoods of Georgia—my grandmother had an old organ, where you'd sit down and pump it, and I used to try to play it.

"I started singing in the church, the Abyssinian Baptist Church on West Kenny Street in Newark, New Jersey. And I stayed there for many years, from the Little Folks Choir to the Gospel Chorus," Smith recalls.

"And I also had a little old gospel group. In fact, Dionne Warwick—this was back in the '50s, before she became famous—and her sister, Dede, have sung background for me on Joe Bostic's TV show. They're from East Orange. Singing groups at that time used to travel from one little town to the next, all that kind of stuff. We used to visit their church and they'd visit ours; we had that kind of relationship." Smith was still in her teens when she made her television debut, on Bostic's WOR-TV show *Gospel Time*, in 1957. That same year, she also made her recording debut, singing with the Back Home Choir at the Newport Jazz Festival, an appearance that was recorded "live" and released on Verve Records.

"Gospel has always been my love," Smith says. "Because everything I sing, you can hear that gospel in it. And anything that a musician plays, you can hear the blues in it. I don't care how far out they try to go—that blues has to creep in there somewhere. I'm talking about the contemporary players or singers—that blues is going to get in there some kind of way. And with my singing, the gospel is going to be in there, somewhere. And many times I tried to cover it up, but you can't do it. Because you're born with it, you know." She listened to much more than just gospel while growing up, of course. Like many of her teenage friends, she listened to rhythm and blues, the black popular music of the day. "I was still in school when Ruth Brown was doing 'Mama, He Treats Your Daughter Mean,'" she says, citing Brown's blockbuster R&B hit of 1953 (which Smith herself had a chance to record many years later). Through the years, though, she listened to a wide range of song stylists, and she has acknowledged as influences not just Bessie Smith (the most obvious one) but also such distinguished, jazz-influenced popular singers as Ella Fitzgerald, Billie Holiday, Peggy Lee, and Dinah Washington, along with two older blues singers, whose names will be less familiar to most contemporary readers: Victoria Spivey and Miss Rhapsody (who also sang sacred music, besides blues). "And of course I knew Mahalia Jackson," she notes. "When she would appear at Carnegie Hall or someplace, our choir would sing background for her."

Carrie Smith first began making a name for herself singing religious music. A fellow member of the Gospel Chorus she belonged to in Newark—Charles Banks—came up with the idea of presenting Smith in concert in New York City. They booked her at Town Hall. "And in 1961, three or four busloads of people went from the church over to Town Hall to see me perform. And I received a wonderful review for the concert—the first review I ever had—written by Robert Sheldon of *The New York Times*. I still have it. He spoke about how much he enjoyed the music. The first song I did was an old spiritual and I sang it a cappella.

Then I had about four singers with me who sang background for me.

"Well, after Town Hall, which was my first concert professionally, I moved out to California. I stayed out there six years. I auditioned for Art Linkletter's show. They accepted me and I did a blues number on the show called 'I'd Rather Drink Muddy Water.' And a fellow by the name of Big Tiny Little was looking at the show, and he was looking for a singer at that time. He contacted the TV station. He wanted to know, was I available? I said yes, and I started traveling with him on the road, with his combo and went into Las Vegas with it, to the Star Dust Hotel and the Aladdin Hotel. Then I had a little trio of my own. I worked at the Aladdin with my little trio in the lounge. Then I went back to Tiny and traveled with him for about three years. I traveled with him about '67, '68, '69—somewhere in there. And then I came to New York with him. At the Empire State Building, they used to have a room called the Riverboat and I sang there. When Tiny left, I stayed in New York, and I started beating the pavement. I would go and sit in at little clubs.

"I'd go to Jimmy Ryan's on 54th Street. Roy Eldridge was working there then, with Eddie Locke and Joe Muranyi. I used to go in there and they let me sit in. And then Tyree Glenn, who'd heard me sing with Roy, hired me to sing with his little combo. Then I started traveling with him. There was Norman Simmons, who is now the pianist for Joe Williams, Slam Stewart was the bass player, Jo Jones was the drummer, Roger Glenn was on the bass flute, and Tyree was on the vibes and the trombone. He could play the sweetest trombone you ever heard in your life. And that was my second band job, around 1970–71."

One thing led to another as she gradually became better known to musicians. "I know just about all of them. I call them all my brothers. And they treat me as if I'm their sister. They call me Bessie—'Don't mess with Bessie,' you know. And so, I've traveled with Buddy Tate and Hank Jones and all of them." Around 1972, she recalls, "I worked with Al Hirt down in New Orleans for about nine months, at his nightclub there. In fact,

Ellis Marsalis—Wynton Marsalis' father—and I were the only two blacks in the band. He was the piano player and I was the singer, for Al Hirt. And we both got fired at the same time! Not because of anything we had done—it was just a financial thing; they were having a lot of problems with the club at that time. I knew Wynton when he was just a boy. And his brother Branford."

Carrie Smith's big break came when George Wein was looking for someone to portray Bessie Smith for a 1975 New York Jazz Repertory Company concert saluting Louis Armstrong. "I was chosen by [music director] Dick Hyman. He had heard other singers audition for him, but he chose me; he said, 'You're the one.' And that's when people really began to know who I was and what I was about. 'Cake-Walkin' Babies from Home' put me on the map." The highly respected critic Dan Morgenstern wrote in *Jazz Journal* (June 1977): "Carrie Smith carries off Bessie Smith more convincingly than any other singer I've heard" (and his assessment goes for me, too). Carrie Smith notes, "You know, there are a lot of people out there who always wanted to do Bessie. I didn't want to do her; I just wanted to sing some of the songs that she did. So, that's how I got into Bessie.

"That concert was recorded live in Carnegie Hall [for Atlantic Records: *Satchmo Remembered—The Music of Louis Armstrong*]. That was the last recording that Ray Nance was on. He played the trumpet for me on 'St. Louis Blues' and 'Cake-Walkin' Babies.' That was a great band. I don't think they'll ever capture that sound again. Well, that Carnegie Hall concert really got me started." The concert was such an enormous success, it was subsequently restaged in locations ranging from New Jersey to the Soviet Union. "And George took me to France—to the [1976 Nice] jazz festival—and I was a big hit in France, and from there I started going to all the different countries; they would call, you know. I got to sing with people like Vic Dickenson, Eddie 'Cleanhead' Vinson, B. B. King, Hank Jones, Budd Johnson. I toured with Cab Calloway—down in Spain and all over the place. And I've been going back to Europe ever since. When I go overseas, boy, they know who I am over there!" She appeared in such well-known venues as Ronnie Scott's Club in London and the Hotel Meridien in Paris, while also finding time to occasionally perform in places less commonly visited by American jazz performers, such as Tunisia. She recorded a number of relaxed jazz and blues sides (including "Nobody Knows You When You're Down and Out," "Confessin' the Blues," and "In the Dark") for the French label Disques Black and Blue, with such highly compatible musicians as Doc Cheatham, Buddy Tate, Budd Johnson, George Kelly, Panama Francis, and Billy Butler.[1]

Back in the U.S., Smith sang at the Rainbow Room in New York, Dick Gibson's famed Jazz Party in Colorado, and the Monterey Jazz Festival. "And once Dick Hyman got to know me, and know that I was so versatile, he would call me for different concerts. Right today, he calls me anytime he needs a singer to do anything—if he wants to go back in time. Like, Ethel Waters—we did a tribute to Ethel Waters at Carnegie Hall. You know how many times I've been in Carnegie Hall? At least six or seven. We did the W. C. Handy concert, at which Handy's daughter, Katherine Handy, appeared. We did the Duke Ellington tribute, where I sang 'Come Sunday.' Joya Sherrill was on it, too; she sang 'Blues Is a Woman.' And so on." Hyman has frequently presented Smith in the Jazz at July concerts he organizes each year at New York's 92nd Street Y. Smith also sang on Benny Goodman's last TV special, *Let's Dance* (October 7, 1985), and periodically appeared with Goodman's orchestra in concerts (at the Kennedy Center, University of Michigan, Wolf Trap, and the like) up until Goodman's death, singing such numbers as "Gimme a Pigfoot and a Bottle of Beer" (which Bessie Smith had recorded in 1933 with a studio group that included Goodman), "Ja-Da," "You've Changed," and "St. Louis Blues." She favors much the same sort of material on her own jazz club gigs, accompanied by the likes of Bross Townsend (piano), Carline Ray (electric bass), and Bernard Purdy (drums).

"Why do I sing the old songs?" Smith asks rhetorically. "Because I love good music. I'm not going to knock the kids' music today if that's what they love, but I was brought up on

---

[1]The best of the recordings Smith has made in France are scheduled to be released on CD in the United States in 1993, on the Evidence label.

277

this stuff and this is what's gotten me this far. I like the music. I like the words. I like to know what a song means. I won't even sing a song if I don't know what the words mean. Or what it's saying.

"And then a lot of folks say, 'Well, you can't sing the blues unless you've lived the blues.' I say, 'I live it every day.' And I do. The blues don't always mean that your man is gone or your man hit you or whatever. You can wake up in the morning feeling low—about anything. That's what I call the blues—if you want to name it that." The slightly forlorn air that often permeates her singing voice is in her speaking voice now.

If you need any proof that Smith knows the blues, just listen to her eight-minute-long rendition of "Blues in the Night" on the Stash album *Highlights in Jazz, Twelfth Anniversary Concert* (recorded "live" at NYU in 1985). She finds more substance in that song than most singers do. Her ad-libbed patter with the audience while the band vamps—conjuring up an image of a woman seeking solace in alcohol while waiting for a man's call which, she knows, is not forthcoming—is a masterly example of mood-setting. The sound quality on this "live" concert recording is, unfortunately, subpar, but the recording is a valuable document of the "real" Carrie Smith nonetheless. It captures her talent more completely than most of her albums—too many of which have not done her justice. She complains, exaggerating only slightly: "Every record I've ever made was done in a hurry. Somebody chooses the songs for you. You run in there, and half the time you don't know the words and you just put anything on there. And now, today, I'm sorry for that. The only record that I've ever done that was put together right was the one on the [now defunct] label called West 54th. That's the one where I do 'Lush Life.' Budd Johnson wrote the arrangements. And there's George Duvivier on bass, Art Farmer on cornet, Richard Wyands on the piano, and Richie Pratt on the drums." Other songs on that album included "Just Friends," "What a Little Moonlight Can Do," and "When I Been Drinking." A prime goal of Smith's now is to do an album of her best material, accompanied by top musicians. Arranger Luther Henderson and musicians from *Black and Blue* have expressed interest in doing an album with her if a label can be found that would take the care to do it right. While Smith has made a number of appealing recordings, the definitive Carrie Smith album still remains to be produced.

Since *Black and Blue* opened on Broadway in January of 1989, Smith's energies have been primarily wrapped up in that show. But she still has found time to do other things that were important to her, like participating in a tribute to the late Martin Luther King. And when Ella Fitzgerald was honored with a gala night at Lincoln Center, Smith was among those in attendance in the audience. She explains, simply, "Here's a woman every singer in the world wants to be like—the First Lady of Jazz. Every singer in the world should have been there. I've asked a couple of singers I know, 'Did you go see the tribute to Ella?' 'No, I couldn't make it, I was doing something. . . .' I said, 'Well, I went.' I wouldn't have missed that for anything. Just to hear the woman sing one song, you know, kills me to no end. She's one of my idols. When I listen to her earlier records, like with Chick Webb, when she sang 'A-Tisket, A-Tasket' and 'A Little Bit Later On'— oh, man, she was *singing*, you know. Like Sarah was. When Sarah started, she stuck to the melody, which people don't do nowadays. To each his own," Smith says, adding that *she* prefers hearing the melody to some of the far-out improvisations contemporary jazz singers offer.

"I went to Sarah Vaughan's funeral," Smith notes. "I sang in the choir. I didn't make myself known, running in front of the cameras and all that stuff. And this is where people say that I'm wrong, that I should have been in the camera, and should have had something to say. But I was there for a different reason. I knew Sarah. Sarah and I had both come from Newark. And it was sort of like a private thing. I didn't even come in the front door; I came around the back door with the choir. I could have stood and said, 'Yes, Sarah and I did this, and we did that, and bla-bla-bla.' I didn't want to do that. It was a beautiful service. The minister said everything there was to say about Sarah. She was a great, great, great talent."

Going in the back door of the church to humbly sing as a choir member at the service for Sarah Vaughan is characteristic of Carrie Smith. She doesn't have that overwhelming interest in self-aggrandizement and self-promotion too often found in stars. Her *Black and Blue* dressing room, for example, was decorated with surprising simplicity, without the prominently displayed plaques, honors, or write-ups that so often greet visitors to stars' dressing rooms. I recalled Smith had been honored a few years earlier with a Carrie Smith Day in Newark, and wondered why no reminder of that was in sight. "At the theater everybody has their proclamations up on the wall. I don't have mine there; I leave them at home. What does it mean, collecting dust there?" she says. For that matter, she doesn't "act" like a star, generally. I dropped by Ruth Brown's dressing room the evening she was awaiting word as to whether she had won a Grammy Award for her album *Blues on Broadway*. That night, Smith shared with Brown some dinner Smith had cooked—fried chicken with greens—but she didn't hang around to hone in on the publicity Brown was getting. (Indeed Smith, unlike some performers I've known, has never asked me to give her coverage.) When Brown received the phone call telling her she had won the Grammy, she went to Smith's dressing room to share the good news; by that point in their careers, she and Smith had developed a friendship. (By contrast, Brown and Hopkins remained rivals, wary of one another; that evening Hopkins offered Brown luke-warm congratulations on the Grammy victory. Standing in Brown's doorway—she didn't enter the room itself—Hopkins said she had gotten back her lost cat and Brown had won the Grammy, so they had both had a good day.) Brown also asked me if I could please give Smith some publicity, saying Smith didn't receive the attention from the press she deserved. I thought that was an unusual gesture on Brown's part, and said so to Smith.

"Yeah. I've heard her tell the producers, too: 'Every time you send some publicity out, you never mention Carrie!' She does this," Smith affirms. "Ruth told me, 'I want to help you, because, you know, when I was out of the business, I went and washed clothes and did this and that. And now that I'm back in the business, I'm helping other people. And I'd like to help you as much as I can. Anytime you see me, stick your face in the camera, too, because I'm there as a friend.' And there are not too many show people that would do that. Because everybody's for themself—and I've learned this on Broadway.'' And Brown, Smith acknowledges, has a clear sense of her own worth and entitlement to the attention she is receiving. Indeed, Smith recalls the way Brown really gave it to the producers when *Black and Blue* ads began appearing on the sides of New York buses that showed young dancers from the show rather than the stars, Brown, Hopkins, and Smith. These young dancers, Brown knew, hadn't even been born when she started paying her dues as a performer, doing one-nighters in the racially segregated south of the late '40s and early '50s. "Ruth told the producers: 'I want you to know one thing: I rode in the *back* of the bus so these young performers can ride on the *side!*' Well! I'm sitting there, listening. Ruth can be very witty, you know." What Brown was doing was more than being witty, of course. She was asserting herself, standing up for her rights as a performer in a way that would not come easily for Smith. Ruth Brown and Linda Hopkins both received Tony Award nominations (best female starring performance in a musical) for their work in *Black and Blue*; Brown, deservedly, won the award. If Brown and Hopkins have received greater press attention than Smith for their work in *Black and Blue*, it may be due to the fact that, as strong a performer as Smith is, Brown and Hopkins are even stronger.

Still, Smith admits she feels hurt that the producers of *Black and Blue* have not gotten more publicity for her. She is quietly resentful. "I feel they haven't done anything for me, and I don't intend to do anything extra for them. Like, they called me today and told me Ruth is going to be out Wednesday, and Melba Joyce, who is the understudy for Ruth, Linda, and me, is going to be on vacation. Now I can never understand why they only have one understudy for three people. So they asked me, would I take Ruth's role for that Wednesday? And I said, 'No. I'm not an understudy. You have an understudy.' 'But she's going on vacation.' 'That's your problem. You should have another one there. If it was an emergency, I'd be liable to do it for you. But it's not that; it's just for your convenience.' 'Yeah, but see, you'll be singing "St. Louis Blues," *on Broadway.*' I told them, 'Broadway is fine. I've had a year and five months of it, and I know what it is.'" She reflects with a humble laugh that now here *she* is, like everyone else on Broadway, wishing she was getting more publicity for herself. While understudy Melba Joyce, she adds, would no doubt give anything to receive as much publicity as *she* has received! It's easy to get caught up in that bottomless need for public attention, Smith acknowledges.

"You know, once most people get on Broadway, they don't think about anything else. Like I look at Linda Hopkins. Linda wants to do *Me and Bessie* again [the award-winning Bessie Smith show in which Hopkins starred on Broadway for two years] so bad she could just taste it. This is her hopes and her dreams. Everything with her—and with so many people on Broadway— is 'Look at me, look at me, look at me.' Watch Linda on stage. Every gesture she makes is to keep the focus on her—at all times." Smith mentions the ribald way Hopkins will sometimes pull part of her dress up between her legs for a laugh, making it clear from her expression that she would find it demeaning to make such a bid for attention. "And even when everybody in *Black and Blue* walks down and takes their bow together, she'll do something that says: *Look at me.* I don't like that. We're all supporting each other in the show, supposedly.

"But once people get on Broadway, they don't think about any kind of sports, they don't think about—their whole *life* is being right there on that stage. I want to keep our music going, but show business is not my whole life. And I love to do other things besides talk about myself all the time. And people do that in this business. Don't talk about yourself all the time! Talk about somebody else, talk about other things. Talk about going to the basketball game, talk about anything. But this is their whole life, so they don't know anything else to talk about. It's not mine. I love entertaining, but that's not all there is."

What might she rather be doing sometimes?

"I love fishing. Have you ever gone fishing, Chip?" she asks. "That's the most peaceful thing you can do. I want to buy me a boat and go fishing."

1990

Those "Late, Great Ladies . . ."

"I'm an *interpreter*, not an imitator. I'm doing characters," says Sandra Reaves-Phillips of the touring one-woman show she has devised, *The Late, Great Ladies of Blues and Jazz*, in which she offers capsule portrayals, via words, actions, and songs, of the likes of Ma Rainey, Bessie Smith, Ethel Waters, Josephine Baker, Billie Holiday, Dinah Washington, and Mahalia Jackson. "It's as if an actress takes a copy and says, 'What would be believable here?' And you take a poetic license here and there to make it entertaining, yet being as honest as you can with the interpretation. Because there is no way I could imitate Billie Holiday or Dinah— none of these greats; the audience would get offended if they thought that I said I was imitating them. But I give enough of the nuances and the essence and the physicalities. I've never seen these great ladies 'live,' you know. So it's a matter of taking things that you've learned in reading about them and listening to them. Or if you see a little video clip, you snatch as much off of that little minute as you can and incorporate it into what you're doing and broaden it a few times."

When she's not busy with that show, Reaves-Phillips is frequently cast in roles that are in the Ma Rainey–Bessie Smith mold. She has, on occasion, actually portrayed on stage both Rainey (in a production of *Ma Rainey's Black Bottom*) and Smith (in a production of *Champeen*), but more often has been called upon to portray fictitious characters drawn from their tradition (such as the exuberant, bawdy, blues-singing star "Big Bertha" in productions of *One Mo' Time* and *Further Mo'*). She has sung old-time jazz, blues, and pop songs in such off-Broadway shows as *Blues in the Night* and *Stompin' at the Savoy*, and in the original Paris production of *Black and Blue*. Although she occasionally does other things, from straight dramatic roles to singing rhythm and blues, she always gets pulled back, before too long, to vintage jazz and blues. After she was hired for a dramatic role in the film *'Round Midnight*, for example, the part was rewritten to allow her to sing a Bessie Smith song she wanted to perform.

As I chat with Reaves-Phillips this afternoon in her dressing room at New York's Village Gate, I am curious as to how she wound up becoming a professional singer—and, more specifically, one specializing in old-time jazz and blues songs.

"I didn't start out wanting to become a singer; it just was a way of our life. I sang in church and the little children's choir when I was in Mullins, South Carolina, a little place, down near Myrtle Beach," Reaves-Phillips recalls. She sang constantly, too, as a migrant worker in her youth. "All day long in the fields when we worked—I worked alongside my grandmother—we sang hymns and spirituals and blues. From miles around you could hear the natural voice. So I learned to sing without music. Well, I've got a big old raggedy voice today, so singing outdoors in those fields must have helped—'cause I mean, I can go! And I can tackle many different styles. Ooh, I'm not a trained artist at all, but God's given me my voice. It's not the prettiest—but it feels good. It feels *good*." She laughs, richly and freely. There's a kind of overflowing quality to her laughter, and to her personality, generally. I'm warmed by the timbre of her speaking voice. "You know, I've had to do shows with mikes and without mikes—and when a mike goes out, you've still got to sing. So all of that singing as a child did help a lot. And people have categorized me not so much as a contralto-alto or a legitimate singer—they say I'm an *earth singer*. Maybe that's a new category!"

I wondered if Reaves-Phillips—who can, in addition to her

jazz and blues portrayals, also get into the fervent religious spirit of a Mahalia Jackson quite well—sang a lot of gospel as a child.

"I'm a *learned* gospel singer. I learned that later on in life because in the church we just sang choir songs, little hymns. That was Cradle Rock Choir in Ebenezer Church in Mullins, South Carolina. It was African Methodist Episcopal at that time. I'm a Baptist church member now. But I did hear gospel. So some of it must have kind of recorded itself within me back there— because when it comes out of me now, it comes out as if I was a real gospel singer all my life." But her own church, she makes clear, was rather restrained. "Yeah, it was a nice, quiet, harmonic thing there. They didn't break down and shout. You know, that's where Mahalia got into many problems with church members because she was one of those [Reaves-Phillips' arms begin waving ecstatically] *physical* people, and they went, 'My God, she's—' you know, when she's just gyrating here in church. And I guess that's just me!

"It was back in the early and mid '50s that I was growing up down South. During that period, I came to New York City for a short time to visit, and then I went right back to Mullins. It wasn't until I was 15 years old that my mother made me settle down in New York, to finish school, to get a good grip on education. And that's where I graduated, in Brooklyn, New York. My senior year I dropped out of high school. I went back a year later, after I'd started my family, and got my diploma. But during that time, I had been going to talent shows at theaters and nightclubs and hanging out on Wednesday nights, doing guest spots. It was one of the Wednesday amateur nights, when I was 16, that I got my first gig. This was at the Brevoort Theater, which is no longer there, in the Bed-Stuy section of Brooklyn. I was seen there by a scout and he hired me to do four nights at the Brooklyn Baby Grand nightclub. Fifteen dollars a night, three shows a night, four nights a week: sixty bucks a week—and they took tax out of that. So I was a high roller! This was in the '60s; that's how my career actually started." She was trying to make it as a singer of pop music and R&B. "By 18, I was recording my first song for a little company, Sue Records. And I was on the Broadway label itself. I made a song called 'You Succeeded' written by J. J. Jackson. And on the other side was a demo we had made at somebody's house called 'Midnight Comes.' They put that demo on the flip side of this record. One was a ballad and one was an up-tempo Motown sound, a very swingy sound—a very nice song.

"Then I started doing clubs, little gigs around. I started filling in little dates for other performers who were missing dates. They called that, at the time, the chitlin circuit. You were not making money; you'd go way out in the country somewhere, maybe make $25 a night and then sometimes when you got ready to get paid, the promoter was nowhere around, so you had to hitch-hike, get a ride any way you could, back into the city. That was the rough part of the paying-dues period.

"I'd be playing in Pennsylvania, Washington, D.C., way out on Long Island, Virginia—you know, just wherever somebody would say there's a gig; you just took it. You sometimes didn't even know where you were going to stay when you got there, but you wanted it and you did it. But most of my work was around in the New York area. Then by age 21—I was still singing in the clubs—I was doing a second record. By then I was going to Epic, which was part of CBS Records. I did four sides for Epic, including an old Chuck Willis tune called 'Pack Your Bags'— which I think they shelved—and 'Wish I Hadn't Known About You'—a Detroit tune. Those were the days of working and recording and trying to be a star, but you were just being put on shelves. So a lot of my work is just sitting on shelves somewhere. And finally, around age 23–24, I joined Canyon Records and did an album, the only album that was put on the market. I didn't make a dime! It's real weird how people just take your talents and the artists don't get it, but I found those records were being sold in Europe. As a matter of fact, a gentleman over in Paris has every record I've ever made. It put me to tears when I went over there to do *Black and Blue* several years ago and this man had every record I ever made and *I* didn't even have them. And on some of the records, my name had been changed to a fictitious name like Sandra Johnson. Well, the companies don't pay you. But they figure, if they use another name, who's going to say anything?

"We were just trying to make records, hoping for a hit. But I didn't know where they were being distributed—or *if* they were. I thought they were just sitting on the shelf, but some of them were being distributed in Europe. And I never got a dime. Never! So I quit the business. I absolutely quit singing for a very long time. Ten years. I did bookkeeping, I did office work, and so on. I had another child. I have two children, who are now young adults and there they are up on the wall [she points to photos]. My son, who is 27, was on the telethon the other night with Phylicia Rashad, dancing. And my daughter, 24, is an artist also. So I'm a happy mom. And they toured on the road with me when I sort of got into acting. When I did, finally, leave the work force—after having been a barmaid, a bookkeeper, whatever I could do to feed my kids—I was encouraged to go to acting school up in Harlem. This was about 1970. A friend of mine told me to come to acting class. I did. I studied for about two years and saw this ad in *Backstage* or *Show Business* for a blues singer, for a play off-off-Broadway. I went in to audition. I didn't have music; I didn't even know how you go for an audition, OK? I went out, sang 'Fever' and 'At Last' a cappella. Because I had always sung a cappella. So for me it was like going home, you know. And that went well. I got the gig, appearing as an alcoholic blues singer in this show off-off-Broadway called *Little Bit*. So an agent saw me in that show and submitted me for a play starring Bette Davis—*the* Bette Davis—with Nell Carter. It was called *Miss Moffett* and everyone thought it was going to be a megashow. I got hired as an ensemble member and as Nell Carter's understudy. I took my children on the road with me; that was the first show that we toured together. My son was in that production, too; that was his first show. My part wasn't big, of course, but I remember standing in the wings on the night we opened at the Shubert Theater in Philadelphia, watching Bette Davis get a five-minute standing ovation, and thinking, 'God, one of these days I would love to be in that spot.' That was a pre-Broadway run. The play, as it turned out, never did make it to Broadway.

"I auditioned for the Broadway show, *Raisin*, to understudy the leading role, Mama Younger, and to play the character actress, the comedienne. I got that. Then we went on tour for almost two years and when the star, Virginia Capers, who won a Tony Award, left, I took over the lead, playing Mama. That was my first real big role. So that's how I got involved in theater. My head never said I was going to be these things. It's just somehow the finger of fate led me in all the places that I was supposed to be. Theater primarily took over my life." She appeared in national tours of such stage shows as *One* and *The Best Little Whorehouse in Texas*. She was featured off-Broadway in *Sparrow in Flight*, *Basin Street*, and *Opening Night* (which she coauthored). She took especial pride in her stage performances in *American Dreams*, with the Negro Ensemble Company; *Champeen*, for which she won an Audelco Award for Outstanding Female Performer; and the Citadel Theatre production of *Ma Rainey's Black Bottom*. She sang rhythm and blues in New York clubs, too, ranging from Sweetwaters to the Bitter End. And she landed a recurring role on the soap opera *Another World*.

In between the work in theater, television, and clubs, she began carving out a career for herself as a concert artist, doing salutes to departed jazz and blues greats, and developing the one-woman show, *The Late, Great Ladies of Blues and Jazz*, with which she has been touring, off and on, for more than eight years. "I guess I'm best known for that show," she acknowledges, as she recalls its evolution. "Well, about eight or nine years ago, I was doing some rhythm-and-blues work at the Cotton Club up in Harlem. And my friends who had seen me time and time again said, 'God, you remind me of Bessie Smith when you sing certain ballads. Do you ever do her material? Why don't you do her material?' But I didn't know Bessie then. And I didn't care to know. For that matter, I didn't like Billie Holiday, either, back in the '50s and '60s when I was listening. It was just not— my mind was not in that area. Well, finally, I started to listen to Bessie Smith. And I started to fall in love with the lyrics, the naughtiness, the aggressive attitude that she used in the music. When I heard Bessie's lyrics, it was the naughtiness that fascinated me first because I had not listened to double entendres before, but also, her voice was very much similar to mine. And even my stature and my look—people were saying, 'You favor her when you do certain things with your hair.' And then I read the book that was written about her and I said, 'I like this lady; she has style.' I'm closer to her, in totality, than to any of the other ladies I do.

"And then, learning there was a relationship with Bessie and Ma Rainey, I said, 'Well, let me listen to Ma. Let me check out this lady.' Ma, I realized, was a little more laid-back, a little more earthy. When I read about how earthy Ma was and how family oriented she was, I said, 'You know, I'm a lot like that, too.' Because I get into my audience and I like to participate with people. I don't like to be isolated; I like having people around me. And I become people's mother, whether they want me to or not; I just naturally become a mother when I'm in a group of people, taking care of people, wanting to do this.

"So after getting a little more involved and finding out that Europeans knew more about these various ladies than I did, I went on a little minisurge, learning about them. And I said, 'I'm going to do a two-night tribute of some music of the foremothers.' What started out as a two-night tribute has turned into an eight-year love affair! All I was doing, at first, was some songs that had been made popular by these ladies. I incorporated into the show Ma Rainey, Bessie Smith, Ethel Waters, Billie Holiday, Dinah Washington, and Josephine Baker—well, lately, I've taken Josephine out and have put in Mahalia Jackson instead. I just added one after another.

"Like, for instance, in reading about these ladies of the past, I read that there was a little rivalry between Bessie and Ethel Waters. You know, Bessie called Ethel a northern bitch and said she couldn't sing the blues. So I said, 'Ooh, that should be in the show. Bring in Ethel, who's a little feisty!' Ethel was very feisty and she just spoke what was on her mind—but she was refined with it. She'd say, 'I'm not a shouter,' you know. So I said that would be nice, a little color. And then, later on down the road, there was that little edge between Ethel and Billie. So I found all these interesting people from the past that nobody was talking much about anymore. And instead of just talking about them, in my show I actually act as if I *am* them. And that has been the real challenge for me as an actress and performer, and then to write something that the audience really accepts.

"I wanted to do Billie, too, you know. But initially I said, 'Billie Holiday—well, that's a tough one because physically I'm nothing like Billie. And tonewise, I'm heavy; the voice—*nothing* like her.' I was afraid to tackle Billie Holiday, so she was the last one that I tried as a character. But I would talk about her and sing her music until finally I said I must try this. And one night I just went into the tone. I had studied the records and listened to her speak and had captured as much as I could in essence of Billie. And that night, when I put the flower in my hair, the way she wore it, and I bowed my head and took that hit of cocaine [Reaves-Phillips pantomimes snorting coke off her hand] before the audience—they didn't know where I was going! [And now Reaves-Phillips, rather startlingly, begins talking in the slurred, somewhat bitter tones of the aged Billie Holiday.] And all of a sudden the voice went there—and the place just went, 'Oooh.' It was like the place stood still. The goose pimples jumped on. I froze. When I did that [she strokes her forearm], it was like ice covered my body. It was like all of a sudden I was no longer there. And I just *knew* it was the right choice. That became the highlight of the whole two-hour show, Billie Holiday.

"And, as I studied the ladies, I admired Dinah Washington, too, because she was so versatile. She was so outrageously flamboyant, yet she could sing any kind of song and with such style. I liked that, so I incorporated Dinah.

"I used to open my second act with the comedic side of Josephine Baker when she was further on in years. And that's what you see, the further-on-in-years of these ladies because I just felt like, to give each one 20 minutes or whatever, I can't go the whole gamut of their career, so I picked the part that would be most believable for me to portray, which was the latter part of their life, when they were trying to go up again or were going out. So that's where you see it. Dinah comes in bitching that she's late but she doesn't give a damn. She's just all over the place. It's grand! I do about three, four songs of each lady. And we close our evening with Mahalia—the gospel. That was a later decision for me, to do Mahalia. I just felt like for someone to make that kind of commitment to a music that she made, and to stick with it, no matter what kind of temptations were offered her to do other things—that took a certain strength. And her thing was to leave people feeling uplifted and with hope that there is more, that there is a better tomorrow. And that's the way I chose to leave the audience—that no matter what we go through, the blues or the degradation or the suffering, there is always hope. And so when we leave that theater, we've got people on their feet. And it has never failed, whether it was a white audience or European—whoever it was, it has been the same kind of reception, give and take. People who could not even explain in English what they were feeling would come and say [she goes into an accented voice, struggling to get the words out], 'I feel something and I'm just crying,' you know, and they're trying to explain what they're feeling and I'd say, 'I know, I feel it with you. Thank you.' Audiences have responded well everywhere. I mean, this show is taking me around—to some places I've already been back to for the fourth time. I'm booked all through the next year—dates in North Carolina, Texas, Arizona, New Mexico, Kentucky, South Carolina. All over."

Are most of the people who come to see her show old enough to have known the performers to whom she pays tribute?

"No, not at all. But you have a lot of people who are record collectors. Then you have the young college group who might be doing studies in jazz or blues, who are curious. When you go back around and you see them again, they say, 'You know, I've found a Dinah Washington record that was out of print' or 'I found—' so you know these kids are really getting into the music and you appreciate that, because my desire is to not let the legends die. And to pay tribute to my foremothers. I'm very *fulfilled*, doing this show." And indeed she sounds fulfilled— grateful, in a way, to be able to do the show. Veteran trumpeter Bill Dillard (born 1911) usually tours as part of her otherwise undistinguished five-piece band, adding a welcome touch of authenticity. He saw most of the artists whom Reaves-Phillips salutes perform "live," and occasionally worked with Billie Holiday, among others, in the old days. Because he was *there* when these women were stars, Reaves-Phillips is proud to have his endorsement of her work. "Mr. Bill told me, 'You would have made these ladies proud because you're doing so much of what they did, the way they did it.' And [rhythm-and-blues pioneer] Nellie Lutcher came to see my show when I was at the Houseman Theater and she said to me, 'My darling.' I asked her, 'Is there anything that you could share with me to help me?' She said, 'Just do more of the same, just keep going.'" Reaves-Phillips hopes to be able to keep going with the show indefinitely, perhaps changing it from time to time as the spirit moves her. "This weekend when I do the show in Winston-Salem, North Carolina, I will do a small mention of the late Pearl Bailey. I will do just a little bit of a song that she did, 'Tired,' in my introduction of the show. I won't *do* her because I haven't perfected it enough. But I will mention her, do a bit of her song, and then continue with the great ladies."

The show has led to many other opportunities for her. As an example, she notes that Vernel Bagneris, who created *One Mo' Time*, a high-stepping evocation of 1920s black show business, and its sequel, *Further Mo'*, became aware of her from seeing her perform *The Late, Great Ladies* at the Cotton Club in Harlem. *One Mo' Time* proved such an enormous hit when it opened in New York in 1979 that plans were soon made to organize a national touring production, to play major theaters. "Well, Vernel and the producers came to see me at the Cotton Club, and cast me as one of the stars of *One Mo' Time*. I toured for about a year and a half, playing Big Bertha. And then also, later on, I filled in for a young lady who was doing Bertha in the smaller, bus-and-truck touring production of that show, after she got injured. When I originally toured with that show, our opening engagement was at the Shubert Theater in Philadelphia. And what was so wonderful was, that was the same theater where I had started in my first play, *Miss Moffett* starring Bette Davis. So the night when we opened *One Mo' Time* on that stage, it was like instant replay. I remembered how I had watched Bette Davis from the side and wished I could have stood where she was standing. And so when I stepped on that stage that night, it felt like I was standing in that same light. Of course when I walked on, I didn't get the five-minute standing ovation she had gotten, but just to be standing in that spot and remembering that Bette had stood there in my first show—it was a moment that no one else knew about but me and God. And I was almost in tears."

Returning to the Cotton Club for another series of performances of *The Late, Great Ladies*, Reaves-Phillips was seen by Hector Orezzoli and Claudio Segovia, who were putting together a stage revue celebrating old-time jazz, blues, and black entertainment in general, called *Black and Blue*. They had vague hopes of bringing their show to Broadway someday, but their only firm plan was to open at the 3,000-seat Chatelet Theatre in Paris for an eight-week limited engagement in the fall of 1985. Reaves-Phillips was delighted when they invited her to go to Paris with them, to costar in *Black and Blue* with such gifted performers as 1950s rhythm-and-blues queen Ruth Brown (whom Orezzoli and Segovia correctly identified as being ripe for a comeback), gospel and blues shouter Linda Hopkins (best known for her hit one-woman stage show saluting Bessie Smith, *Me and Bessie*), singer/organist Jimmy "Preacher" Robins, and veteran hoofers Bunny Briggs and Jimmy Slyde. With such an abundance of talent and a score rich with jazz and blues classics, in retrospect it appears like the show couldn't miss. But Reaves-Phillips had seen other shows that everyone "knew" would be big hits die quick deaths instead, and so she prudently lined up bookings for *The Late, Great Ladies*, to begin right after *Black and Blue*'s projected run. She sang such numbers in *Black and Blue* as "Am I Blue," the boistrous "My Daddy Rocks Me with One Steady Roll," and "Black and Tan Fantasy." (When the show was restaged for Broadway, "My Daddy Rocks Me" was eliminated, and "Black and Tan Fantasy" was converted to a music-and-dance production number, sans vocal.) The show proved such a hit in Paris that an original cast album (not to be confused with the later original *Broadway* cast album that is available today) was hurriedly recorded and pressed for distribution. "It's not the greatest recording in the world, because they did it 'live' at the theater—but I'm proud to have been a part of that," she says. "I enjoyed doing the show very much. But when it was time for me to move on, I moved on." The show's original limited engagement was extended; it wound up running the whole season.

Most cast members rearranged their plans to remain in the hit show.

"I stayed over in Paris for three months—the others stayed there for another five months—and then I had to come back and do a tour of *Great Ladies* to which I had committed myself. When the producers later got ready to take *Black and Blue* to Broadway [where it opened in January of 1989], they never called me." The producers replaced her with Carrie Smith. (While I enjoy them both, I consider Smith to be stronger overall than Reaves-Phillips.)

"But anyway, it was OK the way things worked out with my leaving *Black and Blue*, because by not being in that show, it turned out that—after I toured a little with *The Late, Great Ladies*—I was able to do the films *Lean on Me*, in which I played Mrs. Powers and sang the title song, and *'Round Midnight*, in which I played Buttercup. I was not originally scheduled to sing in *'Round Midnight*, but out of joking around and cutting up, the director, Bertrand Tavernier, said, 'Oh, we've got to find a way to get you to sing something. What would you like to do?' And I said, 'Well, I like Bessie Smith.' And he said, 'Oh, great, great, what do you know?' And I did 'Put It Right Here.' Right in the middle of the film, there it is! I haven't done any other films since then, but I have a dramatic role—no singing—on an upcoming segment of *Law and Order*, on NBC-TV," Reaves-Phillips notes.

She has sung in jazz festivals, including the North Sea Jazz Festival in Holland, the International Jazz Festival of Berne, Switzerland, and the Montreal Jazz Festival. She has toured in Europe and North Africa with an all-female band, including such musicians as saxist Wilene Barton, pianist Lillette Jenkins, bassist Carline Ray, and drummer Dottie Dodgion. "It was strange, to some people, to see all women on a stage," she notes. But audience reactions were enthusiastic, despite barriers of language and culture. She played in North African cities that were new to jazz. "And the people in the audiences would chant. In many places, they would chant while we were performing and I thought something was wrong. But somebody came to me and said, 'They're relating. They're celebrating.' It was incredible. And sometimes we played among ruins—just some columns left, and people were sitting on the mountainside, where seats had been carved into the sides of the mountain. And we were surrounded by all this stone, with maybe half a column left standing. And there were pits, lion pits, down below—oh, for me it was like, 'God, I can't believe I'm here.' Places like Tunis, Carthage, Tabac. . . ." She has brought her "Great Ladies" to clubs ranging from the Village Gate in New York to Jaylin's in Switzerland. But of all the different venues in which she has performed in the United States and abroad, none has meant more to her personally than Harlem's famed Apollo Theatre. "For me, the Apollo was like coming home. Because every artist wants to be known where they live and work. When I got on that stage, I was as nervous as all hell. I stood on that stage and I thought of all the times that I'd dreamed of going back there as a big pro. And the people just *brought me home*; they wouldn't let me move! I mean, it was like between almost every song, I had to wait. Between every lady, I had to wait. It was just incredible. Someone said, you know, people lined up around the Apollo like they used to do in the days when James Brown came to town; it made me feel good. The management wanted to do two shows in one day. But this *Great Ladies* is not a show you want to play two-a-day; I couldn't handle that. I'm on for two hours in the show, speaking, singing 20-some songs. If I've got to do it twice in one day, then somebody gets cheated. So I just did one show. But oh, God, that was incredible." She was acquainting many in the audience—who may not even have been born when Bessie Smith or Billie Holiday or Dinah Washington played the Apollo Theatre—with aspects of their own heritage.

Reaves-Phillips' salute to those *Late, Great Ladies of Blues and Jazz* is perhaps most valuable to those who are not all that familiar with the recordings of those great ladies. Her interpretations will give the novice listener a general feel for the various individual artists' repertoires, sounds, and styles, and hopefully arouse interest in checking out the artists' original recordings. By evening's end, the listener, having heard Reaves-Phillips offer, for example, the mournful vintage strains of "Blues, Oh Blues" as Rainey, the subtler, more sophisticated pop music sound of "Solitude" as sung by Billie Holiday, and the witty flirting of "Don't

Touch Me Tomatoes" à la Josephine Baker, will have a pretty good idea of what those performers were about, and how each differed from one another. A generous, high-spirited performer, Reaves-Phillips knows how to put across a vintage song with gusto. Almost anyone would get a kick out of hearing her punch out "Strut Miss Lizzie" or "Shake That Thing" regardless of whether one knew she was offering them in tribute to Ma Rainey and Ethel Waters, respectively. And when she does a number like "Shake That Thing," which Waters recorded way back in 1925, she's letting contemporary audiences know that the themes expressed in such "original" R&B top-ten hits of recent years as "Shake Your Body," "Shake Your Rump to the Funk," and "Shake Your Booty" did *not* originate with the present generation.

The more familiar a listener already is with the actual recordings of the performers Reaves-Phillips salutes, the easier it may be to find shortcomings in Reaves-Phillips' interpretations. That is to say, someone who knows Ma Rainey's recordings intimately will be aware when Reaves-Phillips "does" Rainey that there is as much of Reaves-Phillips as there is of Rainey in the mix. She does not really sound or look *all* that much like Rainey. (And indeed, how could anyone expect one performer to be fully capable of looking and sounding exactly like six other quite different ones?) And she sometimes exaggerates characteristics of performers she is portraying, more so than I'd like. But she clearly loves these "great ladies," and if she occasionally smothers them with affection, there is no denying she puts on quite an entertaining and informative show. It's a needed show, too, since it is doubtful that most people today are well acquainted with the work of all of the "great ladies," and their heritage is certainly worth celebrating.

For myself, though, I prefer seeing Reaves-Phillips in a role that allows her to interpret the old-time songs in an appropriately zesty and soulful old-time style, without having to "be" any specific performer. It was a godsend for her, for example, when Vernel Bagneris wrote the shows *One Mo' Time* and *Further Mo'*. As Big Bertha, a fictitious contemporary of Ma Rainey and Bessie Smith (albeit not as successful as either of them), Reaves-Phillips

Sandra Reaves-Phillips (courtesy of Sandra Reaves-Phillips).

Sandra Reaves-Phillips digs into Bessie Smith's "Gimme a Pigfoot" in her one-woman show The Late, Great Ladies of Blues and Jazz *(courtesy of Sandra Reaves-Phillips).*

Sandra Reaves-Phillips salutes Ethel Waters in her one-woman show The Late, Great Ladies of Blues and Jazz *(courtesy of Sandra Reaves-Phillips).*

Sandra Reaves-Phillips, Bill Dillard, and Topsy Chapman in the musical production **Further Mo'** *at New York's Village Gate, 1990 (photo by Carol Rosegg/ Martha Swope Associates, courtesy of Mary Lugo).*

could bring to bear all that she had learned in preparing *The Late, Great Ladies*, expressing her talents lustily in songs from the 1920s and '30s, without having to imitate mannerisms of any particular artist. She established her persona quickly, even before singing, informing fellow characters in *Further Mo'*—with an aggressive, bustling pride that Bessie Smith could have related to—"I *don't* do no harmonies. I go straight for the jugular. It's melody line or bust." With a take-it-from-one-who-knows authority, she advised women in the audience, through song: "Don't Advertise Your Man." She got cute singing a duet with Bagneris, "Positively No." She confided her sorrows on "Trouble in Mind." And she really showed what she was made of in a number that was a high point of the show and an example of the kind of material she revels in: "One Hour Mama." Singing that she was a "One Hour Mama," she projected a bountiful, unconstrained sexuality. There was no suggestion of shame in her tone of voice, choice of words, or body language. She was blatantly erotic, yet jubilantly self-assured. A woman friend who accompanied me one of the times I caught the show surprised me by remarking afterwards that she had never seen a number like that, with a woman's sexual desires so clearly and matter-of-factly celebrated. She didn't quite know how to react; certainly she was struck by the bravura impact of Reaves-Phillips' performance, but was also maybe a bit embarrassed by the forthright display of female sexuality. This bright, professional woman—an Ivy League graduate—had never imagined that back in the 1920s or '30s such a number could have been possible. I was glad to see that—as performed by Reaves-Phillips—a number more than a half-century old (Victoria Spivey and Ida Cox, among others, had sung "One Hour Mama" in the 1930s)—could hit a nerve today. Reaves-Phillips was effectively reviving a type of song— and a way of selling it—that had once been a common part of the black blues world, and is unknown to most listeners today. (Those interested in learning how overtly sexual some of the 1920s and '30s blues records were might want to check out such Stash albums as *Copulatin' Blues* and *Them Dirty Blues*. Songs like "One Hour Mama" were the ancestors of 1950s R&B hits like "Sixty-Minute Man.") By opening a window onto the past,

Reaves-Phillips was providing a valuable service for today's audiences.

Easily the strongest singer in *Further Mo'*, Reaves-Phillips garnered excellent notices. For example, in his rave review of the show, John Simon, one of the most notoriously grumpy of all theater critics, wrote in *New York Magazine* (June 4, 1990), "Sandra Reaves-Phillips, a woman as generously large as her talent . . . belts out songs and softly snarls out conversational zingers with like imperturbability. You get two hours or so of undiluted pleasure and no bad aftertaste, as you so often do in our theater." Mark Gevisser gushed in *The Village Voice* (June 12, 1990), "You'll probably never see a blueswoman get closer to the truth than Sandra Reaves-Phillips doing 'Trouble in Mind' in *Further Mo'*." Well, as much as I enjoy Reaves-Phillips' gifts, I think Gevisser is going much too far. As good as Reaves-Phillips is—and she is a very good, theatrical blues singer—others sing classic blues with greater depth of feeling and sorrow than she does. Ruth Brown, for one, can make you feel her pain, when she wants to, in a way that I haven't heard Reaves-Phillips duplicate. It has something to do with overall temperament and life experiences. Reaves-Phillips, even as we talk, retains a certain sunniness. Brown, some 20 years her senior, has a streak of grim bitterness that periodically surfaces in conversation and gives greater guts to her blues singing; no matter what successes she may encounter today, Brown can't forget the indignities that she suffered from racists during one-nighters in the South in the early '50s, such as being denied the use of a restroom and told to take her "ass out to the woods like the other coons." And Jimmy Witherspoon, whose whole life is wrapped up in singing the blues, can convey a much deeper emotional involvement than Reaves-Phillips does. When he's inspired, he sings the blues in a way that leaves no doubt he's lived what he's singing about. (Bessie Smith, of course, was the incomparable master of that.) Reaves-Phillips doesn't project the same sort of rock-solid conviction.

Recently, she notes, she has begun "touring with two new shows, besides *The Late, Great Ladies*. In *Bold and Brassy Blues*, I do the next generation of blues: the music of B. B. King, Big Maybelle, Jimmy Reed, Muddy Waters—you name it, we're doing it, New Orleans music. And *Heart to Heart—My Rhythm-and-Blues True Confessions* is my doo-wop show. . . . So I get to do quite a bit of variety, alternating with these shows. We change the names of my bands for the newer shows, but we start with the same guys I use in *The Late, Great Ladies;* we just add some instruments. For *The Late, Great Ladies,* we usually carry piano, bass, drums, trumpet, and sax. For the *Bold and Brassy Blues,* we've added guitar, a harmonica player, and a trombone. For the doo-wop show, we add guitar, an extra keyboard, and four background singer-dancers."

Reaves-Phillips has become identified with the older tradition of jazz and blues, and with singing the older songs. I ask her if she feels comfortable with that or would she rather be doing something else?

"Well, I would rather be doing some contemporary music right now because that's kind of like where I started—in the rhythm and blues, the pop field. I would love to do that because people *do* kind of stick you in a category. And I just want to flit—I want to do it all," Reaves-Phillips says. "It might be very hard for somebody to conceive of my being in the pop field now, but I would love to be a recording artist again and get up there and cut up and carry on. Yeah. Tina Turner's doing it, you know." And that's a key difference between Reaves-Phillips and Carrie Smith. Smith would rather be singing the old songs she sings than any other kind of songs; indeed, she doesn't much care for a lot of contemporary pop music. Reaves-Phillips likes the old songs she sings (and for which she has found there is a market), but—all things being equal—she would rather be doing more contemporary songs, making a name for herself as a recording artist today rather than as an interpreter of songs made famous by Bessie Smith, Billie Holiday, and others.

Her album, *The Late, Great Ladies of Blues and Jazz,* will not be found in record stores, she notes. "It's only available where we go to do the show. I send it to radio stations when we're going to go to that city so at least they'll have some kind of copy. I'm looking for a record company. Years ago, in the '60s, I made records, but I don't know where they're distributed now or even if they are. I did *The Late, Great Ladies* album as a self-production.

I went to a couple of record companies but they were not interested at the time. Now that nostalgia *has* grown a bit, though—who knows? I might be able to get something in the future. I'd like to be with a company again because I haven't recorded for a company in maybe 15, 20 years or more. And I think every singer who was a singer wants to record again, once in a while."

1990

From Stockholm to New Orleans

It's doubtful that any of the first generation of New Orleans jazzmen could ever have imagined that the type of music they were creating would be as enduring and spread as far afield as it has. If one of the early jazz pioneers were told that by the 1990s a leading exponent of New Orleans jazz would be a clarinetist from Sweden, I'm sure he would have scoffed. But it's true. Orange Kellin, born near Stockholm on July 21, 1944, grew up to become the first foreign member of the Preservation Hall Jazz Band. Bands he has led or co-led, such as the New Orleans Joy Makers and New Orleans Blues Serenaders, have carried forward the New Orleans tradition on record dates, in clubs, and at festivals. Kellin is currently the musical director of the stage production *Further Mo'*, a sequel to the hit musical celebration of old-time jazz, blues, and vaudeville called *One Mo' Time*—for which he served, along with Swedish-born pianist Lars Edegran, his longtime collaborator, as co-musical director. He has been a key element in both shows, not just for his playing but also for having found and arranged many of the delightful—and often obscure—musical numbers performed in the shows.

We met one afternoon recently at New York's Village Gate—where *Further Mo'* has been playing to enthusiastic audiences since May 17, 1990—and discussed Kellin's career.

305

How did he first get interested in older forms of jazz?

"I suppose like anybody else, you know, through records and visiting musicians in Sweden, when I was a kid," Kellin recalls. "When I was a teenager and before, the so-called Dixieland jazz—for lack of a better word—was more or less the pop music of the day. You may have heard the British expression 'trad boom' as they called it in the '50s—that gave rise to Chris Barber and all those musicians. That's the era I came up in. I never knew that this form of music was something very exotic and soon to be forgotten and considered pretty archaic. They played lots on the radio then. Everybody had kid bands in the schools, like they had rock 'n' roll bands 10 years later trying to do Beatles stuff."

At first, all varieties of traditional-type jazz that he heard on the radio seemed about equally intriguing. "But as soon as I was able to distinguish, I had a strong preference for the American stuff; the British and the Swedish stuff didn't really interest me too much."

When he was 13 or 14, he was soaking up everything, from early New Orleans jazz to latter-day revivalists to big band swing. "I listened to anything. I first was interested in more like Benny Goodman, that kind of stuff. As long as you could tap your foot to it, that was OK with me—anything basically that swung."

How did he come to play the clarinet?

"Well, the sound always intrigued me. After I saw *The Benny Goodman Story*, that was it. I must have been 12 or 11 or something when the movie came out, but boy, that was the most fantastic sound I ever heard! The sound just stuck in my head."

As much as Kellin liked Benny Goodman's music, however, he ultimately found he responded most strongly to the New Orleans idiom.

"I heard on the radio these American Music records—you know, Bill Russell's stuff.[1] And there was a particular record with Albert Burbank and Wooden Joe Nicholas—'Shake It and Break It' [recorded for American Music in 1945]—I thought it

---

[1] Russell (1905–1992) was a New Orleans jazz historian/record producer/violinist.

was fantastic. I was about 15 or 16, and then I started delving deeper into that and thought everything else was totally irrelevant. I was hearing the real thing; everything else seemed like crap.

"I looked for other people that had the same interest and formed a little band—the Imperial Band—and off it went. We were all teenagers and we even made some records, and they sold. The first record—I was 17, I guess. These were 45s, EPs as they call them—two tunes on each side. George Buck has bought up the rights to them—he has them in his vaults—and we're all praying he's not going to issue them! [Kellin laughs.]

"Our band even did tours—we even toured Denmark, before I was 20—and we signed autographs and that kind of stuff. This was before the Beatles era. Lars Edegran and I—we're about the same age—were coleaders. I was in the northwest suburbs and he was in the southeast suburbs of Stockholm; it was at least a two-hour subway ride. So everybody used to meet in the middle, in the center of town."

Their band was popular, one of many trad bands on the scene. "A lot of high schools or colleges used to have dances. One school or another had a dance and there were always a couple of those bands playing, taking turns. And there were private parties, house parties, whatever, all through the '50s up until, basically, the Beatles struck in the '60s.

"Our band specialized in '40s vintage New Orleans jazz. Bill Russell was the big hero; anything he had recorded was the real thing as far as we were concerned. We listened to Bunk Johnson, George Lewis, all that stuff. George Lewis was very big in Europe in those days. I was not a rabid George Lewis fan, though. There were others that were as high or higher on my list. One player of that style, Albert Burbank, hit me more. And I also liked the so-called Creole school of clarinet players, like Albert Nicholas, Omer Simeon, and Jimmie Noone. I liked Edmond Hall very much, and saw him when came to Stockholm.

"I never really tried to play like anyone; I just listened to everything and then let it come. I didn't get one of the old clarinets, although most of my peers did that. They were copying one or another and going for all this romantic stuff, but it never appealed to me. Quite the contrary; it really rubbed me the wrong way, trying to redo something."

At that point, Kellin wasn't much interested in clarinetists working in more modern styles. Artie Shaw, for instance, seemed irrelevant to him then. "Later on, I became a big Artie Shaw fan. He's in the top 50 on my list now. But not in that early stage of the game. I was pretty much rigidly into the New Orleans scene," Kellin notes.

"I always wanted to be a musician professionally, but I never thought it was possible. Everybody told me that it was impossible. In 1966, I was going to Stockholm University and studying aimlessly. And then I went to New Orleans that year— a pilgrimage! I went there with my sleeping bag and a small suitcase and a clarinet. I never went back. I'd been there maybe a month and I was offered to make a record, on the Center Records label, which no longer exists. They put me in the union and there I was, a month after arrival, playing with these old Preservation Hall–type veterans: De De Pierce and Cié Frazier and Earl Humphrey . . . people like that. It was recorded at Preservation Hall. And that was a big deal for me. I was 22. And I started getting jobs and more recordings."

How did the New Orleans jazz veterans treat him?

"Well, it was a very different scene then than it is now. Things have developed in various directions—some not for the better, some certainly for the better. But in those days, people like myself were rare. So they took it as a big curiosity and they were really surprised that anybody from way over in Sweden— which could as well have been Mars, as far as people in New Orleans went—had heard of them and the music and knew all the tunes, so they were flattered in a sense. Now, 20-some years later, things have changed a lot because there have been hordes of musicians from near and far—I mean, from anywhere in the world—descending on New Orleans, and other resentments have developed since then. Well, there's the resentment, for one thing, from people that consider themselves more local than others, meaning that they've lived there longer, and there are all kinds of weird undercurrents going on. But when I first came, it was not like that at all. It was basically a hundred-percent-positive experience."

Kellin already knew the musicians' repertoires when he arrived. "I'd been buying all those records and keeping up with them. And there had been other people that had come back from visits, telling about it and showing slides and all that kind of stuff.

"In those days I didn't work at Preservation Hall as a regular thing. I was there as an occasional sub. So I was playing all kinds of places—dance halls and parades and parties. New Orleans had a superactive scene—much more so then than now. The music was still very much a social function. There were a lot of parties and parades and weddings, which still goes on, but now they may not necessarily use traditional jazz bands and New Orleans–type jazz bands like they did then. So there was a lot of work. There were still a few dance halls around. I played at Luthjen's Dance Hall on weekends for two or three years. That was an old dance hall that existed in more than one location since the '40s, if not earlier. That was an all-white audience. In those days they were still socially segregated. Segregation wasn't permitted by law—it wasn't institutionalized anymore—but people avoided each other."

In the '60s, he played with highly respected New Orleans veterans, including Punch Miller, Percy Humphrey, and Louis Barbarin. "Then in the '70s, I had a band called the New Orleans Joy Makers that included some of these players—the best musicians around then. Lou Barbarin's a fantastic drummer. He's still around. But he doesn't play anymore. I think he's born 1902, so he's way up there. A great drummer. And Percy Humphrey was in the band for a while. And Ernie Cagnolatti and Kid Thomas, and all the famous New Orleans trumpet players, for those who keep up with that scene.

"And they were relatively young then. Percy Humphrey and those guys were born in the early part of the century, so they were in the early '60s maybe. Somewhere in their 60s, which today would be considered pretty spry. Now they're in their 80s.

309

And now Dizzy Gillespie is 70—so they were a lot younger then than he is now. Cagnolatti, I guess, was born in 1910 or so, so he may not have been even barely 60. I played with him a lot. "In New Orleans there is a very perceptibly different culture. The music has a much bigger role; it's just part of living. You know, you read stories about how they had tough day jobs working on the docks or something, and then they will play a long job after it. But playing was considered relaxation; it wasn't considered work. It was like a way of communicating, both for musicians and for the audience—informal dancing and responding, that kind of thing."

He got to see the musicians off the job, too, at times. "I'd go to people's houses and their parties and things like that. One musician that quickly took me and some others under his wing was Johnny Wiggs, an older white trumpet player whose big idols were Bix Beiderbecke and King Oliver. And he could tell stories how he was standing in front of King Oliver's Band, just watching the shape of the fingers of Johnny Dodds, and that kind of stuff. And then to play dances at Tulane University, I guess in the teens. That was pretty amazing to hear, a first-person account of those days. I used to go crabbing with Johnny Wiggs, too."

He was getting a thorough grounding in New Orleans music, from musicians on and off the job, and other old-timers he'd meet. "The true expert in all that is really Bill Russell. He is really a walking encyclopedia. I mean, whatever you want to talk about, he knows more than you. He's incredibly knowledgeable and very, very unassuming."

How did Kellin's family back in Sweden feel about what he was doing?

"Well, they certainly wished I wasn't doing it," he says.

Would they really rather have had him studying aimlessly at the university?

"Yeah, I think so. I think my father is still saying all hope is not lost—that I'll still get a respectable career. [He laughs.]

"I didn't go back to Sweden even for a visit for the first six years. And that was on tour with this band, the New Orleans Joy Makers, with Percy Humphrey and Lou Nelson and Lou

Barbarin and so on. It was kind of an interesting homecoming. We went there for a couple of weeks and we were touring all over Europe at the time—a lot of mixed emotions. It was great coming home with a band like that—it caused quite a stir—but it was also the first time I realized that you can never go home again. Home is only something that exists in your memory. Everything had changed and people had moved on. At the same time, I didn't really feel at home in New Orleans; to some extent, I felt like a visitor. So, it made you feel like you're a permanent visitor anywhere. There's nowhere where you really belong or fit in 100%." Meanwhile, Kellin kept recording, for such labels as Center, GHB, Jazzology, and Vanguard in the '60s and '70s.

"I came to New York the first time in 1970 and I played the Newport festival then. It was a big event in my life because I got to meet Louis Armstrong and play behind him for a couple of tunes. That was for his 70th birthday. We had quite a few New Orleans musicians up—the Eureka Brass Band and Percy Humphrey's Band and the New Orleans Ragtime Orchestra. He did a few songs and they had the whole gang of us back there, backing up as we could. Just to meet Louis Armstrong was like meeting Jesus Christ or something. And Mahalia Jackson was there, too. And so it was very powerful. The next year both of them died." Kellin returned to New York in subsequent summers to play at the Newport Jazz Festival or its successors as it periodically changed names (today it's called the JVC Jazz Festival). He also played in Wallace Davenport's Band, which toured for George Wein quite a few years.

Pretty Baby, the 1977 motion picture that marked the screen debut of young Brooke Shields, also marked the screen debut—if it can be called that—of Orange Kellin.

"Jerry Wexler came to town and he wanted to have some very serious indigenous music for the film *Pretty Baby*, which was set back in the teens. So the New Orleans Ragtime Orchestra was in that show for that. I think the music was very well done. It's all old stuff, old rags and stuff," he says. "But it's done in a a serious way. Not the sort of happy, foot-stomping type of stuff; some of it was kind of heavy-duty stuff.

"Well, there's a scene where they carry Brooke Shields out

311

on the tray. And there's this band in the background and that was us. It's like that long [he snaps his fingers] that you see us. And they had made us up a little browner tint because we're supposed to be Creoles. Bill Russell in brownface was a sight to behold! It looked like we had a pretty good suntan. And we slicked the hair back and tinted it black."

Although the band was not seen for long, it was heard on the soundtrack throughout the movie. The music garnered favorable attention, including an Academy Award nomination for best soundtrack.

Kellin also played in another film around that period, "but it was pretty bad," he concedes. "It was called *French Quarter* and as it happened, they changed the soundtrack for some reason. We had made the soundtrack and then somebody else wound up playing in the movie. So you can just see us playing." Far more significant to his career was an idea for a show that writer/director/performer Vernel Bagneris casually mentioned to him one day.

No one, but no one, could have anticipated the enormous success of *One Mo' Time*. Ultimately it would run for several years in New York and a year and a half in London. There would be additional companies in the U.S. and abroad as well—enough to keep the show's creators involved with it, off and on, over a period of five years. The original cast album, with music arranged by co–musical directors Orange Kellin and Lars Edegran, would be nominated for a Grammy. Not only would the show cast public attention on Bagneris, Kellin, Edegran, and several singers, but also it would revive the career of a long-forgotten Jazz Age trumpet great: Jabbo Smith. And its surprising commercial success would help make possible the subsequent mounting of other shows and concerts dealing with old-time jazz and blues and black entertainment in general, including *Ain't Misbehavin'*, *Black on Broadway*, and *Black and Blue*.

Kellin recalls the show's humble beginnings. "I knew Vernel from New Orleans. He was in the theater and I was in music and there's only a million people in New Orleans so it's not that hard. He used to work around the corner from Preservation Hall

Orange Kellin (courtesy of Orange Kellin).

The top photo shows a late 1970s edition of the New Orleans Joy Makers: Kellin, Frog Joseph, Jabbo Smith, Lars Edegran, Thais Clark, Stanley Williams, and Frank Fields. The bottom photo shows a 1980s edition of the Ragtime Orchestra: Walter Payton, Kellin, Lionel Ferbos, Bill Russell, Lars Edegran, John Robicheaux, and Paul Crawford (courtesy of Lars Edegran).

Orange Kellin with Benny Goodman and Jabbo Smith (in the top photo), and Johnny Letman (in the bottom photo) (both courtesy of Orange Kellin).

Orange Kellin (courtesy of Orange Kellin).

and where I lived. And he came to me with this idea he had, which sounded interesting."

Bagneris wanted a show that would evoke the flavor of a night in 1926 at New Orleans' Lyric Theater, part of the T.O.B.A. circuit of vaudeville theaters for black audiences.[2] Bagneris' grandmother used to go to that theater, and as she told him of the artists she had seen there, he realized there was a world of old-time black entertainment he hadn't known about—a world that was left out of theater history books he'd read. He asked Kellin to suggest jazz, blues, and vaudeville numbers that might have been presented at such a theater in the 1920s.

Kellin found many, perhaps most, of the numbers that wound up going into the show. He knew old-time jazz, blues, and vaudeville music much better than Bagneris did. "Vernel liked the sounds of it and he used to go into Preservation Hall sometimes, but he had no particular knowledge of the old stuff. It was easy to come up with songs—a lot easier for *One Mo' Time* than for *Further Mo'*—because there were songs that were near and dear to your heart and were absolute musts, like 'Cake-Walkin' Babies' and 'Honky Tonk Town' and a few other ones. 'Kitchen Man' had to be done the right way. It had been done before by Linda Hopkins in her one-woman show [*Me and Bessie*], but way too fast—you couldn't catch the lyrics. 'You've Got the Right Key but the Wrong Keyhole' was a must, and various other ones. I played all kinds of records for Vernel. We had fun just picking the songs and trying them out."

Initially, Kellin was involved in the project only in his spare time. He stayed busy gigging as a sideman with various groups in New Orleans, as well as leading a band of his own. "All through the '70s I had the New Orleans Joy Makers. Lars Edegran was the piano player basically, not exactly coleader. Every year there was a new trumpet player. It started with Percy Humphrey on the trumpet. The next year it was Kid Thomas. Then it was Cagnolatti," he recalls. But he found himself devoting more and

---

[2]T.O.B.A. stood for Theater Owners' Booking Association. Black performers who toured on the circuit, working long hours for little pay, said the initials stood for "Tough on Black Actors" or "Tough on Black Asses."

more time to his work with Bagneris, who found singers capable of handling the old-time numbers with the proper spirit.

"Vernel knew Topsy Chapman and Thais Clark; they had been working a lot together in a gospel group [the Chapman Singers, founded by Chapman in 1972]. He just brought them to rehearsal and they came singing unbelievable—I never heard anything like that from somebody of that generation. At the time, they must have been around 30 or so—relatively young to somebody who had been used to working with people in their 60s. That was quite a revelation," Kellin recalls.

"The whole thing was just done as a project, having fun. There was no thought of a commercial success or anything like that. We were thinking of it as something to tour around universities or conventions and things like that, a halfway-educational kind of thing to showcase black culture—I mean, an aspect that had totally disappeared, that was totally ignored at the time. This was before *Ain't Misbehavin'* and nobody had really delved into it.

"All of the songs were old, but they were rearranged. We took pains not to sound like any particular version that you can associate with any particular record or particular singer. After we had gotten the concept of the show worked out a little bit, I needed help with the arrangements basically, and Lars knows a lot more about music than I do, so that's how we got him on *One Mo' Time*. He was co–musical director. We were splitting the duties. The New Orleans Blues Serenaders was the name of the band in the show. It still is, in *Further Mo'*, for that matter.

"We had our first little tryout—I think the show was an hour then—in New Orleans. And it was wildly received. It seemed this was really bigger than we had thought. So we went back to work on it and expanded it a little bit more and showed it again. We were ambulating around town, various locations.

"We had a five-piece band and four actors then. The fifth character—the theater owner—was a later addition. *One Mo' Time* kept evolving. It took quite a while before it settled into a regular, ongoing performing schedule at one theater. Bagneris wrote a slight script to give audiences a sense of what it was like to be a black performer on the T.O.B.A. circuit in the '20s. Because the show was being presented only occasionally at first, the participants spent most of their time on other projects.

Kellin notes, "When we started, that wasn't on a regular basis. I started really working hard on the show the end of '77 and then the first performance was January '78, and then there were sporadic performances all through '78 and most of '79, when I mostly did other things, you know, touring with the New Orleans Joy Makers and the New Orleans Ragtime Orchestra— those were the two bands I played with regularly.

"At the same time, I was also trying to resurrect Jabbo Smith.[3] He was out in Milwaukee doing nothing—working for Avis, parking cars. Paige Van Vorst of *The Mississippi Rag* told me that Jabbo was still around and even played on occasion; Paige had heard him and said he wasn't too bad. I called Jabbo up and asked if he wanted to come to New Orleans, just to practice up and have a few jobs maybe. So he said, 'Sure, no problem.'

"He came down with his trumpet. And he also played the valve trombone. He had a brown paper bag with like 25 mouthpieces and four sets of teeth and absolutely no embouchure. There was no way that his embouchure was going to get built up, so we started checking out the best combination of mouthpiece and teeth. I finally found what he liked the best and what sounded most secure and then decided that he was just going to go with that. And he actually got very good. He built up. He had other problems that made it difficult. He was an alcoholic, I guess.

"We started playing a few jobs around town and he used to come and see *One Mo' Time* whenever we showed it. He got the biggest kick and thought it was the greatest thing he'd ever seen. It was just like the old days, he thought. So Vernel thought he'd write him a part in the show. He wrote Jabbo a part as a janitor with a broom. Jabbo had a few lines, but he never could remem-

---

[3]Smith (1908–1991) was a dazzling trumpeter who in the late 1920s was considered by some to be a rival of Louis Armstrong, but then faded into obscurity.

ber his lines. We already had a trumpet player so we couldn't put Jabbo in the band; we didn't want to fire him. I think we used him on second trumpet for a while."

Kellin also used Smith for a period (around 1978–79, he recalls) as the trumpeter in the New Orleans Joy Makers. "Jabbo was a lot of good times. We did a couple of tours of Europe and made a record in Europe with a lot of his tunes on it, maybe a half a dozen. It never came out here—*Jabbo and the New Orleans Joy Makers.*"

Meanwhile, to the surprise of Kellin, Bagneris, and everyone else involved, *One Mo' Time* was gaining a momentum of its own. Kellin recalls, "It got a great big following; it became sort of an underground thing—wherever and whenever we did it, people used to turn out." Eventually, it began playing every Saturday at one theater, and finally, every night there.

"April '79 is when the D'Lugoff brothers [who later presented the show at the Village Gate in New York] came down to New Orleans, and there were all kinds of notables in the audience like Allen Ginsberg and other people. Somehow or another the word had traveled. And the audiences were wild. It was only a 200-seat theater so it was no big deal to pack it. And we had no idea if the show would translate to New York audiences.

"I remember, I had sent out tapes to various people before they had come down, like George Wein and Jerry Wexler—I sent it to him because we had worked with him when we did the soundtrack of *Pretty Baby* a couple of years before. So I knew him, and he said, 'Oh no, that music will never sell. Nobody will come for that.' He had no interest. And George Wein said, 'Well, I don't know, we could try using New York musicians, you know, and bring up a couple of the girls.' He said, 'No thank you.' And then finally Art D'Lugoff [who runs the Village Gate] says he'll take the whole package.

"The trumpet player didn't want to go to New York so that's how Jabbo came to be in the show. The show had gone on for a year and a half or so, sporadically, in New Orleans, before Jabbo was in it. Jabbo did one of his own compositions, 'Love, Love,' in the first act. I don't know what vintage that number was. It wasn't from the '70s; maybe he wrote it 20 years earlier or something. He had a trunkful of songs, some of them beautiful. And he did one in the second act called 'Yes, Yes, Yes.' That was his song, too. And Jabbo was a huge success, to everybody's surprise."

With his trumpeting and singing, Smith brought to the show a crucial element of authenticity. Whereas the other performers were re-creating, after a fashion, music of a bygone era, Smith was a charismatic survivor from that era.

Whitney Balliett wrote in *The New Yorker*: "He stops the show. It is a kind of singing that is almost gone. It resembles Louis Armstrong in the twenties and thirties, but it is looser, the voice is lighter and it pours. Before he returns to his seat, the trumpeter, almost as an after-thought, takes a short solo. It is a kind of trumpet playing that is almost gone, heavy-toned, daring but uncertain, melodic, lifting, querulous. The playing is as it should be, for the singer-trumpeter is none other than the legendary Jabbo Smith."

The show became a smash hit. Kellin says, "I remember *The New York Times* was the one and only that gave it a poor review, and everybody else, just about, gave it a great review. John Corry in *The Times* said it was offensive and things like that. I think he misunderstood a lot of the black colloquialisms and took them as being offensive to blacks—which they didn't themselves. He couldn't see the fun in it. I guess Vernel's idea was that he didn't want to hide anything that went on. If it went on, you know, he wanted to display it. Which is a lot more interesting, I think, than to rewrite history."

Some 10 months after the show opened in New York, a national touring company opened in Philadelphia. The show went on to become a hit everywhere, from Los Angeles, California, to Sydney, Australia. "At one point, we had five different companies going at the same time. With all the *One Mo' Time* companies, I picked the bands, which was an interesting proposition in various places. Of course the idea is, for theatrical purposes, that it's going to look like a black band. And it's not so easy in Australia and England. In London, we initially had all American musicians—excepting present company—but after six months, the union demands that everybody's replaced with the local subjects. So I wound up with a guitar player who was half Burmese, so he was kind of a little swarthy looking. And the drummer was half Welsh and a quarter Chinese and a quarter West Indian, so he looked kind of strange, too. And the clarinet player was from India—I mean of Indian extraction, actually, but he was born in Kenya. Stuff like that. That clarinet player, he's a guy who's playing in Keith Nichols' big band, so he was fairly well versed." Such restrictions on who can be hired, Kellin believes, are "not good for any artistic purposes. They may be good for, you know, a truck drivers' union or something, but not for performers." The music turned out all right, he notes, but he prefers being able to pick musicians without having to worry about their nationality.

Kellin's last performances in *One Mo' Time* were in a tour of Europe in 1984, which culminated in the show's being videotaped in a TV studio and broadcast on various European television stations. (The videotape, he feels, does not have the excitement that the stage production had.) But that was not the end of his involvement with the *spirit* of *One Mo' Time*. With some personnel changes, the New Orleans Blues Serenaders—the band he and Edegran had co-led in *One Mo' Time*—continued to perform from time to time, notably in engagements at the prominent New York cabaret Michael's Pub, with singers Chapman and Clark from the show's original cast. They did songs they had done in that show, as well as other old-time songs, many of which could have fit very nicely in that show and some of which are now being used in *Further Mo'*. They recorded albums for George Buck (such as *The New Orleans Blues Serenaders, Volumes One and Two*, GHB #221 and #222). Bagneris appeared with Kellin's band, doing some Jabbo Smith rarities—"beautiful stuff" says Kellin—in Europe as recently as 1989.

After *One Mo' Time* ran its course, Kellin lived at times in New Orleans, where he played with the Preservation Hall Jazz Band, and at other times in New York, where if nothing else was happening, he could always play at the Cajun, which offered traditional jazz and Cajun cooking seven nights a week. He periodically toured with the Preservation Hall Jazz Band, as well as with the Riverboat Ragtime Revue. Kellin found more work in New Orleans, and he liked the atmosphere. "New Orleans is a little more easygoing. However, after you spend a long time there, the walls start closing in on you and then it's nice to come to New York. In New York you really have to be involved in a project of some sort to make a living. For me, the kind of music that I'm involved in, it's pretty hard to free-lance." His music, he believes, could be more commercially viable if major record labels supported it. (And there is no question that he plays at least as well in his particular idiom as any number of better-known and better-paid straight-ahead jazz players do in theirs.)

Kellin was also involved, along with Bagneris, in some proposed musicals that never really got off the ground. One was based on the life of Bill "Bojangles" Robinson. Another was a revival of the songs and comedy of the old black vaudeville act "Butterbeans and Susie." Their material, although entertaining in small doses, didn't seem strong enough to hold today's audiences for an entire show. Some of the better material Kellin found for that show later wound up in *Further Mo'*.

When Bagneris first proposed to Kellin doing a sequel to *One Mo' Time*, his idea was to move the action 10 years ahead, to set it in 1936 instead of 1926. "Getting into the '30s there were a lot of good songs and it would have been a totally different thing. We bantered about it, Vernel and I, and Vernel finally decided no, he didn't like it; it was too depressing. It was hard to make something that was fun out of the '30s.

"So then his idea was to do more of the same. I thought that was kind of dangerous. I mean, hardly any sequels work. You're faced with the prospect of picking tunes that were competing with the memory of something that had gone before, not the actual thing. And the memory tends to be a lot larger than the actual thing was. I noticed myself, playing the old tapes back, some of the stuff was kind of rough-and-ready, when I had remembered its being pretty perfect, you know."

But Kellin agreed to work on the project. *Further Mo'* wound up being set in 1927, the action taking place the very last night of the Lyric Theater, which burned down that year. And again, Kellin has helped bring to light a number of long-forgotten songs of the 1920s. Kellin notes, "We tried a lot of tunes and rejected a lot of tunes and finally ended up with what we've got here. Vernel had certain tunes in mind that he wanted to do.

"We had done a couple of albums—an offshoot of *One Mo' Time*—with the Blues Serenaders. I was working with that as an independent unit for a while, with the five-piece band and the two singers. We did it at Michael's Pub a couple of times. We did a couple of albums and Vernel liked some of the songs there. 'My Man' was one that he wanted to do. 'Salty Dog' we had done with the Blues Serenaders in our regular little club act thing. I didn't think it was going to be so suitable but he insisted, and of course he has the final word and it turned out that he was right. Ones I particularly remember putting in this show were 'Alabamy Bound' and 'Hot Tamale Man.' 'Messing Around,' which I picked—it's now the opening number—I knew from the Johnny Dodds version. I was trying to pick songs that hadn't been done very much. 'Shake It and Break It,' 'Sweetie Dear,' 'Pretty Doll,' 'Trouble in Mind,' 'Sweet Man,' 'One Hour Mama' were some others that I picked. 'Boot It, Boy' was on an old tape somewhere that I found. 'Alabamy Bound'—I got the sheet music. 'Salty Dog,' 'Mississippi Mud,' and 'Wild Women' (one that Thais was doing) Vernel picked. 'I Had to Give Up Gym' came in a roundabout way. I think somebody had suggested to Topsy on one of her tours that it was a great song, and she said, 'Well, check this song out.' And we did. I think Vernel had a tape of it and it turned out to be a classic. 'Hot Time in the Old Town' was Vernel's idea—the finale in both shows.

"'Positively No,' 'Home Sweet Home,' and 'Come On In' are from the Butterbeans and Susie show we did a number of years ago, just two actors and a small band. That show was Vernel's idea. Butterbeans and Susie have been overlooked; I went out to Rutgers and dug up their old records.

"'Baby, Won't You Please Come Home' is from an album we did with the Blues Serenaders. 'Don't Advertise Your Man'— we were looking for a new song and we more or less agreed on that one. 'Funny Feathers' came because Vernel needed a chicken song, to go with a costume he would be wearing. I knew 'Funny Feathers' from the recording with Victoria Spivey and Louis Armstrong.

"We started working on *Further Mo'* in late '88. We had the first performance in April '89. We practically did *One Mo' Time* at first. We started working on the musical material and we did a few concert performances where we mixed in some *One Mo' Time* material and the new material just to get an audience. Then we had like a glorified workshop in New Orleans for four weeks. And that went very well. We had another glorified workshop in the fall of '89. *And Further Mo'* is what we were calling the show then. Then we went to the Crossroads Theater in New Brunswick. It was pretty good and it kept getting better."

Kellin found, to his surprise, that he was glad to be returning to the world of *One Mo' Time.* "After we hadn't done this now for a few years, it seemed like such a nice thing to do, because we have so many good memories about the old show. When we started this, it was like coming home again."

His career, he adds, is one he could never have imagined happening. He had no idea when he made that first visit to New Orleans that he was going to settle in the United States, much less make a career out of playing New Orleans–type jazz.

"What I had envisioned of my life was something totally different. I was much more academically oriented in those days and I thought I would study and, you know . . . but I guess deep down I always wanted to be a musician. And maybe there are forces at work that you aren't even aware of in your subconscious, that steer you in the right direction. Either that—" and he laughs, "or you're good at justifying it after it happens."

1990

325

VERNEL · BAGNERIS

One Mo' Time

Although Vernel Bagneris (whose French Creole name is pronounced Ver-NELL BAH-ner-reese) sings and dances to old-time songs with an infectious, offhand charm, I don't think of him primarily as a singer or as a dancer. And although he writes, directs, and sometimes even produces his shows, I can't say I think of him primarily as a writer, director, or producer, either. He is all of those things (and more) at once: a singer/dancer/actor/writer/director/producer with a particular interest in black culture of bygone times. Although he is not a jazz musician himself (but a decided jazz enthusiast), he has done more to further the dissemination of vintage jazz and blues songs than most jazz musicians. He is a revivalist who has sought to give us not just wonderful old music well worth reviving but also the *context* in which that music originated. In so doing, he is providing a rare and valuable service. Moreover, whatever project he is involved in is apt to have a touch of magic, so that audiences wind up *learning* from his shows—about the black experience in times past—without really feeling that someone is trying to teach them something; they are chiefly aware that they're being entertained, and in high style.

I've keenly admired Bagneris's talents since he launched his first show in New York, *One Mo' Time* (which he wrote, directed, and costarred in), in 1979. Described by critic John Simon of *New York* magazine as "part jazz and blues revue, part backstage comedy, and wholly *sui generis*," it ran for more than 1,300 performances at the Village Gate, becoming the fifth-longest-running show in off-Broadway history. In the course of its New York run, no less than seven other companies were created to present the play elsewhere, including a year-and-a-half run in London's West End. And additional productions have been periodically mounted since then. *One Mo' Time* gave people an opportunity to experience a night at a black theater in New Orleans in the 1920s—both the entertainment being served up with gusto to the public and the joys and anguishes being felt by the performers offstage. Its sequel, *Further Mo'*, presenting the same characters on the very final night of the theater's existence in 1927, offered a script that was more pointed and performers—most of whom were veterans of *One Mo' Time*—who were more seasoned and effective. That it did not achieve the same popularity as the first show, despite those advantages, is understandable; as fine as it was, it could not have the fresh impact of the original. If Bagneris gets the opportunity to make a movie version, he says, he will combine the best elements of both shows into one. By conventional standards, both shows were imperfect; their books seemed rather slight, and numbers popped up in a somewhat helter-skelter fashion as if the creator had reached, at times, into a grab-bag to determine what might come next (very much, I might add, in the tradition of shows from the period depicted). And yet, although more than a dozen years have passed since I first saw *One Mo' Time*, and more than two years have passed since I first saw *Further Mo'*, both of those shows glisten in my memory with a new-penny brightness while memories of plenty of bigger, slicker, seemingly more carefully constructed—and certainly far costlier—musical productions have grown faint. They touched me in a way that, for example, the more lavishly produced—but comparatively soulless *Eubie* (a Broadway revue celebrating the music of Eubie Blake, with an all-black cast)—did not. The first question I wanted to ask Bagneris was simple: why and how did he go about creating *One Mo' Time*?

"It was really because, when I studied theater, there was a

lack of any references to blacks in the theater until probably
Lorraine Hansberry," says Bagneris, making reference to the
playwright who won the New York Drama Critics' Circle Award
for *Raisin in the Sun* in 1959. And he knew there was a more
extensive history of black involvement, if only because his grandmother had told him of frequently enjoying shows in her youth at
the Lyric Theater, which had burned down in a fire of mysterious
origins in 1927. The Lyric, she had explained to him, was a
vaudeville theater in the French Quarter of New Orleans where
(using the parlance of the day) colored performers played for
colored audiences. It was one of a number of such theaters, all
of which were run by whites, that made up the T.O.B.A. circuit.
These theaters provided a major outlet for black singers, dancers,
comedians, and musicians—from rising talents to established
stars of the black entertainment world. Bagneris learned more
about that long-gone scene when he talked with a woman who
had been a ticket-taker at the Lyric back in the '20s, and who was
now living just around the corner from him in New Orleans. He
felt a further sense of connection to that era when he saw, on
Bourbon Street in the 1970s, Blanche Thomas, singing the sometimes bawdy vintage blues of Bessie Smith (who had been a
strong influence upon her) and others. Thomas' death in 1977—
her professional career dated back to the mid 1930s—heightened
a sense for him that an era of fascinating old-time jazz and blues
was fading into history, and gave him an impetus to try to
preserve some of the legacy, if he could. He started out on quite
a small scale.

"I originally put together *One Mo' Time* in 1978, as an audio/
visual show with which we could go around and tour colleges
and high schools," Bagneris recalls. He conceived of an hour-
long production, to give a feel for black music and performing
styles of the 1920s. "I thought hopefully we could also make a
little money on the side doing conventions, but basically the
show was for schools because I was on a grant from the N.E.A.;
I had my own experimental theater group in New Orleans then,
which did Ionesco and Beckett. But we used to go into the school
systems and I noticed a big lack—even when I was in college—
a lack of any black theater history, any written text, at that time.

You're making up for that now, Chip! But I decided that instead of trying to write a textbook—I'm not that kind of personality—that I would try to create an audiovisual presentation. So I asked some friends, Orange [Kellin] being one of the first, and Lars [Edegran], and Kuumba [Williams], and they were really excited about the idea of trying to re-create a period and then go off to colleges and show what it had been like. Students could watch our production and learn about a whole period—the 1920s—of black theater history." It was all done on a shoestring budget; Bagneris oversaw who was cast in the show, what they would wear, and so on, with Kellin providing invaluable input on the music. "Well, Orange and I look for different things in songs. I have to double-check with him, because I look for lyrics. I was an English literature major in college. So my whole thing is looking for words. What I do is, if I find a song that I feel is great for characters, in the words, I'll go to Orange and say, 'Does it have a melody line?' because I have no clue what's a good melody line and what's not. I just don't. And sometimes he'll say no and I'll have to skip it, you know. But I'm looking for lyrics; he's looking for music. And the combination seems to work great."

The script he wrote was designed, in its humor and its very pacing, to give a feeling for shows from the period *One Mo' Time* was depicting. "It's evocative. I noticed when I was doing plays that whatever period you're in—like if you're doing a Shakespeare play, the actors backstage will tend to talk in Shakespearean language: 'Why hast thou come in so late?' you know. [He laughs.] So I figure vaudevillians, they'd talk in that same sort of one-liner style they used on stage. The characters in *One Mo' Time* speak my lines, but those lines are formatted in a vaudeville one-liner style. I didn't get the lines themselves from old joke books, but I know the structure of those jokes and wrote in that vein. When I started *One Mo' Time*, I went around to some rare book stores and got some old vaudeville joke books, the sketches and stuff, to learn what that was. And once I got the flavor of what that was, then I was able to re-create through my own humor the same thing. I've got a lot of those old books now—which have coon jokes we couldn't really use today; audiences today wouldn't think those jokes were funny. But I know what the bounce is about, the timing and the meter and all that. And so you use that while you're writing and you do your own with it. Because it has to evoke the period and yet interest and amuse a 1990s audience. By using a '90s sensitivity on this '20s style, that's the magic—the audience thinks they're back there and they're glued into it, but the writing is no more 'period' in a sense than Neil Simon's. The structure is period but the actual statement is today." Bagneris worked extremely conscientiously on a project that he didn't anticipate would have much of a life beyond high school and college auditoriums. If schools accepted his show favorably, he hoped he could return to them with subsequent shows. "I thought that maybe later, after we'd finished with this project, I would do a '30s show, and then a '40s show, and a '50s show. But the popularity of *One Mo' Time* just sort of swung everything out of the waters.

"We decided to do *One Mo' Time*—*for one night only*—at a commercial theater, the Toulouse Theater in New Orleans, just to see what that would be like. And the audience just went wild! The guy running the theater asked could we come back the next week—and the next, and the next. It went from two shows a week, to four, to six, to a regular eight-shows-a-week run. And I had to put another company together when we left to come up to New York. *One Mo' Time* wound up running for six and a half years at that Toulouse Theater in New Orleans. And back during the time when we were running down there just on the weekends, Art D'Lugoff, who runs the Village Gate, and [producer] Jerry Wexler came and they enjoyed the show. And they asked me to come up to the Village Gate in New York. But I thought it was for, like, a week. I had no idea it was going to be an open-end run.

"The show was still running in New Orleans when we opened at the Village Gate. I had to train one [company] so we could leave. And that's what started the whole ball game, as far as I was concerned. But when I went out on the road with it—in the national touring company which I did with Sandra Reaves-Phillips, a year after we opened at the Gate—a lot of people would come up, like when we went to Houston or Philadelphia

or wherever, and they would say something like, 'Oh, my grandmother went to this.' And old people would come up and say,
'Yeah, I remember this—but you didn't have such and such a
thing,' and they would tell me about a certain number or a certain
routine that they remembered. And my own knowledge of the
period started getting better. I started digging after a while. As
an actor playing a character, Papa Du, who was supposed to be
a performer back then, I wanted to know more about the period.
So as an actor I started doing research—even more than I had
done as a writer to put together *One Mo' Time*. And I gathered
such a bulk of material that I thought, gosh, I'll do another show.
So I finally did it—*Further Mo'*—ten years later."

The enormous popularity of *One Mo' Time* with people of
different ages and races alike took many professionals along the
Rialto by surprise. It had been considered "common knowledge"
among people I knew in the theater community, the jazz world—
even in the record industry—that you could not get black audience support for shows dealing with black music of the 1920s
and '30s. Contemporary black audiences, the prevailing thinking
went, were not interested in the black past. I wondered if Bagneris wanted to comment on that.

"Yeah. I think one of the problems has been that most of
the black productions that have been presented have been put
together by white artistic staffs—particularly directors and writers. So, what happens is that there's a bent on it that I think a
lot of black audiences have been turned off to. In our case, we
really stuck for the authenticity. Like you were here on that
Sunday that the older people came, people who had been there
and seen it. And they're excited because they see it again and
they see it honestly and truthfully, rather than seeing 20 chorus
girls in what would have been really more like Palace Theater
costumes, doing routines that were not colored—in quotes—
routines. Generally, if a person had put together a vaudeville
show, even if it had a black cast, they would have put together
a white-styled vaudeville show, very similar to, let's say, *Honky
Tonk Nights*, which Michael Kidd put together two years ago.
That really was not a black show. It had black faces in it and
black talent in it, but it was really just patterned on the norm

331

white pattern. It looked like *Sugar Babies* with brown faces. And I was wondering, when I was sitting there, what was I learning that I didn't already know about black vaudeville? Nothing. So I think black people sour out sometimes on shows because the messages are so predigested for them. That's why you get excited about a Spike Lee film versus some ordinary film that just has a black actor in it. It's coming from a whole 'nother approach that means something a little deeper to you than just seeing Lou Gossett in *Legal Eagle* or something." He notes that although the audience composition for *One Mo' Time* and *Further Mo'* eventually stabilized at about 50% black, 50% white, initial audiences—before word-of-mouth got around and when potential ticket-buyers had only reviews to go by—were "like 99% white. It usually takes a while for black audiences to hear that the show isn't just the typical thing that they would get—and then they start coming and bringing their friends. But they start coming late.

"I'm not saying that people making shows like *Honky Tonk Nights* are racist or trying on purpose to sway people wrong; they're not. People just figure, 'Blacks were doing vaudeville, too, so they must have been doing it like we were doing it.' But they weren't. It was a whole 'nother texture. And I wouldn't know the texture if I hadn't done a little research by talking with my grandmother, who had been to the Lyric Theater, and she turned me on to the woman who worked behind the cash register, and then a woman who was one of the chorus girls. And you start getting a texture and you think, 'Well, this is not what the movies or Broadway have portrayed of that period.' This is something very different, something very solid. This is a performer getting off a third-class train with no hotel, opening up an old leather bag, shaking out a costume and getting it together for that evening and starring solo, like a Bessie Smith. Getting out there, very center-stage sort of thing, without the help of a lot of scenery and chorus girls and huge pit orchestras and all that. There was a need for more individuality.

"There was also a need to communicate things to audiences, things that were not coming to them through the norms like newspapers and radio, things like a new dance that had just broken out in Chicago or St. Louis, where the company had toured and had learned that dance. Well, they'd come down and teach that dance in a song: 'First you put your two knees close up tight, then you swing them to—' and you know, you're literally messing around. The song that opens the show teaches the audience a hot new dance that hasn't come here yet; we're going to show it to you. So people came to the theater to learn and to communicate. And little political things were put in. And it was—I'm using the word 'colored' because it was the period— colored people talking to colored people at these performances. You have to realize that in the South, they couldn't even get together in a little group. Anything more than three was illegal. So to all pile in, the only times that they could do that was at a church, where you had to watch what you said, or at a vaudeville hall, where you could go ahead and kind of say it but not. They did a lot of double entendre politically as well as sexually in the shows. You had to keep the level very broad because it serviced all colored people. My grandmother was only like 14, 15 when she was going to that theater. You know, so beginning with little ones all the way to older ones—they were all in the audience. And that's sort of the fun of this show—that we play to a 9-year-old as well as we play to an 80-year-old."

I comment that some in the audience will never before have seen anything so earthy—a good-natured celebration of sexuality—as some of the bawdy blues numbers included in *One Mo' Time* and *Further Mo'*. They, along with other songs in the show, are delivered in a performing style, exuberant and emotionally rich, that was once common in the black theater world but is totally new to many in the audience today.

"Yeah, I think it got whitewashed—I guess that's a good word. When film and television came in, you know, blacks were rather excluded from all of that. I mean, if you see the films of Oscar Micheaux [pioneering producer/director/writer, who made nearly 30 films with black casts, for black audiences, between 1919 and 1948]—the ones Micheaux put together when he had 'black Hollywood' in St. Louis, it's a very different texture from the normal Hollywood films. They were trying to do a specialized colored film. But I would bet that if someone hadn't found those old films in the archives, most people would assume that they were pretty much the same as the Hollywood films. And yet they weren't. So they're documented proof that we had a different need from whites as far as our entertainment was concerned.

"Whites would go to opera and ballet and theater and down the line. Back then, radio was really theirs, in a sense, and the newspapers certainly were. And you had to follow the main course, so when you stepped out, it was a very different feeling; it was a subset but it was very different. And later on in history what happened was that it just sort of died out."

Bagneris has been able to maintain artistic integrity in his shows by keeping costs so low he can retain control. In bigger-budgeted Broadway and Hollywood productions, he notes, the people putting up the money have the ultimate artistic control. "In New Orleans, I produced *One Mo' Time*—the sets, the costumes, the whole to-do was put together. It was a producer's dream. When we opened at the Village Gate, D'Lugoff used our same posters, the costumes. The set was rebuilt, but it was the same show we had done in New Orleans, brought up. I do things that are controllable in size so that I can maintain control and feel very happy and when the curtain's open that, yes, I made every statement that's up there. And through the communication with choreographer Pepsi Bethel, who does the staging, and with Orange Kellin working on the music, and, you know, just the staff and the performers—yes, we have all decided that this is what we want to present. There has been none of the thing you find on Broadway, with someone who has put up money declaring: 'This is my six million dollars, so throw this out and throw that in and fire the director!' Many Broadway shows have four and five different directors that come through, you know, whereas with this, it's a controllable and therefore truthful experience."

Besides performing in and writing his shows, Bagneris notes, "I cast them and coordinate all of the artistic designs, like the lighting and the costumes and the whole bit."

Does Bagneris, then, see himself mostly as a writer, a director, a singer-dancer, or what?

"I see myself as whatever opportunity comes up that I think

is going to be fun and challenging—that's what I do. So to limit myself—I just never have and I'm not comfortable at it. I don't put a label on myself. A writer? I met and talked to Tennessee Williams, James Baldwin—they both were fans of *One Mo' Time*. Like three or four times they came to see it in New Orleans. And *they're* writers. So I can't really call myself a writer. And I've worked with some very good directors. *They're* directors and I don't put myself on that same level. So I don't really label myself one thing. I'm just sort of doing what I feel is necessary for that project to survive. And sometimes you cross those lines, you know."

And yet even if he does not really think of himself as a dancer, I note I find him a marvelously engaging one—loose limbed, eccentric, nonchalant. He's also a much better dancer now—he's developed a real style—than when he first opened in *One Mo' Time*.

He laughs, as if to deflect the compliment, then says, "I guess it's from years of doing it, because I've never had a dance class in my life. When Pepsi Bethel first came to New Orleans to stage the show, I said, 'Well, maybe before I come to New York or when I'm in New York, I should take dance classes.' And he said, 'No, you've got this natural thing and let me just work with it. Don't let anybody really lay anything on you because you're going to get stiff. They'll teach you how to keep your legs straight and you've got a natural bent for jazz.'

"I draw upon Pepsi a lot. He's in his 70s. He was a Broadway dancer, in shows and clubs and stuff. And I've observed a few of his classes. He teaches at Clark Center. He has his own Pepsi Bethel Authentic Jazz Dance Ensemble. And he travels a lot, getting like these medicine shows in the South and all that. But he really is just a fountain of information. And he's clear. So he's a gold mine for me as a performer—as was Jabbo Smith, until he had a stroke and fogged out. Pepsi is glass clear—and he's been there."

Bagneris' dances have a wonderful period feel to them. Is he simply doing what Bethel dictates or sometimes creating his own routines?

"It's a 50-50 thing with us. He structures. I learn that. And

335

then I start breaking it down. But right now, for example, I know stuff like 'Spank the Baby' and 'Fall off the Log' [Bagneris pantomimes bits of dance routines]—after 10 years of working together, I actually know the names of things, so he can say, 'Well, do four Fall off the Logs for that part, and then you're free to kind of fool in there, but then right here you've got to Spank the Baby four times.' So he formats. Different size stages require different things. Performing at the Village Gate, you're dancing on a matchbox. So I mean everything is just in there—'underneath yourself' is what they call it. And then, by contrast, when you go to the Shubert Theater in Philadelphia, or wherever on the road, or to the West End in London, you've got a lot of stage to cover. So suddenly Pepsi has got to give me more and let it fly and all that. So it's different, and it's wider. But at this point, after working so long together and being so elastic about our work, he'll say, 'Now I want this to happen here and that to happen there'—and he'll give me that, and then he'll just say, 'Now put the middle in there for me.' And I do. And if what I do is out of the period in any sense, he'll stop me and say, 'No, we can't do that.'"

Perhaps the scene that took audiences most by surprise in *One Mo' Time* was the one in which Bagneris did a number in blackface makeup. By including the number, he was being authentic to the period. Although many members of today's audience are unaware of it, in the 1920s and earlier, blackface makeup was a common theatrical convention not only among white entertainers—from show-biz leaders such as Al Jolson and Eddie Cantor on down—but also among many black entertainers—from Ziegfeld Follies–star Bert Williams on down. (Those who would like to learn more about the history of blackface are directed to such books as *Blacking Up* by Robert C. Toll and *Blacks in Blackface* by Henry T. Sampson.) In *Further Mo'*, Bagneris once again included a number in which he wore blackface makeup; in fact, he wore the blackface makeup while dressed in a chicken outfit modeled after one Bert Williams wore in a celebrated routine; when the lights came up on Bagneris, in blackface and dressed improbably as a chicken, it was like seeing the most oft-reproduced photo of Williams brought to life. Considering how controversial blackface has become today, with many believing it to be demeaning to blacks, why did Bagneris opt to include the numbers?

"Well, it's about trying to defuse things," he responds. "It was a very innocent, sweet thing. All the kids in the audience, if you ask them—like Bill Dillard's grandson—if you ask them which number in *Further Mo'* did they like best, they all loved the chicken number. Because there's an innocence and a purity there. That shouldn't be a negative, stereotype, never-to-be-seen-again thing that we're going to be defiantly against—because blackface has been doped up to seem as if it were just an evil thing done by whites to absolutely make fun of and kick on black people. I don't know if it started that way; possibly there was a bit of that going on. But at this point, to look back at it and to see it done by blacks in a black vaudeville house—it's the innocence and the fun of it that I wanted to bring back. I wanted to open up the closet door and say, 'Hey, this is just a sheet hanging on a broom; this is not a ghost.' To defuse what had been a rather powerful smack: 'If you're not good, we'll bring the blackface out on you.' [He laughs.] So, it was all about finding peace; that's why I brought it back."

He has gained considerable respect, he adds, for what pioneering black entertainers who performed night after night in blackface (some willingly, some rather unwillingly) went through.

"Physically, it's very difficult on me as a performer, putting this black gunk on my face every night. Even the dresser's helping and she gets a little bit on her and it's like 'ughh,' you know, because it's a mess. And to put it on your skin and go through the little eruptions that'll happen because of it—personally, I'd rather cut it from the show, but it's a necessity to have it because it's the truth. It was there; it was harmless; it was part of it. And why skip it like it was something evil and harmful? So instead I just lay it there. And it's more casual," he says. "You know, it's amazing—it's maybe a minute and a half out of a two-hour show. But if you were to put that blackface scene out in your publicity pictures or in a TV commercial, it would cause more hell, just for that moment, because people are conditioned to think that it's something that's absolutely horrible rather than something that came out of a certain innocence and fun. Zany—that's what it is."

Although the chicken costume he wore was modeled upon one Bert Williams wore, Bagneris notes he did not sing the actual number that Williams sang while wearing that costume, selecting instead a stronger number that was also from approximately the period depicted ("Funny Feathers," originally recorded in 1929 by black blues singer Victoria Spivey with backing by Louis Armstrong and others). He explains: "The number Williams originally did would be dry today. So instead we picked out something that is comfortable in that chicken outfit and yet is fun for the audience of today. Because I don't want to be a moldy fig about all of this. That's been the big feat."

Bagneris did not mind if he raised some eyebrows by including the blackface scenes. If people wanted to take those numbers purely as entertainment, of course they could. But if seeing Bagneris in blackface—and lines in the play indicated his character did not *like* having to wear it—also pushed emotional buttons for some viewers, prompting some reflection about racial stereotyping, that was all right, too. Bagneris didn't see the past as something to be buried; he always preferred exposing it to the light. In fact, as patrons entered the Village Gate, they saw on the walls photos of early black vaudeville performers, some of whom were in blackface. He wanted that history to be seen, not buried, and those pioneering performers who struggled in hard times to be respected.

Although most who saw Bagneris' shows were enthusiastic, he did receive criticisms from some people who thought that his presenting scenes in blackface (as well as his use of the words "mo'" rather than "more," and "colored" rather than "black") constituted an inappropriate revival of stereotypes. But he felt that enough time had passed to look at the past honestly, without rancor.

"It's like *Amos 'n' Andy*, you know. At the time when the NAACP fought to keep it off television, it was the only black show on television. So they said if that's the only blacks you're going to present on TV, black vaudevillians doing this—because they *were* all vaudevillians in the cast of TV's *Amos 'n' Andy*—if you're *only* going to present that to represent blacks, then take it off. But now, with everybody everywhere—blacks in all sorts of roles—what would be the big deal about doing a show like *Amos 'n' Andy*? I mean, that was more than 25 years ago but people still think, 'We're not going to let *Amos 'n' Andy* back on television!' You know, it's an empty argument at this point."

He can understand why the NAACP fought to get the show bounced from the air in the early 1950s. If its exaggeratedly comic, word-mangling characters were the only images of blacks on TV, they did tend to reinforce stereotypes—even if the humor presented was actually very much like that one could have found black comedians offering in black theaters. From its earliest days in radio, *Amos 'n' Andy* always had many black, as well as white, fans, who enjoyed the humor without feeling the characters represented all blacks. With so many different black images in the media today, Bagneris sees no harm in the broad comedy and all-too-human foibles of *Amos 'n' Andy*. He believes people could enjoy their comedy today without having to feel they were intended to represent all blacks. In fact, Bagneris hopes to direct and/or costar in a proposed Broadway musical comedy version of *Amos 'n' Andy*, to be called *Fresh Air Taxi*, if sufficient backing to mount the show properly can be obtained. Stephen M. Silverman, former chief entertainment writer for *The New York Post* and the author of several film biographies, wrote the original script (using vintage *Amos 'n' Andy* radio scripts as source material) and recently brought in Bagneris as a cowriter. The score is by legendary jazz trumpeter Jabbo Smith, who made a comeback in Bagneris' *One Mo' Time*—a mix of vintage Smith numbers dating back to the 1920s and more recent ones, including instrumentals to which new words have been added. Mounting of the show has repeatedly been delayed, first in a drawn-out legal effort by CBS to block the show. CBS argued copyright infringement, contending that it owned all rights, although a judge eventually determined that all pre-1948 *Amos 'n' Andy* radio scripts had fallen into public domain. The real issue seemed to be that CBS, remembering past NAACP objections to *Amos 'n' Andy*, did not want *Amos 'n' Andy* revived at all, lest it stir up old charges of racial insensitivity. Finding sufficient financing for the show has likewise been hampered by the fears of potential backers that the show—even with a black cast, a black director/coauthor, and a black composer—might be perceived as anti-black. Yet Bagneris is confident he could help create a show that everyone could enjoy, without reviving negative stereotypes. He'd like to reclaim those characters. "There's no news yet on whether the show will be produced on Broadway. We'll see what happens. I'm hoping for it. Stephen wrote a damned good script. And Jabbo's music—*really!* Stephen once contacted Cleavon Little about the possibility of appearing in it and he was extremely interested. And Ruth Brown said, 'Oh, yes, that's one of my favorites.' If we get it together, the show would be great. It's just getting the money together, because everybody says, 'Oh, we don't want to offend black people.' *The money* says that.

"That's why I do small shows—because they're *my* business. I've never really gone for doing a big thing, unless I knew it was going to be well controlled. That's why I've never directed a Broadway musical yet or tried to step out in any large way. I find it more peaceful for me in my life to have controllable elements. Like *Staggerlee* was pretty small. And *One Mo' Time* and *Further Mo'* were small.

"I know the other side from an actor's point of view, having performed in the film *Pennies from Heaven*, which cost like $25 million. There you're hired as an actor; you just do what you do. But when it's something I wrote or something I want to direct, then it's my turn to plan. I accept that I have not reached a point career-wise where somebody is just going to write out a check for $4 million for me. I've reached up to a budget of a million so far. You go a step at a time." But simply having loads of money to spend does not necessarily ensure a better production, he points out. "My theater experience is through Jerzy Grotowski—this sort of avant-garde Polish director—that is always aiming towards a poorer theater, to strip away, to let creativity come forth, not only from the artists and the director but also from the audience. Let them use their imagination a little bit. So I don't know if I want the bigger budget yet. I'm really enjoying having to keep a cap on it."

Has Bagneris always wanted to be involved in the theater, I inquire? He takes the time to give that a proper answer. Born July 31, 1949, he does not recall having any interest in performing until in the seventh grade he had to sell chocolate bars in a school fund-raising project. "You see, I sold the most chocolate bars in the whole school and won the grand prize, a tape recorder. And it was the damnedest thing I'd ever seen! Nobody had a tape recorder in that neighborhood at that time. I couldn't believe my voice was coming back, you know. So I made these concert tapes. I remember singing into it and then rubbing the microphone on the grass to make the sound of applause. I'd sing and there'd be this applause, and I'd say, 'Oh, thank you so much.' And that was my first little try at performing. For several years, that tape recorder fascinated me to no end."

His interest in music evolved naturally. Very much into the traditions of New Orleans, as a youth Bagneris strutted and danced to the music of the brass bands at every possible opportunity: weddings, funerals—wherever there was a street parade. Music played an important role in the rich cultural heritage of the city, and he absorbed it gladly. Of course, there was a downside to life in New Orleans; when Bagneris was born, segregation was still very much the order of the day. He recalls, for example, having to ride in the back of the bus as a little boy. But he never bought into the bigots' idea that he was some kind of second-class citizen. His parents instilled in him a fine sense of self-worth. "My father and mother met when they were 17 and 15, and got married at 19 and 17, and they were lovebirds straight through. I came from a very, very loving family. There was never any talk of divorce or 'I hate your guts. . . .' So my brother and my two sisters and I are very close. We enjoy being together, and they're really proud of what I'm doing. My sister, next year, will be a medical doctor. My other sister is an assistant principal at a school in New Orleans. My brother is a politician in New Orleans. Everybody loves to get together for Christmas and Thanksgiving and Mardi Gras and jazz festival. There's about 12 to 14 legit occasions in New Orleans to get together and we tend not to miss them."

Bagneris says that his interest in the theater really emerged while he was studying English literature at Xavier University. "Part of the course was reading Shakespeare, and I started getting into drama from a literary point of view. Then they actually did a Shakespeare play and a girlfriend of mine wanted to audition but was scared to go by herself and asked me to go with her. At the auditions the guy said, 'Well, I don't really need any girls because we're packed; I need men.' So I did a role, and it was a lot of fun. The next semester I did another role, and then I decided to double-major in drama and English literature. And I started writing my own pieces that I would present for the school, sort of in that '70s black-awareness-hippy-and-all-that state. I got independent courses—three hours for directing and three for lighting and three for playwriting. I would write and direct it and present it at the school. I got to say a lot and the students were really interested; they'd really come. It cost them like a dollar or something to get in. And I thought, *This is great. I'm getting this college credit and they're letting me keep the box office.* Because of that, I was able to move away from my parents into my own apartment. I thought, *This is the life.* I never really stopped since."

It was while in Europe, where he headed for further study in theater after graduation from college, that his enthusiasm for older forms of jazz grew. He went to jazz festivals in Norway, Sweden, Switzerland, and Italy, seeing more American jazz performers in Europe than he had in New Orleans. And they seemed to be treated royally; they were truly appreciated. He periodically returned to New Orleans, taking a nondemanding job until he could finance another trip abroad, where he could study with such avant-garde theater notables as Grotowski and Artaud. Back in New Orleans, he formed the New Experience Players in New Orleans, an experimental, multiracial theater company, where he directed and/or performed *A Day in the Death of Joe Egg, Endgame, The Lesson, Tiny Alice, Who's Afraid of Virginia Woolf? The Laundry,* and *Passacaglia.*

"*One Mo' Time* just happened to be something that exploded. But I think if I hadn't done that, I'd still be in New Orleans, sort of writing something and trying to direct it. Find some actors and rent a theater and see what happens," Bagneris notes. That show won him widespread praise in theatrical circles. Bagneris has been inducted into the Hall of Fame of the Southwest Theatre Conference and given a formal letter of appreciation by the governor of Louisiana. But none of the praise he received meant more to him than the expressions of pride and approval he received from his grandmother, now in her 80s, who had attended the Lyric Theater in her youth.

After extensive national and international touring with *One Mo' Time*, Bagneris (in collaboration with musician Allen Toussaint) created and directed the hit off-Broadway musical fable *Staggerlee*; a film version is now in preparation. He would also like to make a film combining the best of *One Mo' Time* and *Further Mo'*. "The story continues from *One Mo' Time* to *Further Mo'*; I'd like to slap them into one big story for a movie version. There was a movie years ago that I liked a lot called *The Night They Raided Minsky's*. My movie would be like sort of *The Night They Burned Down the Lyric Theater*. You'd get music from both shows. And I'd have my three different story lines: Bertha's in love with Papa Du in the first one, and the theater owners want to burn down the theater for the insurance money, and Thelma wants to take over her own company."

Since the success of *One Mo' Time*, many projects have been offered to Bagneris. "Around 1981, I did an eight-week workshop as a director for a show Charles Strouse and Sammy Cahn were working on called *Bojangles* [based on the famed black tap dancer/singer/actor of the 1920s, '30s, and early '40s, Bill "Bojangles" Robinson]. And Walt Disney Productions called me to see if I'd like to write a script for a Creole folk tale they hope to animate. This guy had seen *One Mo' Time* and *Further Mo'*, and he asked me, 'Would you be interested in writing this screenplay?' I'm thinking about it." Bagneris has also been hired to portray Bert Williams in a play, *American Vaudeville*.

And he has plenty of projects of his own he is interested in developing. "I've written an hour-long teleplay on Jelly Roll Morton, which I'd like to see produced. It would have Jelly Roll's music, of course. And I would love to play Jelly Roll Morton. I mean, he's everything that I know, as far as New Orleans, Creole, and all that stuff. People have told me I look like him. And he's long been one of my big favorites musically. For my 30th birthday in 1979, Morten Gunnar Larsen, who was the pianist for the national company of *One Mo' Time*, gave me the two volumes I was missing of the eight-volume set of Jelly Roll Morton's Library of Congress recordings. And sometimes Morten and I would get together after the show—there would be a party or something—and we would do a couple of Jelly's numbers. He'd play and I'd sing. Morten loves Jelly's music. There are three pianists in the world that I know of who *are* Jelly Roll Morton's fingers today: Bob Greene, Butch Thompson, and Morten Larsen.

"I first worked on a theater piece about Jelly Roll Morton six years ago. I pretty much just did the Library of Congress Jelly Roll Morton interview tapes, on stage. Art D'Lugoff gave me the upstairs room at the Village Gate for free. He said, 'Just go upstairs and see what you can do.' For six weeks it was like a workshop on my part. I wanted to see what I could come up with. *Dull, dry, boring!*"

Now Bagneris goes into the voice he uses for his portrayal of Morton, uttering lines taken from Morton's 1938 Library of Congress interviews: "'As far as I can understand, my folks was in the city of New Orleans long before the Louisiana Purchase . . . bla bla bla bla bla.' I did that dry, moldy fig stuff," Bagneris says. The show, originally titled *Mr. Jelly Lord* (and known in its most recent incarnation as *Jelly Roll Morton: A Me-Morial*), may have needed some reworking but it was *hardly* as dull, dry, and boring as the self-deprecating Bagneris suggests.

In the original production, Bagneris talked, sang, and danced as Morton while Terry Waldo provided the piano playing. Bagneris was true to the spirit of Morton both as a man and as a musician. Moving about eccentrically but with a sly sense of style as he sang "Jelly Roll Blues," Bagneris projected an irresistible self-confidence. Moments later, explaining how he believed his bad luck was due to someone's having put a voodoo spell on him, he captured the pathos that was no less a part of Morton's makeup. Bagneris was a natural for the role of Morton. And his workshop production helped to convince others that there was theatrical potential in Morton's life.

344

Vernel Bagneris, alone (top photo, courtesy of Terry Lilly) and with his co-stars in the musical production Further Mo'*: Sandra Reaves-Phillips, Frozine Thomas, and Topsy Chapman (bottom photo, by Carol Rosegg/Martha Swope Associates, courtesy of Mary Lugo).*

Above, and on facing page: Vernel Bagneris as Jelly Roll Morton, at Michael's Pub in New York City, 1992 (photos by Chip Deffaa).

Vernel Bagneris and pianist Morten Gunnar Larsen (photo by Chip Deffaa).

Producers Margo Lion and Pamela Koslow asked Bagneris if he would be interested in writing a Broadway show based on the life of Jelly Roll Morton, to serve as a vehicle for Koslow's husband, acclaimed tap dancer Gregory Hines. Bagneris met with Lion and Koslow but their concepts did not mesh. For one thing, they wanted a script that would enable Hines to express various emotions through tap dancing, and Bagneris did not see how he could do that. The producers subsequently hired George C. Wolfe to write and direct the show, which, titled *Jelly's Last Jam* and starring Hines as a rather nasty, bigoted Morton, became the smash hit musical of 1992. It was a striking theatrical production but took extreme liberties with Morton's life and music. Denying the uniqueness of Morton's genius, the script depicted Morton—the first important composer in jazz—as doing little more than setting down the music he heard all about him in New Orleans. (Morton's strikingly complex and cohesive music, of course, never sounded like "typical" New Orleans music.) Adding insult to injury, the show then offered music that had been so freely "adapted" in conventional Broadway fashion by arranger/composer Luther Henderson as to bear, for the most part, little resemblance to anything Morton had actually created.

Bagneris, meanwhile, had not forgotten about Morton. Although he was not able to get his teleplay produced, in 1991 he presented his two-man tribute to Morton (with Morten Gunnar Larsen at the piano) at the Oslo, Norway, Jazz Festival. The following year, he and Larsen returned to Oslo to perform the show, in a revised form, at Ridhuset, part of the National Theater of Norway. The show then opened, to glowing reviews, at Michael's Pub in New York, in the fall of 1992. And Bagneris continued improving it after its opening.

Catching the show during the first week of its five-month run, I found it beguiling, if all too brief at 50 minutes in length. Returning several weeks later, after Bagneris had fleshed it out with a couple of other songs and bits of dialogue, I found it as entertaining a show as any I'd seen at Michael's Pub in years. Bagneris' *Jelly Roll Morton: A Me-Morial* serves as a welcome—and needed—corrective to the historical and musical misrepresentations of *Jelly's Last Jam*. Bagneris and Larsen ought to be able to tour with this show. It would certainly be an asset to any jazz festival or party. It would also be a natural for television or home video.

It's a treat to hear Bagneris (as Morton) trying to impress a woman with the splendor of his many different suits: "Listen, baby, I can change like this every day for a month and never get my regular wardrobe half used up. I'm the suit man from suit land." Those two authentic lines of dialogue alone have more life and color than any lines in *Jelly's Last Jam*. And Bagneris effectively uses Morton's words to both tell Morton's life story and set up his musical numbers. After relating how he used to impress the women with his many suits, for example, Bagneris explains that he would wind up gambling with their men friends, experience great "luck," take his winnings and move on. Some woman, dejected over his departure, would inevitably plead as he left town—and at this point in the show, Bagneris begins singing a plaintive Morton song that fits the context perfectly— "Don't You Leave Me Here," to which he would reply (singing a snatch of another Morton song) that he was "Alabama Bound." Beautiful. Not all songs are introduced quite so adroitly—and Bagneris will no doubt continue refining the show—but there is always a reason for Bagneris' moving from speech to song, and we're carried along with the forward momentum of the show. Larsen interprets Morton's music with great playfulness, as well as accuracy. And Bagneris' stylized, at times sensuous, moves to the music fascinate. The producers of *Jelly's Last Jam* doubted that Morton's own music could hold the interest of contemporary audiences. Bagneris proves them wrong.

Am I right in inferring, I finally ask Bagneris, that in working on such varied projects as *One Mo' Time*, *Further Mo'*, and *Staggerlee*, and in portraying such artists as Bill "Bojangles" Robinson, Bert Williams, and Jelly Roll Morton, his common goal is to try to bring back to light some black culture that's been forgotten?

"Yes," Bagneris acknowledges. "And bring it back in the '90s perspective, in such a way that a black and white audience with no racial tension, with brotherhood, can sit down and watch it and everybody would be comfortable. Remember in the '60s how you used to go to a black play and you'd know you weren't supposed to be there? As a white person, you knew they were talking about you bad and you weren't really supposed to be there. Well for my stuff, what I'm saying is that I'm bringing peace to something. *Everybody* should be there because it's about history and it's about a modern perspective on what that was."

1990, 1992

Appendix:
"Revivalists" of Another Sort—
Restorers of Vintage Recordings

One thing most of the traditionalists and revivalists profiled in this book have in common is that they came to know the jazz tradition via reissues of older recordings. The availability of good-quality reissues is essential if new fans—and new players—of older styles of jazz are to emerge. Because the engineers who work on reissues of vintage recordings play such a crucial—and often overlooked—role in preserving our jazz heritage, I thought it would be appropriate to get the observations of a few respected members of this field.

"So many of the CDs they're making from old jazz recordings are disappointing. Some are devastating. The people making these CDs often aren't working hard enough to get all of the sound which is on the original discs out in proper fashion. And that is really tough—because once they put it out in CD form, it isn't likely that they're going to do it again and do it better," declares Jack Towers. And his opinions merit serious consideration. At 77, he is the dean among restorers of vintage recordings in the United States—an engineer to whom some savvy reissue producers turn when they place a higher priority on getting the sound quality just right than on getting a job done as fast as possible. He has remastered important projects ranging from Charlie Parker's Savoy recordings to the Smithsonian Institution's acclaimed History of Jazz series.

I've also spoken to others now making names for themselves in the record restoration field who use approaches different from Towers', including Harry Hirsch, 63; Robert Parker, 58; and Steven Lasker, 38. Each of these conscientious professionals has valuable input to share regarding the preservation of our recorded jazz heritage. Towers, as elder statesman of the field, gets the floor first.

"If I have to transfer a shellac 78 or an acetate, I first clean the record with a mild detergent and a little brush made out of goat hair I got from John R. T. Davies in England," Towers notes. Cleaning vintage 78s of all dust and dirt before making taped copies may sound like an obvious first step, but it is one that Towers knows unfortunately is *not* always taken. "Then I find a stylus that gives it the best play. I don't just use one stylus. I have various size styli for 78s—small ones that go towards the bottom of the groove and bigger ones that ride up towards the top. If you have a lot of them, you can find a place on the groove wall that plays the best. And you start with that." Among technical tools at Towers' disposal in his workshop at his Maryland home are a Packburn unit for avoiding ticks that may be only on one side of a groove wall, a Berwyn transient noise eliminator to take out additional ticks and pops, and a notch filter known as a "little dipper" to diminish high-frequency hiss.

"Then, when ticks remain after using some of the technical equipment that gets rid of them, I use a device—invented by John R. T. Davies, who's really a genius in this field; we've all learned so much from him—with which I can locate the tick and mark it precisely. Then I very carefully etch the oxide away from the base of the tape, just where the tick is. I etch just enough to bring the tick down so you don't notice it anymore."

It is this painstaking handwork—along with a superb set of ears and knowledge of how the music *should* sound—that has earned Towers his reputation. He notes, "If I've got noisy source material to work with, locating and etching away ticks by hand for just one number might take me all morning or all day."

Computerized noise-reduction systems such as NoNoise and CEDAR, now commonly used by major labels, can certainly yield quicker results—but not as consistently pleasing ones, in Towers' judgment. Technicians are coming up with some wonderful computer equipment, he believes, but he is concerned that people using such systems often "try to do too much with them and they affect the music. They fight to get every trace of surface hiss away. And in my case, I do leave some in rather than do away with part of the music. The reissue CDs really vary. In some cases, they've just taken out the ticks nicely and the music sounds great. But oftentimes it's gone way downhill."

What does he think of Australia's renowned engineer, Robert Parker?

"He does marvelous transfers, but—you know, I'm from the old school—I'm bothered by the artificial stereo and the reverberation that he adds. However, he may make the music that he's working with—which includes some of the oldest recorded music—appetizing enough so that some younger folks will listen to it who otherwise wouldn't." And that, indeed, is why I sought out Parker. For while I believe it is vital to preserve archival copies of vintage recordings with no artificial stereo effects imposed, if his alternative versions can entice additional younger listeners into the jazz fold, I'm for them.

Parker's "Jazz Classics in Digital Stereo" CDs were introduced in Australia in 1984 by ABC Music; they are now being distributed in the United States and Canada by DRG Records of New York.

Why does Parker opt for a stereo effect?

"I'm trying to give a better feeling for what it would have been like to have been in the studio when the recordings were made. I put the sound into a stereo sound field to make it more easy for the listener to hear the detail in the performance—the delineation of the instruments or sections of instruments. If you can present the brain a sense of stereo which is in any way reasonably convincing, it will then allow you to concentrate on facets within that sound stage in the way that you would if you were at a live performance, much more easily than if you're trying to concentrate on a single watch of sound."

Parker's stereo effects, while controversial, are markedly superior to the simulated stereo effects that were widely tried (and subsequently abandoned) a generation ago. "There were various engineering flaws in early simulated stereo systems, which didn't work very well. They'd have a phase difference between the two speakers, which gives an effect of spread but unfortunately also creates confusion in the mind."

One reason Parker's reissues have the laudable impact and vibrant presence they do is that, as he notes: "All of the albums I've done are recorded directly from disc to digital, without going through analog tape at all. I wanted to preserve particularly the dynamics of the original recordings. The sound gets more soggy sounding if it goes onto analog tape. Also you're adding a little bit more hiss to an already hissy recording.

"It takes a tremendous amount of time and patience to extract the maximum information from the early records. Quite a lot of the problems that you hear in conventional reissues stem from the fact that they are done in a great hurry. Most reissues do not give a true indication of the vitality of the original performance. To get that last *nth* degree requires a lot of time and patience. You can't just feed sounds into a computer and expect to come up with the most convincing representation of the original performance. You have to listen to it and make all sorts of fine adjustments.

"If you want to get rid of surface noise, hiss noise, you've got to accentuate certain frequencies, which you find by experimentation, to compensate for the deadening effect of the noise reduction. I hate with an intense hate the leaden deadness of 78 records that have had all of the surface removed by computer systems like NoNoise and CEDAR. It totally destroys the enjoyment of the performance. I can't listen to the stuff. I don't use NoNoise or CEDAR. I've done long experiments with them. Both systems have problems when you use them for automatic click removal. Unfortunately, both systems are also capable of adding distortions or problems to the sound. I've made up a demonstration CD—before-and-after examples of CEDAR and NoNoise— which conclusively proves to my satisfaction that both systems are fatally flawed. And I've also got graphs that I've made from my computer's looking at it. You can see the distortions on the waveform, which in the case of NoNoise are horrendous. I think this is a very important problem. We are in the position now where we're getting a one-off chance at what's left of the recording archives. And it's being wrecked for us, quite frankly, for future generations."

Harry Hirsch, Vice President of Technical Services at Digital House, comments, "Most archivists look upon the addition of arificial stereo or reverb to vintage recordings as being in bad taste. Recently I transferred 80 V-disc 78s, recorded in the 1940s, for Warner Brothers—for a set being direct-marketed by Time-Life Music called *V-Disc, the Songs That Went to War*. I told Warner Brothers that if they wanted reverb or artificial stereo, to get somebody else! What's the sense of cleaning the discs up and then putting dirt on them?"

His chief advice for other sound engineers is: "Don't look at dials! Trust your ears." While he will examine grooves of 78s microscopically to get an idea of what size stylus should play best, he will experiment with slightly larger or smaller styli to determine which actually yields the best sound. He notes that prior to 1954, when the RIAA curve was adopted as an industry standard, different companies recorded at different curves. Using an Owl disc filter system to determine proper de-emphasis curves for playback, Hirsch turns the dial with his eyes shut— judging purely by his ears, not by dial indications, when the sound is right.

Assuming that one's hearing is still good, he notes, an older engineer has an advantage over a younger one in transferring vintage material because he knows the music better. "I've played in big bands myself. I *know* how big bands should sound in a way a 19-year-old engineer won't.

"NoNoise and CEDAR can be very valuable—but in the hands of the wrong person they're treacherous! Some engineers will say, 'I had 30 decibels of compression and no one noticed.' That's ridiculous. If you have licked the noise problem, stop there! You have so much power with these instruments, you can start getting oversynthesized. You wind up with a false sound— not a good sound—and you take the soul out of the music."

Traditionalists and Revivalists

Most of us who have done any serious listening to recordings have encountered some reissues so dismaying as to make one almost wonder if this country is losing the ability to produce decent reissues. I think of Duke Ellington and Muggsy Spanier reissues in which introductory bars of music were actually lopped off. Did whoever was responsible have any interest in the music being remastered? Or I think of one Bix Beiderbecke reissue with so much high end taken off that I had to wonder about the hearing ability of whoever was responsible.

But then something comes along like *Billie Holiday: The Complete Decca Recordings* (GRP) that is so well done—it could serve as a model for a major-label reissue—as to restore some optimism. You can appreciate the tonal quality of Holiday's voice much better on that reissue than on the thin-sounding, echoey simulated-stereo reissues that had been released in the '70s. (Holiday was one of two major Decca vocal stars who had been particularly ill served by bad simulated-stereo remasterings, the other being Al Jolson.) Steven Lasker was coproducer (along with Andy McKaie) of that Grammy-winning Holiday CD reissue, and he did all of the disc transfers. MCA has been keeping him busy doing disc transfers for many reissues, and he's done occasional work for other companies as well. He appears to be someone to watch in the field. He has good ears; he is open to both using new technology and taking advice from his elders (he acknowledges with gratitude guidance he has received from both Jack Towers and John R. T. Davies); and he is abundantly enthusiastic. A record collector before he got into record production (I first heard of him as an Ellington authority, at a Duke Ellington Society gathering), Lasker treats older jazz with respect.

Transfers of 78s that previously would have been done in-house at MCA on a turntable with just one stylus and no variable-pitch capacity, are now being done at Lasker's Venice, California, home, using any of his 20 different styli and a turntable on which he can make pitch corrections (since some early 78s were not recorded at exactly 78 revolutions per minute). Lasker has also had notable success in preserving high frequencies, which have all too often been lost (due to excessive filtering or other problems) in the transferring of 78s to CDs. And he has succeeded in using NoNoise more intelligently than others before him. I haven't generally been impressed by computer systems like NoNoise. (To my ears, no one has gotten better sound quality on reissues than John R. T. Davies does, working by hand.) But I *have* been favorably impressed with some of the results Lasker has gotten, and was eager to learn his views.

Lasker comments, "I hated NoNoise, up until about a year and a half ago. I loathed it with a passion. I thought it was doing much more harm than good, by a long shot. However, they have developed a decrackler mode that is wonderful. It is invisible weaving; you cannot tell that anything was done. The denoising can help if used judiciously. As Andy McKaie has said, 'As with any other tool, if you use it wrong you're going to bang yourself on the thumb.' Unfortunately, it has been overused. It has tended to change the timbre and the tonal effect of some instruments, particularly pianos. And as far as denoising goes, it astonishes me that it can't do a very good job on just simple hiss—which cheap analog denoisers get rid of very nicely.

"On the Billie Holiday set, we used the decrackler extensively. But we used the denoiser on only a handful of tracks, and very judiciously." Lasker, it should be noted, uses the decrackler in a very labor-intensive way; he does not just set it on autopilot. "For one 20-track CD, it takes me about a week of studio time to decrackle. Everything else for that CD—the denoising, EQ-ing, and assembly—is one day. But that decrackling—you put it on an automatic pass and then you go over it manually; and that's what takes time, going after everything."

And that is one point—that you have to be willing to invest time if you want decent results—on which all four restorers agree.

1992

Bibliography

Allen, Frederick Lewis, *Only Yesterday: An Informal History of the 1920s.* New York, Perennial Library/Harper and Row, 1964.

Balliett, Whitney, *American Musicians: Fifty-six Portraits in Jazz.* New York, Oxford University Press, 1986.

Berger, Morroe, Edward Berger, and James Patrick, *Benny Carter: A Life in American Music.* Metuchen, N.J., Scarecrow Press and the Institute of Jazz Studies, Rutgers University, 1982.

Berton, Ralph, *Remembering Bix.* New York, Harper and Row, 1974.

Bruyninckx, Walter, *Sixty Years of Recorded Jazz, 1917–1977.* Mechelen, Belgium, n.p., 1978.

Carmichael, Hoagy, *The Stardust Road.* New York, Greenwood Press, 1969.

Charters, Samuel B., and Leonard Kunstadt, *Jazz: A History of the New York Scene.* New York, Da Capo Press, 1981.

Chilton, John, *Who's Who of Jazz,* fourth edition. New York, Da Capo Press, 1985.

Collier, James Lincoln, *Duke Ellington.* New York, Oxford University Press, 1987.

Condon, Eddie, and Hank O'Neal, *The Eddie Condon Scrapbook of Jazz.* New York, St. Martin's Press, 1973.

Condon, Eddie, and Thomas Sugrue, *We Called It Music.* New York, Henry Holt and Company, 1947.

Dance, Stanley, *The World of Duke Ellington*. New York, Charles Scribner's Sons, 1970.

Dance, Stanley, *The World of Swing*. New York, Charles Scribner's Sons, 1974.

Deffaa, Chip, *In the Mainstream*. Metuchen, N.J., Scarecrow Press and the Institute of Jazz Studies, Rutgers University, 1992.

Deffaa, Chip, *Swing Legacy*. Metuchen, N.J., Scarecrow Press and the Institute of Jazz Studies, Rutgers University, 1989.

Deffaa, Chip, *Voices of the Jazz Age*. Urbana, Ill., University of Illinois Press, 1990.

DeLong, Thomas A., *Pops: Paul Whiteman, King of Jazz*. Piscataway, N.J., New Century Publishers, 1983.

Eberly, Philip K., *Music in the Air*. New York, Hastings House, 1982.

Feather, Leonard, *The Encyclopedia of Jazz*. New York, Da Capo Press, 1985.

Feather, Leonard, *The Encyclopedia of Jazz in the '60s*. New York, Da Capo Press, 1986.

Feather, Leonard, and Ira Gitler, *The Encyclopedia of Jazz in the '70s*. New York, Da Capo Press, 1987.

Giddins, Gary, *Satchmo*. New York, A Dolphin Book, Doubleday, 1988.

Goodman, Benny, and Irving Kolodin, *The Kingdom of Swing*. New York, Frederick Ungar Publishing Company, 1961.

Gourse, Leslie, *Louis' Children: American Jazz Singers*. New York, Quill, 1984.

Hadlock, Richard, *Jazz Masters of the Twenties*. New York, Macmillan, 1965.

Johnson, Grady, *The Five Pennies*. New York, Dell, 1959.

Keepnews, Orrin, and Bill Grauer, Jr., *A Pictorial History of Jazz*. New York, Bonanza Books, 1966.

Kernfeld, Barry, ed., *The New Grove Dictionary of Jazz*. New York, Grove's Dictionaries of Music, 1988.

Lax, Roger, and Frederick Smith, *The Great Song Thesaurus*. New York, Oxford University Press, 1984.

Miller, Tari, ed., *The Princeton Recollector*. Princeton, N.J., 1980.

Morgenstern, Dan (text), and Ole Brask (photographs), *Jazz People*. New York, Harry N. Abrams, Inc., 1976.

Ramsey, Frederick, Jr., and Charles Edward Smith, eds., *Jazzmen*. New York, Limelight Editions, 1985.

Rust, Brian, *Jazz Records, 1897–1942*. Chigwell, England, Storyville Publications, 1982.

362

Sanford, Herb, *Tommy and Jimmy: The Dorsey Years*. New York, Da Capo Press, 1980.

Sanjek, Russell, *From Print to Plastic: Publishing and Promoting America's Popular Music (1900–1980)*. New York, Institute for Studies in American Music, Conservatory of Music, Brooklyn College of the City University of New York, 1983.

Schuller, Gunther, *Early Jazz*. New York, Oxford University Press, 1968.

Schuller, Gunther, *Musing*. New York, Oxford University Press, 1986.

Schuller, Gunther, *The Swing Era*. New York, Oxford University Press, 1989.

Shapiro, Nat, and Nat Hentoff, eds., *Hear Me Talkin' to Ya*. New York, Dover Publications, 1966.

Shapiro, Nat, and Nat Hentoff, eds., *The Jazz Makers*. New York, Rinehart, 1957.

Shaw, Arnold, *52nd Street: The Street of Jazz*. New York, Da Capo Press, 1977.

Simon, George T., *The Big Bands*. New York, Schirmer Books, 1981.

Simon, George T., *Simon Says: The Sights and Sounds of the Swing Era, 1935–1955*. New York, Galahad Books, 1971.

Stearns, Marshall, *The Story of Jazz*. New York, Mentor Books, 1958.

Stillman, Edmund, and Marshall Davidson, *The American Heritage History of the 20's and 30's*. New York, American Heritage Publishing Co., Inc., 1970.

Sudhalter, Richard M., and Philip R. Evans, with William Dean-Myatt, *Bix: Man and Legend*. New Rochelle, N.Y., Arlington House, 1974.

Whitburn, Joel, *Pop Memories, 1890–1954: The History of American Popular Music*. Menomonee Falls, Wis., Record Research, 1986.

Whitcomb, Ian, *After the Ball: Pop Music from Rag to Rock*. New York, Limelight Editions, 1986.

Acknowledgments

I am greatly appreciative of the generous help that has been provided by Dan Morgenstern, Director of the Institute of Jazz Studies at Rutgers University, and his associates, Ed Berger and Vincent Pelote. In my research on music, they have always been there for me, to answer questions or suggest avenues to explore. And the institute's renowned collection of jazz clippings, oral histories, records, and books has been an invaluable source of background information for me.

My thanks, too, to the editors of the various publications for which I originally wrote articles about musicians in this book: Leslie Johnson of *The Mississippi Rag*, V. A. Musetto and Sue Byrom of *The New York Post*, Mike Joyce and W. Royal Stokes of *JazzTimes*, Bill Smith and John Norris of *Coda*, Ed Shanaphy of *Sheet Music Magazine*, Art Lange of *Down Beat*, Chuck Creesy of *The Princeton Alumni Weekly*, Warren Vaché Sr. of *Jersey Jazz*, Michael Schnayerson and Bret Watson of *Avenue*, and Dennis Matthews of *Crescendo*.

Earlier, shorter versions of the following profiles in this book first appeared in *The Mississippi Rag*: Joe Muranyi, September 1985 issue; Orange Kellin, October 1990; Sandra Reaves-Phillips, May 1992; Peter Ecklund, July 1992; Marty Grosz, January 1993. I profiled Vince Giordano in *The Mississippi Rag*, November 1984,

364

as well as in *Avenue*, December/January 1984/1985, and *Sheet Music*, February 1986. I profiled Richard Sudhalter in *Down Beat*, October 1985, and in *The Mississippi Rag*, March 1991. I profiled Ed Polcer in *The Princeton Alumni Weekly*, March 26, 1986. I profiled Carrie Smith in *JazzTimes*, December 1990, and in *The Mississippi Rag*, December 1990. I profiled Dan Barrett for *Coda*. The appendix originally appeared, in slightly different form, in *JazzTimes*, June 1993. The profiles of Eddy Davis, Terry Waldo, Vernel Bagneris, and Stan Rubin were written expressly for this book.

I appreciate the assistance in various ways provided by Nancy Miller Elliott, Joe Franklin, Lars Edegran, Rich Conaty, Joe Boughton, Alan Roberts, Mat Domber of Arbors Records, Merilee Trost of Concord Records, Marilyn Lipsius of RCA, Michael Bloom of GRP, Didier Deutsch of Atlantic, Wendell Echols and George Buck of Jazzology, Bob Erdos of Stomp Off Records, Jeff Nissim of MusicMasters Records, Charles Bourgeois of Festival Productions, Phil Evans, Jack Kleinsinger, Lloyd Rauch, Ian Whitcomb, Earl Kunzig, Ruth Brown, Matthew Flamm, Sune Johnsen, David Hajdu, Marilyn Levine, Denis Carey, Herb Freedman, C. A. Tripp, Tari Miller, Andrew Mytelka, Terry Lilly, Roy Hemming, David Gersten, Gil Wiest, Rebecca Reitz, Ellison Photos, Edward Enck, Ron Neal, Chuck Mann, Pat Meyer, Kristi Bockting, George Boyle, Danielle Salti, Aya Betensky, and Andreas Johnsen. My thanks to the ever-thoughtful Bernice Doyle of *The New York Post* for her kind assistance. Princeton's Ferris Professor of Journalism Emeritus Irving Dilliard and Lanny Jones have my appreciation for their guidance early on.

My special thanks to Frank Reuter, who has played an invaluable role as first reader and copy editor of this book and its predecessors in the Studies in Jazz Series, and to Frank Jolliffe, who has done likewise as proofreader.

Finally, of course, I'm indebted most deeply to the musicians who made this project so pleasurable for me, and to my family.

Index

Wettling, George, 156, 159
Wexler, Jerry, 311, 320, 330
WFUV-FM, 11, 19
"What a Little Moonlight Can
  Do," 278
What a Wonderful World, 162
"What Cha Gonna Do When
  There Ain't No Jazz?" 43
"What's New," 131
"When Day Is Done," 98
"When I Take My Sugar to Tea,"
  148
"When I Been Drinking," 278
"When the Saints Go Marching
  In," 236
White, Al, 112
White, Michael, 101, 191
Whiteman, Paul, 10, 11, 16, 22,
  29, 100, 129, 173, 187, 236
Whiting, Richard, 103
Whoopee, 89
Who's Afraid of Virginia Woolf?
  342
"Why," 56
Widespread Depression Orches-
  tra, 204
Wiedoft, Rudy, 192
Wiest, Gil, 95
Wiggs, Johnny, 30, 310
Wilber, Bob, 29, 135, 143, 144,
  157, 179, 243
"Wild Women," 324
Willcox, Spiegle, 29, 180, 190
Williams, Bert, 336, 338, 343, 350
Williams, Clarence, 35, 156, 269
Williams College, 12, 176, 226,
  237
Williams, Cootie, 133, 150, 153,
  190
Williams, Jackie, 208, 213
Williams, Joe, 222, 275
Williams, Kuumba, 329

Williams, Sandy, 160
Williams, Stanley, 314
Williams, Tennessee, 335
Willis, Chuck, 286
Willis, Danny, 62
Wills, Bob, 27
Wilson, Chuck, 23, 49, 50, 58,
  208, 213, 216, 256
Wilson, Earl, 240
Wilson, John S., 39, 45, 49, 55, 56
Wilson, Smilin' Jimmy, 76
Wilson, Teddy, 198
Windhurst, Johnny, 159
"Winter Light," 209, 210
Winters, Jonathan, 77
Wiseman, Fred, 117
"Wish I Hadn't Known About
  You," 286
Witherspoon, Jimmy, 302
Wizard of the Keyboard, 45
WNEW-AM, 256
Wolf Trap, 206, 207, 277
Wolfe, George C., 349
"Wolverine Blues," 230
Wooding, Sam, 64, 129
Woods, Carol, 71
Woodyard, Sam, 75
WOR-TV, 273
World's Greatest Jazz Band, 159
WQEW-AM, 19
WQXR, 70
Wright, Bob, 35, 71
Wright, Laurie
"Wrong Side, The," 70
Wyands, Richard, 278
Wynn, Al, 77

Xavier University, 342

Yale Collegians, 225
Yale University, 106, 152, 206,
  225, 226

About the Author

Chip Deffaa, a jazz critic for *The New York Post* and England's *Crescendo*, has written for such publications as *Entertainment Weekly*, *JazzTimes*, *Living Blues*, *Down Beat*, *Modern Drummer*, *Sheet Music*, *Keyboard*, *New Woman*, *The Mississippi Rag*, *Video Review*, England's *Storyville*, Canada's *Coda*, and Japan's *Swing Journal*.

He is the author of *Swing Legacy* (Scarecrow Press and the Institute of Jazz Studies), *Voices of the Jazz Age* (University of Illinois Press), and *In the Mainstream* (Scarecrow Press and the Institute of Jazz Studies), and is at work on *A Jazz Portrait Gallery*.